The *Secrets*
of
Men's Clothing

Ivan M.C. Chen, Ph.D.

*This book can be ordered through createspace.com, other
websites, or any bookseller worldwide.*

Contents

Screenshot, fair use.

Mark Twain said, "Clothes make the man. Naked people have little or no influence on society." If you wear clothes, why not wear the right ones correctly? The problem is that most men do not know what the right clothes are or how to wear their clothes properly. Many men think they know enough about the clothes they wear every day. Chances are they do need help. The accountant says in the movie, The Confession, "It is not hard to do the right thing. It is hard to know what the right thing is. Once you know what the right thing is, it is hard not to do the right thing." I hope that this book will help you find what the right things are and help you dress better.

Introduction

Alan Flusser, a prominent fashion designer and author, said, "During the past 25 years, men have spent more money on clothing for themselves than in any other period of modern history." Nevertheless, most men buy or wear wrong clothes. Men can only wear what they buy and buy what are available to them. It is impossible for a man to dress well if he keeps buying the wrong clothes.

The problem is serious.

In an ad during WWI, Hart Schaffner & Marks urged consumers to buy the company's products and save. In truth, people waste their money more on buying the wrong size clothes or wearing the clothes incorrectly than on buying bad quality clothes. Flusser once claimed that 90% of all men wear their jacket sleeves too long. Jacket sleeve is one of the most visible parts of a man's ensemble. If a man can make

This country can't afford waste in food or clothes— neither can you. Our clothes wear long and save

1

mistakes on jacket sleeves, he is likely to make more mistakes on other areas. For those 10% of men who wear the correct jacket sleeve length, do you think they will do everything else correctly? I have sold men's clothing for more than a decade and have hardly ever met a man who bought the right articles of clothing and wore them correctly. The problem is dead serious. What is worse is that most men do not even realize that they know little about the clothing they wear every day.

Manufacturers and retailers are uninterested in teaching their customers.

You think manufacturers and retailers will promote their products vigorously in order to sell more products. Ironically, they are not enthusiastic in educating consumers. The reason is obvious. Clothing stores are filled with mediocre or poor quality clothing items, which must be sold. How will retailers be able to sell bad quality clothes if they teach you how to detect good ones?

No designers will admit that they also make bad quality merchandise. So, they raise the prices of inferior products to match the prices of better ones, hoping that consumers will not discover the difference. A polo shirt made of 80's 2-ply double mercerized cotton and colored in fiber-reactive dyes is far superior in quality than a traditional polo shirt made of 40's 2-ply regular cotton and colored in pigment dyes by the same designer. The price difference is only a few dollars.

Fashion books often mislead consumers.

Contemporary fashion books are ineffective to help consumers make the right choices. Most books copy old ideas and known information from one another; some keep spreading erroneous beliefs. Every book lists every variety of men's clothing items but cannot suggest which variety is preferred. Fashion experts claim that the spread collar is dressier than the point or button-down collar, but no one explains why. Experts also suggest that a shirt collar should fit the neck snugly, yet few of them know how tight the collar should be. Few books explain how the collar should be fitted. Many authors give wrong suggestions such as measuring the neck over the Adam's apple or adding half an inch to the neck size. Manufacturers already did so when the shirt was made.

Many men buy a brand new suit and have the suit pants cuffed at the wrong width, which is the best way to cheapen a suit. Most men dry clean their wool suits or slacks regularly and have their garments damaged by washing with harsh chemicals or by machine pressing. They do not realize that wool is known as the miracle fiber and wool garments require minimal care.

Consumers are uninformed partly because fashion experts keep hiding important facts or keep giving false information. Manufacturers spend millions of dollars each year to put important information, such as *80's 2-ply* and *super 100's*, on the labels of their products. Few consumers know what these terms mean. Contemporary authors avoid such terms perhaps because these terms are too technical. Some authors dare to take on the task, only to give the wrong explanation. Esquire's *The Handbook of Style* declares that the thinnest wool yarn is called Super 100's. In the 18th century worsted count system, the yarn count ran from 30's to 100's, which was the finest wool yarn available at the time. Today a 100's wool yarn is no more than an ordinary wool yarn. A book presented by AskMen.com in 2007, *The Style Bible*, mistakes yarn size for thread count and claims that the

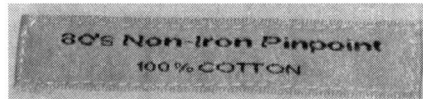

finest Supers are in the range of 450. Super 450's wool yarns do not exist under current technologies. The finest wool yarns are about 250. In several spring 2005 issues of Ralph Lauren's publication, *Polo Revue*, 80's/2-ply was defined as "80 horizontal and 80 vertical threads per square inch and two plies of yarn twisted together before weaving." This definition is unbelievably inaccurate. Many consumers and fashion experts including Alan Flusser believe that fabrics made of two-ply yarns are superior to those made of single-ply yarns. This is another serious misconception. How will consumers be able to make sound shopping decisions if they are misled constantly? It is difficult, if not impossible, to buy good quality garments without basic knowledge of fibers, yarns and fabrics.

Many consumers are content with less quality clothing.

John T. Molloy, author of *Dress for Success*, advised consumers to buy the best quality clothing they can afford. In truth, the goal of our life is often not to pursue the "best" but "satisfactory" results. It is impossible and unnecessary to own every article of clothing in the best quality even if they exist. Most men choose clothing items that are "good enough" for them. The problem is that many men have a low standard. They are easy to be content. I am not suggesting that a man should search all over the city for a better article of clothing every time he needs a simple item, nor am I suggesting that a man should be in debt to buy better quality clothing. What is silly is that consumers often ignore good quality clothing items in front of them and buy other less quality ones for higher prices. Shirley Temple said in one of her movies, "Everything has two prices, one for the fool." It may be reasonable to buy less quality merchandise if it saves you money. In reality, less quality garments are unnecessarily cheaper. Why buy the wrong items for the same or higher price?

Consumers rely too much on salespersons.

Most consumers do not believe it is complicated to pick up a clothing item in the store. If they need help, they can always rely on salespersons, they think. John T. Molloy gave five main reasons for businessmen's dressing for failure. One is that men let their favorite salesclerks choose clothes for them. Salesclerks in men's clothing stores are generally poorly trained or not trained at all. Mortimer Levitt, a custom shirt maker, once declared that "Salesmen in the country's best stores do not know how to take a measurement for collar size." This is alarming. Each time I told a customer that he was wearing and buying the wrong size of dress shirt, I usually got scolded with insulting words, such as "I have worn dress shirts before you were born." Many customers were offended and told me that they had just been measured at another clothing store. Some had their shirts custom made. Over a decade, I have seldom met a customer who dresses correctly. It is not an exaggeration when Flusser claimed that 90% of all men wear the wrong jacket sleeves alone. Millions of consumers are given the wrong clothes every day without noticing the problem. What is funny is that they keep thanking salesclerks for selling them the wrong clothes.

Secrets you need to know

Clothing stores nationwide are filled with mediocre or poor quality clothing items because consumers keep buying them. There is more merchandise in the store that does not fit than that fits a particular individual. It is much easier to sell a customer the wrong articles of clothing. Alan Flusser suggested that a man can learn from a failed purchase. My experience told me otherwise. Most consumers do not learn. In truth, they do not even realize there is a need to learn more about the clothing they wear every day.

Consumers keep buying the wrong clothes because they lack practical knowledge. Over the years, I have spoken with tens of thousands of customers. They have been impressed by the information I provided. Many customers commented that they had never heard what I told them. Everything I taught is like a secret to them.

People tend not to give a man credit for the quality of his clothing because they know he did not make any of the clothes he is wearing. People will, however, give the man credit if he coordinates his clothes well and wears his clothes correctly. Wearing the clothes correctly is as important as wearing the right clothes. For this reason, I have collected a number of trade secrets, which not only teach you how to buy the right articles of clothing, but also teach you how to wear them correctly. Many of the secrets have never been reported in previous literature. Some of the biggest secrets in men's clothing are not included in this book because they have been discussed extensively in many of my previous books. These secrets include the following.

a) How to arch out a tie without using a collar pin or vest. (See *the Art of Arching out a Tie.)*
b) Why is it unwise to tie a four-in-hand, half Windsor or Windsor knot? (See *the Art of Arching out a Tie.)*
c) Why is it unnecessary to clean wool slacks regularly? (See *a Pair of Perfect Pants* or *the Etiquette of Suits and Sport Coats*)
d) What are the advantages of wearing a spread collar shirt? (*The Essentials of Dress Shirts*)

The ancient Greeks define "philosopher" as a "lover of knowledge." As a doctor of philosophy and lover of knowledge, I have been disappointed by the conducts of fashion manufacturing and publishing industries. They continue to give incomplete or erroneous information and to spread fallacious beliefs about men's clothing. I have written a series of books to correct many pervasive misconceptions. Despite the non-cooperation from the fashion and retail industries, it is the ultimate responsibility of each individual consumer to learn how to dress properly. The ideas and methods presented in this book have been proven effective by tens of thousands of customers, whom I have served. I am confident that readers will find this book practical, enlightening and different from other fashion books in the market.

1.   *What is a well-tied tie?*

What is a well-tied tie?

Oscar Wilde once said, "A well-tied tie is the first serious step in life." But, what is a well-tied tie? Fashion experts believe that a well-tied tie should have a forward arch beneath the tie knot, but they have no clear idea how to accomplish this goal. All they can suggest is to pull the tie firmly against the collar. Alan Flusser said, "The necktie should be pulled up into the collar so that it is tight enough to arch out slightly from the neck." Thomas Fink and Yong Mao, the authors of *The 85 Ways to Tie a Tie*, wrote, "A properly executed knot causes the tie to protrude slightly from the neck, forming a hollow before it returns to the chest. This effect may be achieved by gently tightening the tie around the neck and pulling the knot up into the collar."

An arch beneath the tie knot

It is unthinkable less than a century ago that any well-dressed man would not attempt to arch out his tie. Old photos show that it was common for men to arch out their ties. What methods did these men use? They used a collar pin or a buttoned vest or jacket to support a pulled out tie. These methods do not always work.

As collar pins and vests become endangered species these days, most men wear a flat tie that falls straight down from under the collar, producing a dejected look like the branch of a willow. The arching of the tie becomes a lost art.

Fair use   by Carl Van Vechten

Fair use   Fair use

Hollywood's biggest stars arched out their ties with a vest, a collar pin, or both.

PAT F. GARRETT
The most famous peace officer of the Southwest

It was unthinkable in the past for a well-attired man not to attempt arching out his tie.

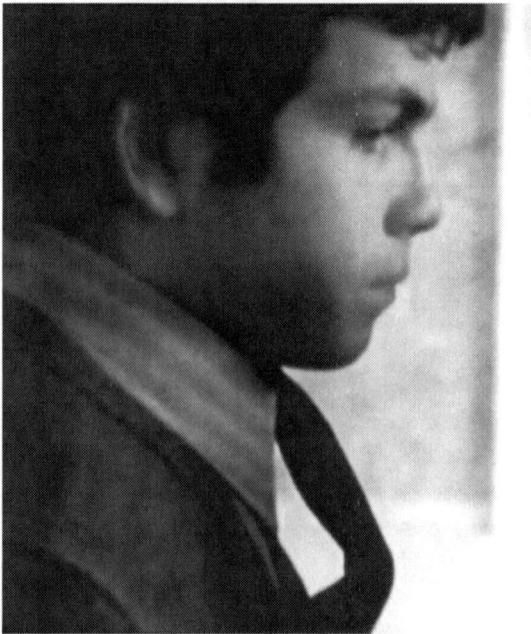

Even a child knows how to pull out his tie so that the tie will not lie flat and lifeless.

Screenshots, fair use.

It is ineffective to use a collar pin or tab to arch out the tie. The method does not always work and often creates a wrinkled collar. Here are samples of failed attempt.

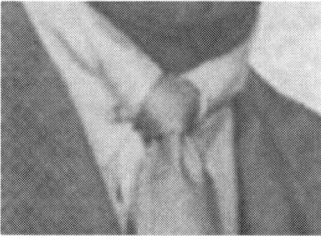

TV screenshot, Fair use

13

Screenshots, fair use.

A man entered into a dining room and kept touching his tie to draw attentions to his tie. The tie arched out alright but the collar was terribly wrinkled. There are better ways to arch out a tie naturally without using a collar pin or a buttoned jacket or vest.

14

Steven Spielberg
by Alan Light

Some men use a buttoned vest or jacket to pull out the tie a little. This method works only when the vest or jacket opening is cut high. Or, the tie will protrude at the middle of the chest instead of arching from under the tie knot.

Why can't men arch out their ties?

Fashion experts blame everything on the making and construction of the ties. Fink and Mao wrote, "The extent to which a knot will cooperate depends on its backing, the bulk of material in the back of the knot." In truth, whether a tie can arch out or not has a great deal to do with the type of tie knots. Every fashion expert promotes the three most popular tie knots in the world, the four-in-hand, half Windsor, and Windsor. These three knots are the main reasons that billions of men cannot arch out their ties.

This rare photo shows that LBJ arched out his tie slightly. Do not know how he did it. Other photos indicate that President Johnson could not arch out his ties even with a tab collar shirt. There are many factors that influence how a tie hangs. With the right construction of the tie and the right knot, a man may be able to arch out his tie without knowing why. Fashion experts call it, "Accidentally looking great." A good dresser should make sure that his tie is well-tied all the time regardless of the quality or style of the tie.

Arch out a tie naturally!

"**Ideally** the tie should arch slightly away from the shirt front rather than laying flat and lifeless," wrote Susan Bixler and Nancy Nix-Rice, authors of *The New Professional Image.* They said "ideally" perhaps because it is rare that a man is able to arch out his tie without any special support. In 2008, I published the world's first and only book, *The Art of Arching out a Tie*, in which I demonstrate that it is easy to arch out a tie if you use the right method. The book examines the very factors that influence the arch of a knotted tie. Now you can arch out your tie effortlessly without using any artificial device regardless of the quality of the tie.

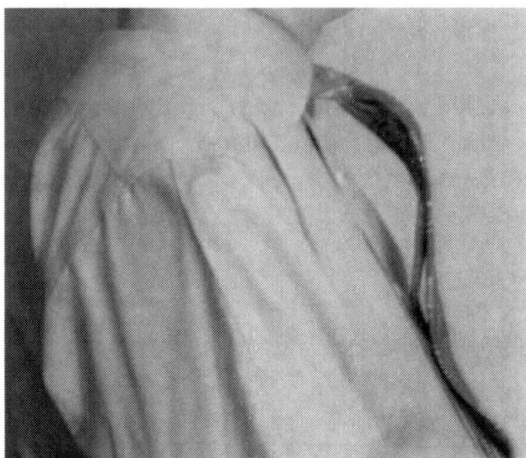

Billions of men live on earth. Few men can arch out the tie without the support of a collar pin, collar tab, or vest. The above picture shows the author of this book arches out his tie without using any device. The picture beneath shows the author wears the same shirt and tie, but the tie is weeping. The key secret is in the--tie knot. There are about 100 tie knots. Some knots are more effective in arching out the tie. The two pictures show the stunning difference between the world's simplest knot, the Oriental (above), and the second simplest knot, the four-in-hand (below).

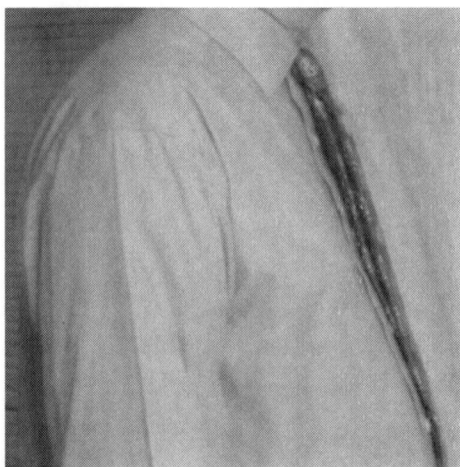

Do not assume that the tie will arch out automatically if you use the right knots. There are other factors that affect the arch of the tie. The factors are presented in Ivan M.C. Chen's revolutionary book, *The Art of Arching out a Tie.*

18

2. Why do so many men wear a crooked bowtie?

Photo of David Lynch, Jerry Seinfeld, Don DeFore, Rob Morrow, John Corbett, Michael Jeter and Tim Curry by Alan Light. Photo of James Marsters by Raven Underwood, licensed under Creative Commons Attribution (CC-BY) 2.0.

Many men are afraid of wearing a bowtie because they think it is too complicated to tie a bowtie. So, they give up the idea of wearing one, or buy pre-knotted bowties. Alan Flusser wrote, "There is no point in sporting the bow tie unless you plan on tying it yourself. Place a mathematically perfect pre-tied bow under your chin and you forsake all individuality. The hand-tied bow's moody loops and unpredictable swirls give you that subtle insouciance, that desired aplomb."

Flusser observed that the bowtie was once considered "a garment that combines confident flourish with absolute respectability." There is nothing to show respect if the bowtie is worn incorrectly. Why do so many men wear a crooked bowtie? One possible cause is that they wear a wrong bow. The residual twisting force, created by using the wrong knotting method, pulls the tie in the vertical direction, resulting in a crooked bowtie.

In truth, it is easy to tie a bowtie. You tie the bowtie the same way you tie your shoes. The difference is that you cannot see what you are doing when you are tying a bow on your neck. Many men tie a bowtie in front of a mirror. This may create more confusion for a beginner because everything you do appears in the opposite direction in the mirror. For a beginner, it is probably easier to practice a few times on the upper leg. Tie the bow and go to a mirror for adjustment. To get the right size bow, you may have to try several times. Many men wear pre-knotted bowties, which are often sloppy, not "mathematically perfect" as described by Flusser. One serious drawback of using a pre-knotted bowtie is that the width of the bow may not go well with the wearer's face. If this is the case, I suggest the wearer re-knot the bow. The width of the bow should finish within the outer edges of the eyes and the outside lines of the face or shirt collar.

Each time I mention to customers it is as easy to tie a bowtie as to tie a shoe, they are amazed. Many of them would buy the tie and be willing to give it a try. The problem is that many men tie their shoes with a vertical bow instead of a horizontal bow.

horizontal bow   *vertical bow*

The problem with a pre-knotted bowtie is that the width of the bow may not correspond to the wearer's face. If this is the case, the bow should be re-tied.

21

THE BOW TIE

Every man should know how to do this

1. Make a simple knot with both ends, allowing slightly more length (one or two inches) on the end of A.

2. Lift A out of the way, fold B into the normal bow shape, and position it on the first knot you made.

3. Drop A vertically over folded end B.

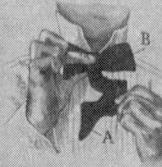

4. Then double A back on itself and position it over the knot so that the two folded ends make a cross.

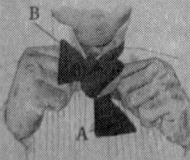

5. The hard part: Pass folded end A under and behind the left side (yours) of the knot, and through the loop behind folded end B.

6. Tighten the knot you have created, straightening any crumples and creases, particularly in the narrow part at the center.

– 150 –

In Esquire's *The Handbook of Style*, the subtitle reads "Every man should know how to do this." The handbook then illustrates the wrong method of tying a bowtie—the vertical instead of the horizontal bow. It seems that the correct subtitle should read "Every man should not do this."

22

Despite the plea from fashion experts that gentlemen should tie their own ties, Spencer Tracy had his bowtie knotted by his maid. The result was a crooked bow.

(Screenshots from *Cass Timberlane*, fair use)

23

Two Methods to Tie a Horizontal Bow

Method One

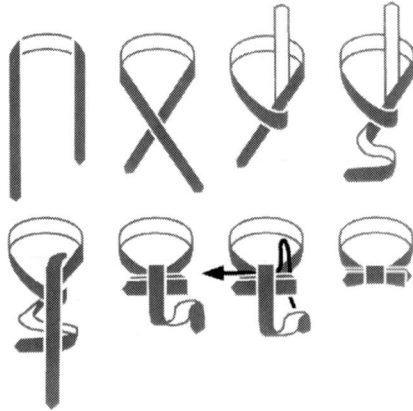

by Chris 73, CC-BY 2.5.

Method Two

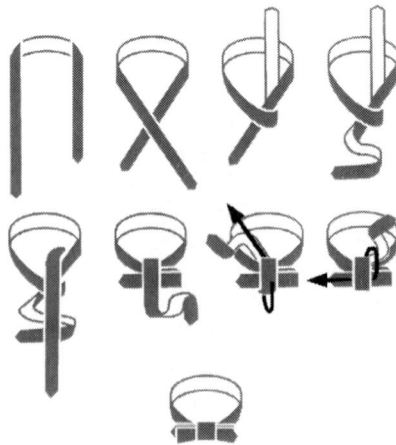

How a Vertical Bow Is Created?

When tying a tie, only one end is moving around. The moving end is called the active end, and the other passive end. If the active end of the tie wraps the passive end from the wrong side, a vertical instead of a horizontal bow is created. The following procedures explain how a vertical bow is produced.

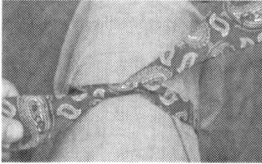

If the active end is on the upper side of the loop

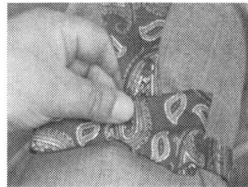

and you begin the knot by wrapping the passive end from the lower side,

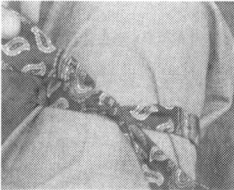

or if the active end is on the lower side of the loop

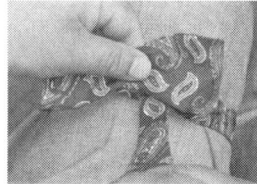

and you begin the knot by wrapping the passive end from the upper side,

you will create a vertical bow.

How to Knot a Horizontal Bow

The following procedures demonstrate the correct way to tie a horizontal bow using Method One.

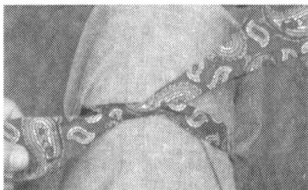

Version One:
Presume that the two ends are crossed in such a manner that the active end is on the upper side of the loop.

Start the knotting process by placing the active end on top of the passive end from above.

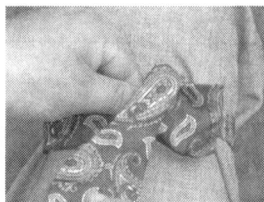

Version Two:
Presume that the two ends are crossed in such a manner that the active end is on the lower side of the loop.

Start the knotting process by placing the active end on top of the passive end from below.

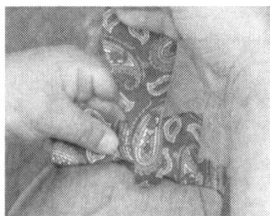

Both versions will produce a horizontal bow.

Who would wear both a bowtie and a long tie in the same outfit in public?

3.   *How long a tie should be knotted?*

The Pervasive Belief

The conventional wisdom is that the tip of the tie blade should cover the belt buckle or reach the waistband of the trousers. By doing so, the tie divides the wearer's upper body into two sections, known as gores in fashion design. This seems to be a good idea. The problem is that the majority of men wear their pants a few inches below the waistline. Contemporary trousers have a lower rise than those in the old days. Many men feel it is more comfortable to wear pants on the hip than on the waist. As a result, their torso appears to be out of proportion. It makes no sense to wear a tie length that reaches the hip. Experts claim: if a tie does not hang to the waistband, it will expose a patch of the shirtfront and lure eyes to the midriff. I do not understand how these experts think. To lure eyes to your midriff is much better than to lure eyes to your private part. No one complains that a man exposes a giant patch of the shirt front when the man wears a bowtie.

An ideal man has a torso about two lengths of his head. The torso starts at the bottom of the neck and ends at the waistline, which is the smallest part of the torso. In my humble opinion, a tie should hang to the waistline, which is near the

29

navel for most men. If a man wears his pants correctly at the waistline, the tie should touch the pants. If a man wears his pants several inches below the waist, there is no reason to lengthen the tie a few inches just trying to cover his mistake. A tie that drapes below the belt and points at the genital area looks unbalanced and intrusive.

Some people have a long torso. They wear high waisted pants to reduce the volume of the upper body. Some people do not have a long torso but wish to create the image of having longer legs by wearing high waisted pants. When the waistband of the pants is higher than the actual waist of the body, the tie is better worn short enough just to touch the waistband. Or, the extra tie length will contradict the effect created by the high waisted trousers.

Most short men are short because of their short legs. Since short men cannot make their legs longer, they should reduce the volume of their upper body by wearing high waisted pants and short ties. If a short man is unwilling to wear high waisted slacks, he will still look better with a short tie.

I have met a number of tall men who insist on wearing an extra long tie. In most cases, they really do not need one. Some of them wear a shirt collar that is too big for their neck, most of them use the Windsor knot, and, worst of all, they do not know the proper length of a knotted tie. Most tall men are tall because they have long legs, not because they have a long torso. Unless a man has a very large neck or very long torso, a regular size tie should be long enough for the man if he uses a simple tie knot. Some men have a large belly; they think they need an extra-long tie to go around their belly. How ridiculous it is!

Sometimes customers ask for extra-long ties because they want to tie the Windsor knot. Obviously, these men do not know how to wear a tie either. Why buy the wrong tie to tie a bad knot that does not produce a well-tied tie?

There has never been any golden rule, suggesting that the tie must cover the belt buckle.

At one time, Men including big and tall ones wore a short tie.

Screenshot, fair use.

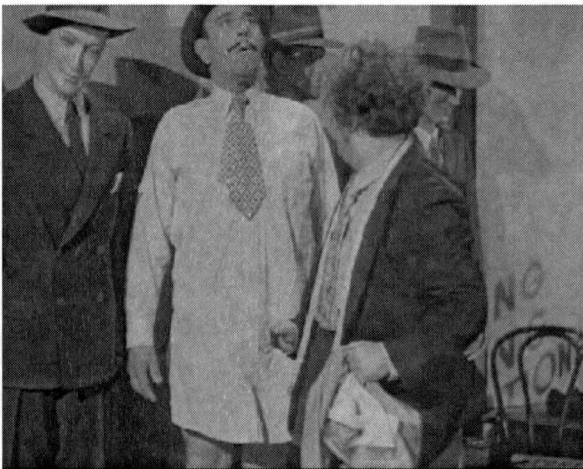

Duke of Windsor, the trend setter of the early 20th century, did not shy away from wearing a short tie. The small end extended beyond the tie blade, indicating that it was intentional to wear the tie in such a manner.

Fair use.

Salvador Dali, Spanish Painter, wore a short tie in the same manner that the Duke of Windsor wore his.

(photo by Carl Van Vechten)

James Stewart and Spencer Tracy could wear their tie long but they chose not to.

Screenshots, fair use.

When a man sits down, his upper body bends and his torso gets shorter. Thus, every man tends to have his tie length wrong when he sits. For those men who sit most of the time, they should wear their ties one or two inches shorter than they normally wear when they stand up.

Some heavy men do not have a long torso but they buy extra-long ties because they mistakenly think they need extra length in order for the tie to hang over their large belly and reach the belt buckle.

Adjust tie length to head length.

Fashion experts maintain that the width of the tie should not exceed the widest part of a notched jacket lapel, and the width of the jacket lapel should be proportional to the head size of the wearer. No expert ever suggests that the length of a knotted tie should relate to the length of head. The ideal human body has a torso about two times the length of the head. It is my recommendation that any man should not wear his tie longer than twice the length of his head, especially if the man has a relatively small head.

Neckties belong to the neck; it is better to wear them short than long.

It is a shame for a man to choose wearing a tie but wearing it at the wrong length. It reminds me of a book title, "Today gentleman is no more." I hope that I have argued forcefully about the correct way of wearing a tie. If a man is incapable of wearing a tie at the right length, he ought to consider that the full name of a tie is "necktie." This means neckties belong to the neck. A man would rather wear a tie too short than wear it too long if he cannot hang it right. A long tie lures eyes downward and ruins the proportion between a man's face and his torso.

Any man who wears high waisted slacks and any man who sits down a lot should wear his tie short. Short men should also wear short ties.

The proper length of the tie has more to do with the length of the head than the location of the waist.

Tie Length and Head Length

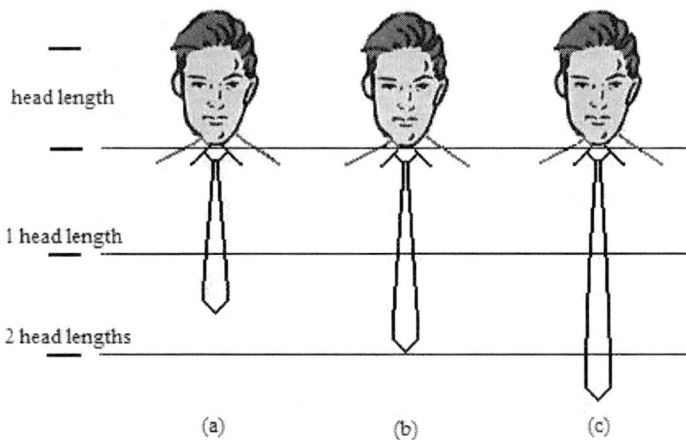

head length

1 head length

2 head lengths

(a)   (b)   (c)

The great masters of art have found that the relation of one part to another is very pleasing to the human eye if the ratio is about 5 to 3, or 1.6 to 1. This visual proportion is known as the Golden Section, Golden Mean, or Golden Ratio.

(a) *The best tie length is about 1.6 times the length of the face based on the Golden Ratio.*

(b) *Nevertheless, an ideal man has a torso of two head lengths. It is wise not to wear a tie length that exceeds two head lengths.*

(c) *A tie length that exceeds two head lengths will diminish the face.*

It is ridiculous to wear a tie length that exceeds far more than two head lengths.

A man with a small head should wear a short tie.

Why do so many men wear too long their ties?

You may think men will wear a tie length that is proportional to the length of their torsos. They do not. Most men wear a tie according to the length of the tie fabric, ranging from 53" to 60". Although the average tie length varies according to the fashion trend of the time, most ties are made about the same length during the same season. Consequently, it seems like every man is wearing the same length of tie. This is wrong. Each man should wear the right length of tie based on the height of his face and top body; he should not wear a certain length of tie only because tie manufacturers make him do so.

Manufacturers have the tendency to produce clothing items that fit most of the consumers instead of an average consumer. Hence, most ties are made too long for an average man.

What should you do if your tie is too long?

Fashion experts, including Alan Flusser, suggest a man can tuck his tie inside his trousers in the style of Fred Astaire or the Duke of Windsor. I do not know why all of the experts with a brilliant mind would come out with such a bizarre idea. The tie belongs to the neck, not the pants. The tie should never be put inside the pants. Tucking the tie inside the trousers not only will damage the tie but also will affect the movement of your top body. What is more, a tucked tie looks tacky and objectionable.

How can any tie be too long? A man can always adjust the length of the tie by knotting the tie at any place he desires. It is impossible for a tie to be too long unless the man wants it to be long. Men wear a long tie because they have a wrong presumption that is the small end (back piece) of the tie should never extend beyond the large end (front blade) of the tie. Indeed, the back piece of the tie should be covered by the front piece. So, why not hide the back piece? A man should hang the front blade of his tie to his navel. If the small end of the tie exceeds the length of the large end, he has several options. 1) He can cut the offending excess off. 2) He can hang the extra length over the tie tag. 3) He can fold the small end a few inches up and secure the fold with a safety pin or with a few stitches of thread. Or, 4) he can use the military style by inserting the small end between any two buttons of the shirtfront, as done by the Duke of Windsor. No one will notice what the man has done as long as the small back piece is hidden behind the large front piece.

An image consultant, JoAnna Nicholson, posted a question, "When is the short end of your tie too short?" She suggested that a man can move up the bar tack or self-loop as much as 4" if the small end of his tie is too short to fit through the bar tack or loop. This is a bad advice. If the small end becomes too short to fit through the loop, it is likely that the man knots his tie in the wrong section of the tie. He ties his tie too close to the narrowest part of the tie. There is insufficient width of fabric to form a decent knot. The man should tie his tie shorter or use a longer tie.

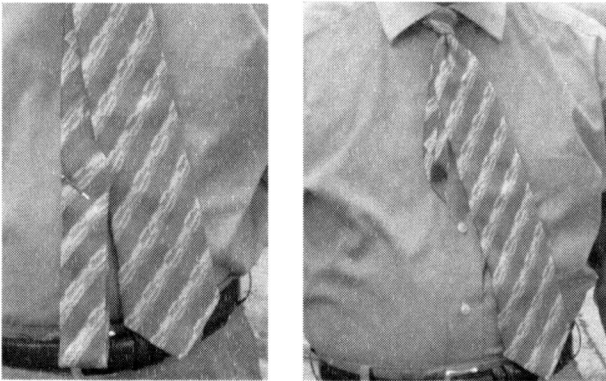

You can hide the extra-length of small end by folding the back piece or inserting the back piece inside the shirt.

41

4.   How to tie unusual knots

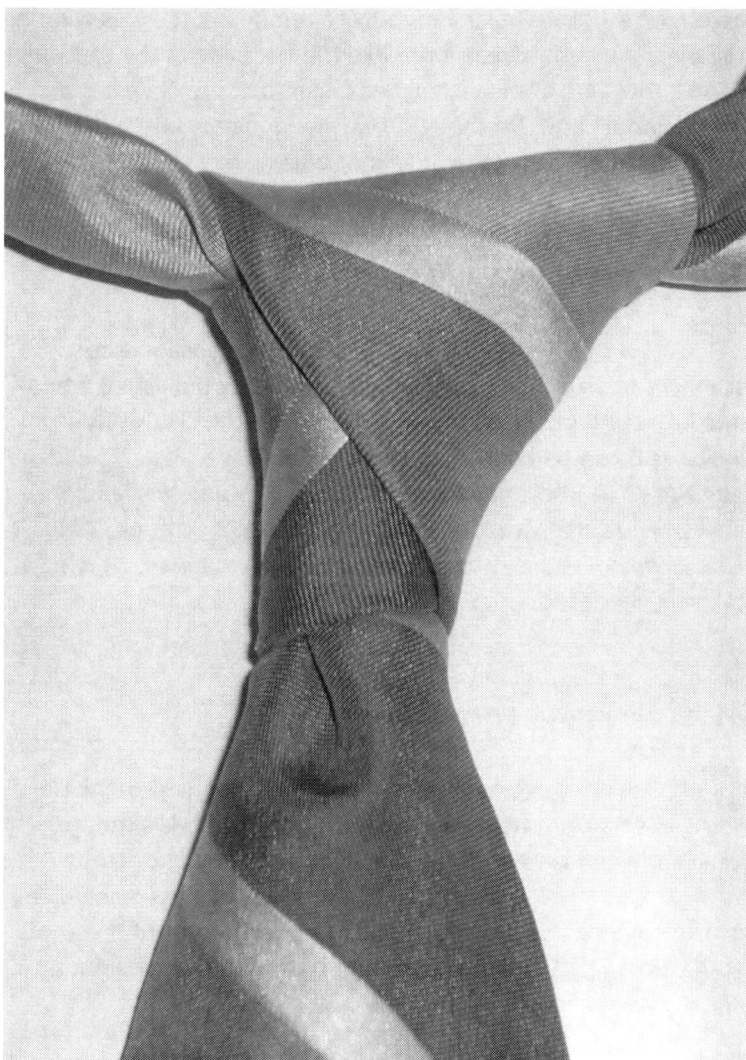

Diagonal knot

While shopping in the store, a customer kept complaining to his friend about how boring men's clothing was. All of a sudden, the customer shut his mouth after he saw the tie knot under my collar. The customer said he had never seen such an unusual tie knot. He apologized for his comment and asked me if I could teach him how to tie the knot. I was wearing the diagonal knot, which looks like the backside of the four-in-hand knot. One of my colleagues laughed at me once he saw my diagonal knot. He thought I was wearing my knot backward. I wished I knew how to tie any knot backward.

100 different ways to tie a tie

Two physicists, Thomas Fink and Yong Mao, used scientific approaches to study tie knots. They published a book in 2000, entitled *The 85 Ways to Tie a Tie*. The book only includes those tie knots involving nine moves or less. The actual number of tie knots can exceed 100 if we include more complex knots. In Davide Mosconi and Ricardo Villarosa's book, *188 Facons de nouer sa cravatte,* over 180 different ways of tying a tie were recorded.

Most tie knots are useless.

Except the diagonal knot and the Onassis knot, all tie knots have a plain triangle shape, even though each knot may be slightly different in size and in symmetry. I wonder why it is so significant that scholars had to spend years in studying every possible way of tying a knot, especially when most of the knots are useless. Isn't it more important to find out which knot or knots work the best?

A useful tie knot should not be merely a method of holding the two ends of the tie together. The ultimate goal of a useful tie knot is to produce a well-tied tie as Oscar Wilde has called for. Every man only needs one method to tie a knot each time he puts on a tie. It is unproductive to be able to tell people how many methods are possible but be unable to tell which method or methods are preferred. If we want different results and if different knots can deliver different results, we may need a variety of knots to fulfill different purposes. Many men, including experts, think they need different tie knots to adjust the size of the tie knot and the length of the tie. This approach works only on the same tie. But, most men do not wear the same tie all the time. If you think the Windsor knot will produce a larger knot for every tie, you are mistaken.

To prove my point, I am providing the following photo, containing the images of six different tie knots (not in order): the Oriental, four-in-hand, half-Windsor, Windsor, Prince Albert, and Pratt. Can you match up each of the tie knots? Most tie knots look similar under a shirt collar. If the result is the same or similar, why does it matter to use different knots?

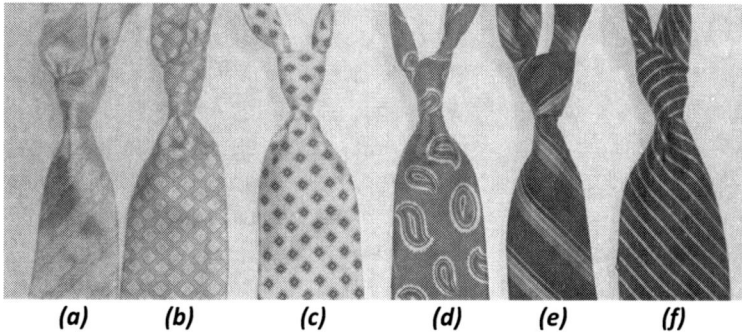

(a)   (b)   (c)   (d)   (e)   (f)

Answer: (a) half-Windsor, (b) four-in-hand, (c) Windsor, (d) Albert, (e) Pratt, and (f) Oriental.

Why does the complex Windsor knot appear smaller than some of the simpler knots? This is because the sickness and width of the tie affect the size and shape of the knot.

Use the thickness and width of the tie to adjust the size and shape of the knot.

I have written two books on ties and have argued that it is better to use the thickness and the tapering of the tie to adjust the size of the tie knot. The Duke of Windsor preferred large knots. So, he used thick ties with the four-in-hand knot to achieve his goal. Most ties are too long for an average man. If a man ties the front end of the tie to the correct length and hides the excessive length of the narrow end, he has no need to use a complex knot to shorten the length of the tie. Too much twisting can damage the tie. Why do we need so many different knots when the result is similar and disappointing--a spiritless tie that weeps like the branch of a willow?

There are good ways and bad ways to be different.

Unlike women's, men's clothing items lack variety. Many men are dissatisfied with the uniformity of their clothing and search for different ways to dress differently. Frequently, I met customers who looked for collar pins or tab collar dress shirts. I asked them why. They said they did not like the way their tie sat on their shirt collar. They were unaware that it is ineffective to arch out a tie with a collar pin or tab.

When I met customers who wanted to buy shiny satin ties to go with their nubby sport jackets, I mentioned to them that fashion experts often suggest the texture of ties should match the weave of jackets. Some of them got offended and said, "But, I want to be different." Some men just do not listen well.

There are good and bad ways to dress differently and better than other men. The best way is to dress correctly since the majority of men are dressing improperly these days. The best way to wear a tie is to arch out your tie naturally and lively. If you are bored with the same shape of tie knot, you may try a couple of unusual knots.

The Diagonal Knot

The diagonal knot was created by Italian designer, Davide Mosconi. The knot is probably the most difficult one to execute. In my book, *The Art of Arching out a Tie*, I revolutionarily classify the tie knots into two categories, the Type-A and Type-B knots. The original diagonal knot is a Type-A knot and tends not to protrude from the neck. Nevertheless, I am able to transform Mosconi's diagonal knot into a Type-B diagonal knot, which can arch out more easily if your tie has the correct construction. You may call this new knot the Ivan Chen knot.

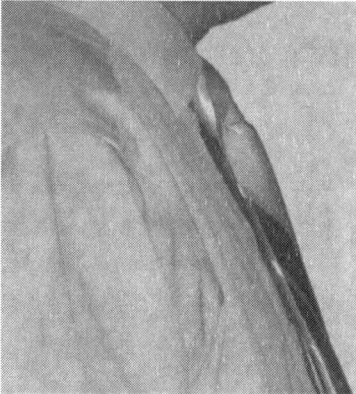

Mosconi's diagonal knot   *Ivan Chen's diagonal knot*

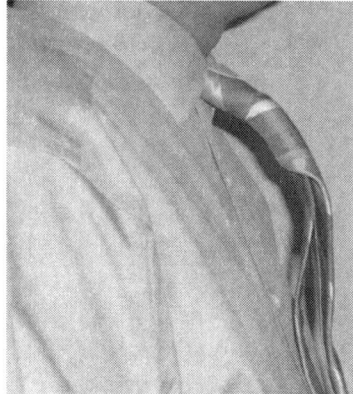

How to tie the Ivan Chen Knot

The procedures to knot the Ivan Chen diagonal knot are as follows.

(a)　Cross the two ends with the wide end inside-out under the narrow end.

(b)　Bring the wide end above the narrow end horizontally to the other side.

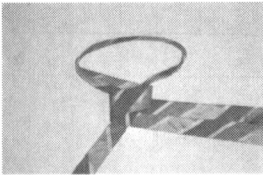

(c)　Wrap the wide end around the narrow end a half turn.

(d)　Bring the wide end from the front up through the neck loop so that the wide end comes outside the neck loop with the seam facing out.

(e)　Bring the wide end down sideways through the front loop without passing through the neck loop.

(f)　Shape the knot into a triangle by twisting it slightly as you draw the knot tight by pulling the wide end downward.

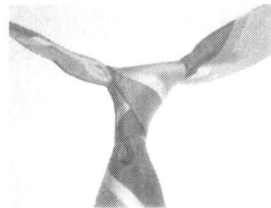

48

The diagonal knot is the only knot that is completed by pulling the wide end through the front loop sideways from outside the neck loop. All other knots are completed by pulling the wide end down through the front loop from the center of the neck loop. Because of this tricky way to completion, the diagonal knot can be executed more successfully with a narrower tie.

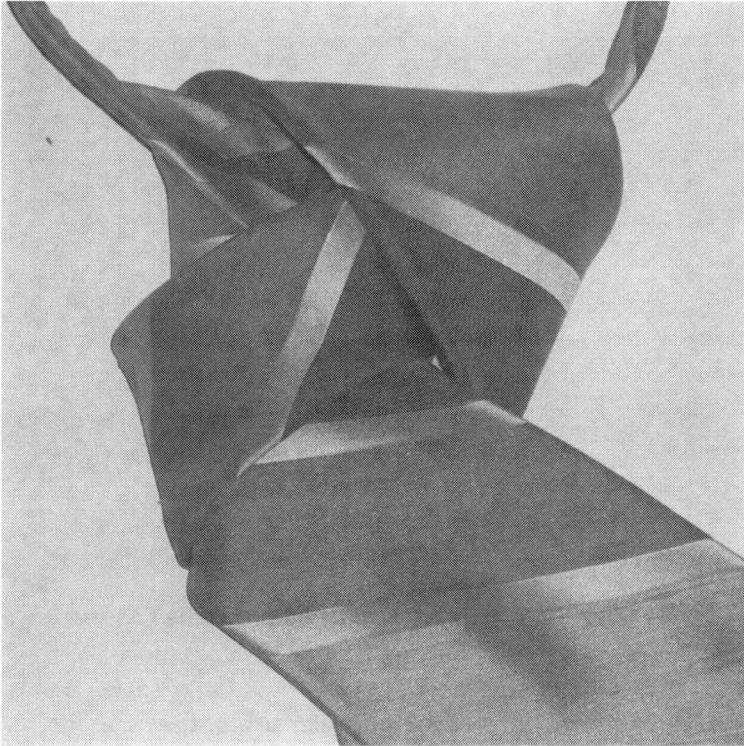

The Onassis Knot

The Onassis knot is a trademark of the Greek shipping magnate, Aristotle Onassis. The knot is accomplished by bring the active end of the finished four-in-hand knot behind to the right (or left) and out through the center. Fink and Mao treated the knot as an extension of the four-in-hand instead of a

49

separate knot. The triangle knot is completely hidden from view. Hence, any knot besides the four-in-hand can achieve the same look of the Onassis. "The result is satisfactory only when used with a collar sufficiently spread to accommodate the full width of the tie. The Onassis 'still has a certain popularity along Seventh Avenue' in New York, reported the *New York Times* in 1989," wrote Fink and Mao.

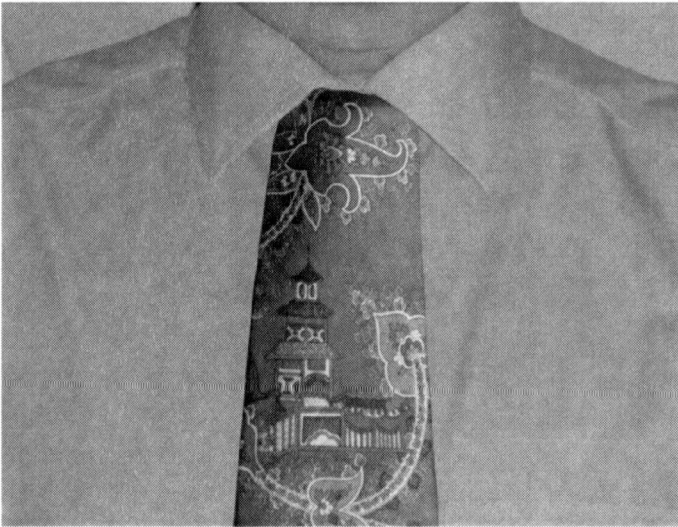

I question whether this method should be considered a knot. It is a sloppy way of tying a tie. A tie looks more attractive with a triangle knot than without the triangle. Don't you agree? The Onassis knot looks like an ascot without the elegance. Some may say the knot looks more like the napkin that Laurel and Hardy tucked under their chin when they sat down to eat. The knot says the wearer is running out of ideas about his tie and is desperate to make something new or different. There are better ways to be different--arching out the tie or wearing a real unusual knot.

Wearing two ties at the same time

I sometimes tie two ties together to create two separate colors and patterns, one color and pattern for the tie knot and the other for the tie blade. To create this effect, you tie two ties together using any of your favorite knots. At the last move, you bring the top tie down through the front loop first, and then you pass the second tie down through the front loop with the second tie on the top of the first tie.

The Cross Knot

The cross knot, also known as the Christensen knot, was popular around the turn of the twentieth century when equal-ended straight ties were fashionable. This knot was presumed dead perhaps because the "cross" effect of the knot can only be displayed by using narrow strip ties. As contemporary ties have evolved into a tapered wide end, this stylish binding is no longer visible.

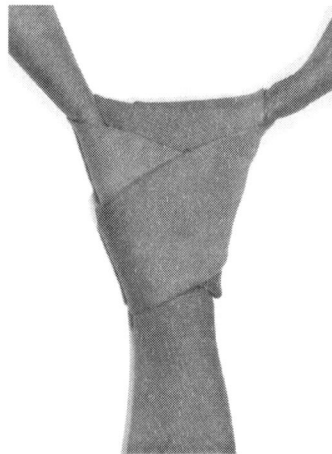

If you wear this knot with a tapered wide tie, no one will notice it.

How to tie the Cross Knot

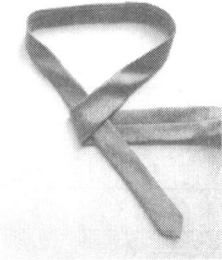

1)   Cross the two ends with the wide end on top. Wrap the wide end behind the narrow end with the seam facing out.

2)   Fold the wide end up from the front and through the neck loop so that it points to the other direction with the seam facing out.

3)   Turn the wide end from the front to the other side.

4)   Wrap the wide end behind the narrow end to complete the first revolution.

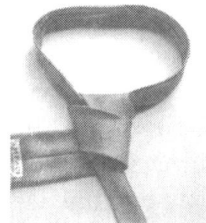

5)   Fold the wide end once more to the other side.

(Step 3, 4 and 5 are the points where the "crossing" occurs.)

6)   Pull the wide end up from behind and through the neck loop.

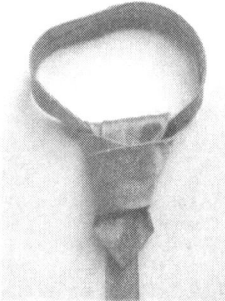

7)   Bring the wide end down through the double-wrap just made.

8)   Tighten and adjust the knot so that the "cross" wrapping is visible if you use a narrow tie. The double wrapping will not be shown if you use a wide or overly tapered tie.

The Atlantic Knot

Despite that there are about 100 methods to knot a necktie, most tie knots look similar--a plain triangle shape. This is no surprise. Contemporary long ties have two uneven ends. The large end is called the blade or apron. When knotting a tie, only end is moving around. The moving end is called the active end, and the other passive end. Most of the traditional tie knots use apron as the active end. When knotting, the width of the tie gets wider and wider toward the end movement of the knot. To complete most knots, the active end is wrapped over the front, then underneath to the center, and finally through the front loop just made. The wider band in this final move covers up the trail of all previous moves, resulting in a plain triangle. In order to show the path or sequence of the knot, a man can wear the tie backside out. But, the narrow end will be in front of the wide apron end, which is unbecoming. Another way is to use the narrow end as the active end. The Atlantic knot is an example of using this approach.

How to Tie the Atlantic Knot

1)   Cross the ends with the smooth side facing out and the narrow one on top of the wide one.

2)   Bring the narrow end up from behind the wide end, through the neck loop and to the front.

3)   Fold the narrow end from behind to the other side.

4)   Bring the narrow end up from the front and through the neck loop.

5)   Tuck the narrow end through the back loop just created and tighten the knot.

The Merovingian Knot

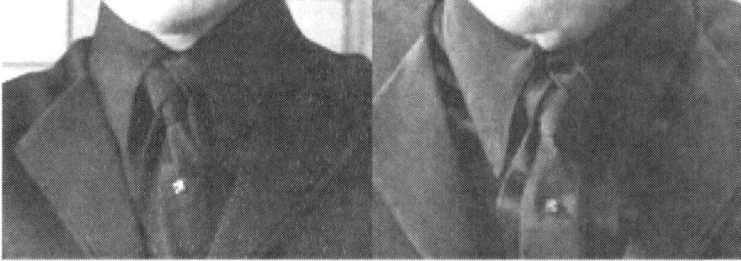

The Merovingian knot looks similar to the Atlantic but is more complex to execute. The name comes from the character Merovingian, who wore the knot in the movie *Matrix Reloaded (2003)*. There are different ways to tie the Merovingian knot. One way is to tie a Windsor knot and then wear the knot backside out. This will result in the narrow end appearing in front of the wide apron as shown in the movie. To avoid showing the center back seam of the tie, you should tie the Windsor knot in reverse, meaning the backside facing out. Another way to tie the Merovingian knot is to use the narrow end as the active end.

How to Tie the Merovingian Knot: Method One
(The Turn-around Reverse Windsor)

There are twelve derivatives to tie the Windsor knot, but not all versions will produce the Merovingian knot when you turn the Windsor around. The following version will produce the Merovingian knot.

1)   Cross the ends with the backside (seam) facing out and the wide end on top of the narrow end.

56

2)   Bring the wide end up from behind the narrow end, through the neck loop and to the front.

3)   Fold the wide end from behind the knot to the other side.

4)   Wrap the wide end around the small end a full circle as in Step (2).

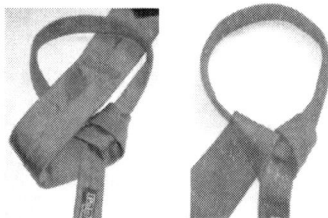

5)   Fold the wide end from the front to the other side.

6)   Bring the wide end up from behind the knot through the neck loop, and tuck the wide end through the front wrap just created.

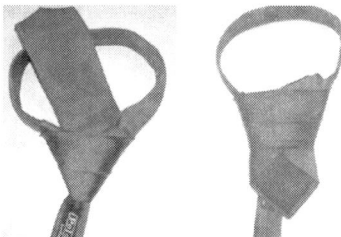

7)   Tighten the knot and turn the tie around.

How to Tie the Merovingian Knot: Method Two
(using the narrow end as the active end)

1) Cross the ends with smooth side facing out and the narrow end on top of the wide apron.

2) **Bring the narrow end up from behind the wide end, through the neck loop and to the front.**

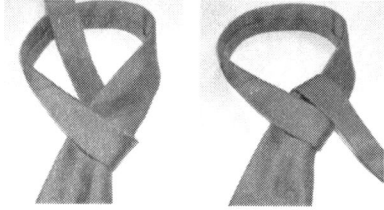

3) **Wrap the narrow end from behind to the other side.**

4) **Wrap the narrow end around the passive end a full circle as in step (2).**

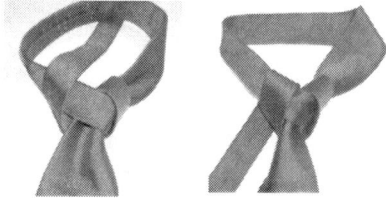

5) **Fold the narrow end from the front to other side.**

5) **Repeat Step (2) and (3).**

6)   Bring the narrow end up from the front and through the neck loop.

7)   Tuck the narrow end through the back loop just made and tighten the knot.

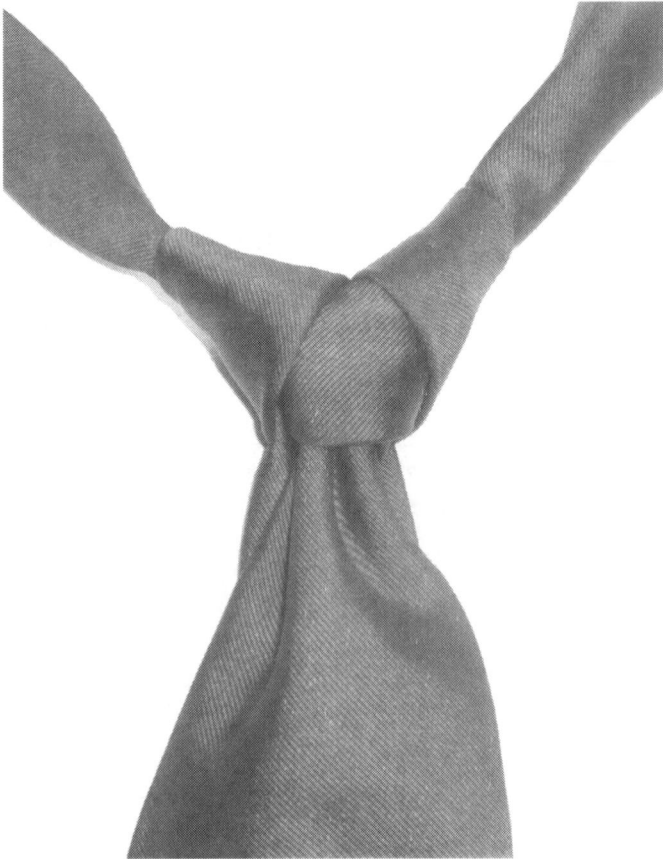

The Artichoke Knot

I created the following strange knot by using the narrow end as the active end to wrap around the passive end left and right alternately and repeatedly until the narrow end is used up. I do not have a name for this knot. We may call it the artichoke knot since it looks a little like the vegetable. The process of tying this knot is rather tedious. The knot tends to be outsized and is unlikely to protrude under the collar. Hence, I am not enthusiastic about this knot. I showed the photo to a few customers and received a mixed review. I post it just to show that it is easy to create an odd shape of tie knot by using the narrow end as the active end.

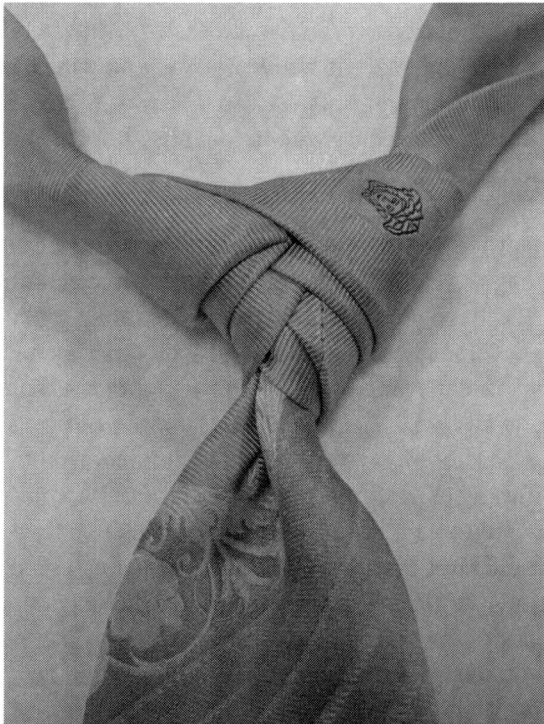

It is impractical to use the narrow end as the active end.

After the knot is completed and tightened, the position and length of the active end remain constant while the position and length of the passive end change as the knot is moving up and down. There are shortcomings of using the tie blade or apron as the passive end. The location of the passive blade is less predictable, making it more difficult to knot the tie at a desired length. The tie blade may be damaged more easily as it comes in and out of the knot constantly. The point where the wide end or narrow end comes out of the knot is called the "neck." The neck opening for the passive end is formed in the first several moves of the knotting process whereas the neck for the active end is created in the last wrap or wraps. Consequently, the neck opening for the passive end tends to be smaller. The tiny neck opening restricts the wide blade to such a degree that the apron often has excessive wrinkles or dimples and is unable to conceal the active narrow end, which is behind the apron. For these reasons, it seems unwise to tie a knot using the apron as the passive end, despite that the method will produce an unconventional knot.

I learned some time ago that the progress of our knowledge is not from simple to complex or from complex to simple, but is from vogue to profound. A strange-looking or complex knot does not make the knot look more elegant or interesting. Oscar Wilde indeed had the right idea that a tie should be "well-tied." Fashion experts unanimously agree that a well-tied tie should have a forward arch beneath the knot. There is nothing in ties that is more profound than having a spirited, arched tie. It requires much more skill to tie a lively, arched simple knot than to tie a lifeless, weeping complex knot. None of the Atlantic, Merovingian and Artichoke knots can protrude under the shirt collar. They are lifeless like most tie knots. If you desire a strange-looking knot, try the Ivan Chen knot.

5. *It may be dangerous to use apron as the passive end.*

Some of my clients work in a mental facility. They told me that they wear clip-on ties instead of regular ties. Mental patients sometimes grab the ties, which action can cause a serious injury if the tie does not come right off. Since the early 1900s, wearing a pre-knotted tie has been considered an act of sartorial terrorism. The pseudonymous author of a 1900 guidebook *Clothes and the Man*, "Major", said the following.

> Of course no gentleman ever does wear a made-up tie
> . . . I consider it part of the duty of every father to tell
> his son this on leaving school . . . The young man who
> always tries to get a tie of the same material and colour
> as her dress doesn't make such a fool of himself as the
> young man who goes to a shop and lays in a stock of
> ready-made ties.

Pre-knotted ties are now uncommon in the market these days perhaps because knotting a tie is a rather simple task--no more complex than tying a pair of shoes. There is no excuse for any able person not to learn how to tie a tie. The funniest thing is that the majority of men cannot tie a nice tie perhaps because they take the simple tie knots for granted. Hardly any man will give much thought on knotting a tie. Many men only know one method. Some men do not even know how to tie a tie at all.

Occasionally, I encounter customers who want to buy a pre-knotted tie for their children or for someone who has Parkinson decease and is unable to knot a tie. Many children's ties are pre-knotted and adjustable by pulling the zipper on the small end. Zippered ties are more secure than the clip-on ones.

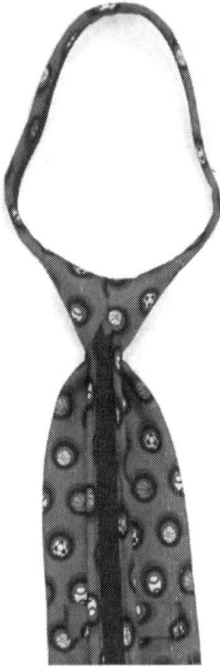

On the other hand, they are less flexible in adjusting the neck size. Depending on the length of the zipper, each tie only fits neck sizes within a certain range. Additionally, zippered ties are more dangerous for young children to wear. The only way to take off a zippered tie is to unzip the small end and lift the tie loop over the head. It is difficult for young children to complete such a task in an emergency situation when the tie is caught or grabbed by a person or machinery such as a car window. I have warned parents to teach their children how to release and take off the tie.

In the previous chapter, I have described several unusual tie knots, including the Atlantic, Merovingian and Artichoke knots. What gives these knots an interesting look is that the knots use the tie apron (wide end) as the passive end instead of the active end. The passive end is the one that moves up and down controlling the width of the tie loop that fits the neck. With traditional tie knots, the small end is the passive end hidden behind the tie apron. When the apron is pulled, it does not tighten the neck loop. Hence, it is fairly safe to wear a tie in such manner. With unconventional knots using apron as the passive end, the knots are potentially dangerous to wear even for normal adults. If the tie apron is pulled too tight, either intentionally or accidentally, the wearer will be choked instantly and can be fatal. For this reason, I strongly advise that this type of knots should not be given to young children, disable adults or seniors.

6. *Why do some ties fray easily?*

When shopping for ties, most people are more concerned with the colors and patterns than concerned with the texture of ties. Some people do pay attention to the weave of ties, but they do so mainly for aesthetic reason. The structure of ties affects the function and durability of ties and should be taken into consideration when choosing ties. It is pointless to buy a tie that cannot be tied into a nice knot or will be damaged after a few wears. When I mentioned that certain tie materials tend to snag or fray easily, many customers began to confess that they did own a number of ties that wore out quickly. They wondered why.

The majority of ties are silk ties. Silk fiber has a luster partly because it is a filament instead of a staple fiber and partly because the shape of the fiber is triangle, which reflects light the same way a prism does. To highlight this unique property, manufacturers tend to use dense weave with a maximum number of "float" to produce a fabric that appears rich, luxurious and shining.

Most ties are made of woven fabrics, which are produced by interlacing warp (lengthwise) yarns with weft (filling or crosswise) yarns. Whether a fabric shines or not has a great deal to do with the weave of the fabric. To be more specific, the sheen of a fabric is caused mainly by the "floats" of yarns. The float is the portion of warp or filling yarns that cross two or more of the opposite yarns.

There are three basic weaves: plain, twill, and satin. In a plain weave, each weft yarn goes alternately over and under each warp yarn. In a twill weave, each weft yarn passes over at least two but not more than four warp yarns. In a satin weave, a warp yarn passes over more than four weft yarns in a staggered pattern. A plain weave contains the greatest number of interlacing. More intersections create more gaps between yarns and allow more light passing through. Hence, plain weave fabrics do not shine. A satin weave contains the least number of interlacing per area, allowing less light to pass through. Some of the light reflects back and shines. The high number of floats gives the satin weave its characteristic sheen.

Many tie fabrics snag or fray easily.

The floats also weaken the strength of the fabric. Once the supporting yarn is broken, the floating yarns come apart. The breakdown of the structure not only causes the fabric to snag and fray, but also causes the fabric to lose its sheen. The loss of sheen is often referred as "deluster" in fabric care industry. If you wear one of these delicate and fragile ties, be sure that you avoid rubbing the tie against rough or hard surfaces and keep the tie away from sharp objects.

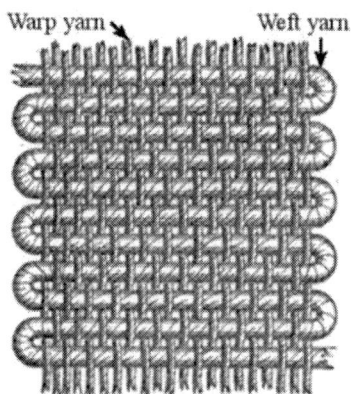

plain weave

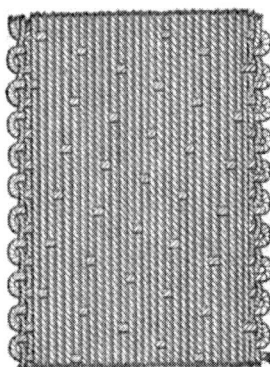

satin weave

Just as you will not wear a tuxedo to work, you should not wear a dressy tie for business unless your work is in entertainment. Several categories of ties are considered dressy and should be worn to a party, to any formal occasion or after 6:00 p.m.

1)   Satin (a basic weave with long warp floats) or Sateen (a weave with long weft floats)
2)   Peau de Soie (a matte-finished satin)
3)   French Natte (a basket weave satin)
4)   Jacquard (satin patterns on a plain background)

If you are unable to recognize the above fabrics, just keep in mind that any fabric that is shiny tends to be dressy. Avoid wearing these groups of ties to work. Or, they may not last.

Wear shimmering ties for evening or party.

7. Better to choke than to be vulgar

Lincoln wearing a sloppy loose collar and a crooked bowtie.

Most Men wear the wrong size collar.

I have sold men's clothing for more than a decade and have been stunned by the fact that a great majority of men wish to wear a dress shirt collar size that is bigger, in many cases far bigger, than their actual neck size. They do so because they feel it is more comfortable this way.

Few men know how to measure the collar width correctly.

Many men do not know their collar size. They often have to ask a salesperson for measurement. It is difficult these days to find a salesperson who knows how to measure correctly. Mortimer Levitt once sent his executives to several of the better men's stores in New York City to have their collar size verified. He then declared, **"Salesmen in the country's best stores do not know how to take a measurement for collar size."** It is even more difficult to find a salesperson who knows how to convert neck size into collar size.

Many fashion publications suggest that the tape must be placed against the Adam's apple when taking the measurement. I doubt the accuracy of this assessment. Not every man has a prominent Adam's apple. Besides, the shirt collar may not sit at the same location as the Adam's apple. No man will enjoy wearing a stiff collar over the Adam's apple.

Most authors also recommend that the collar width is half an inch bigger than the neck size. This is terribly wrong. Many men buy a larger collar for fear that the shirt may shrink. Manufacturers already anticipated the potential shrinkage and added half an inch or more allowance when they made the shirt. A 16 ½" collar on a brand new shirt is actually a 17". As technology improves, manufacturers these days are able to produce shirt collars that guarantee little or no shrinkage.

When a collar becomes too tight, it is probably because the man has gained weight, not because the collar has shrunk too much. If a man changes his weight frequently, don't you think the man is better off to own a few shirts of different sizes so that he will always have the correct size shirts to wear?

Why should a man not wear an oversized collar?

Many men believe that they need extra room around their neck so that they will feel more comfortable and be able to breathe. When the collar is too tight, a man can recognize the problem right away because he can hardly fasten the top button of the shirt. But when the collar is loose, a man may not realize the consequences of wearing a collar that is too big for the neck.

Source: The Archive of the Chancellery of the President of the Republic of Poland, under GNU Free Documentation License (GNU).

Bill Gates wore a collar that was too large.

71

President Obama's collar rose up while Tiger Woods's sank.

First, the collar of the shirt will find a place to rest on the neck. When it is tight, the collar rises up and parallels the chin line. When it is too loose, the collar sinks down not only leaving a big hole at the bottom of the front neck, but also ruining the parallel between the collar line and the chin line.

Second, a raised collar will show a beautiful side-view of the collar wings standing erect on the chest.

Third, the necktie worn on the collar needs to arch out. To arch out a tie, the tie must hug the neck tightly. When the tie is pulled tighter than the collar band, unsightly wrinkles will appear in the collar and shirtfronts. A sunken collar will push down the tie and make it impossible for the tie to erect.

Jay Leno's loose collar puckered when it was squeezed by the tie loop.

Fourth, the chest and waist size of a readymade shirt is cut according to its collar size. The bigger the collar size, the larger the chest and waist size. By wearing a collar that is larger than necessary, the body size of the shirt can be overwhelming for the wearer unless the wearer has a relatively large body.

Fifth, when a man grows older, his neck begins to wrinkle and needs a tall and tight collar front to cover the wrinkles.

Photo by Alan Light

Sixth, a large collar diminishes the head.

Finally, the collar of a fine dress shirt is intentionally made to be stiff--which means not to be comfortable. So, why wear a stiff collar shirt and expect it to be comfortable? This reminds me of the conversation between the young Irish girl, Shannon, and her mother in the movie,

Far and Away. Shannon unfastened the top button of her shirt. Her mother yelled, "Shannon, what is your collar doing?" Shannon replied, "It is choking me." "Well, do it up," said the mother, "Better to choke than to be vulgar."

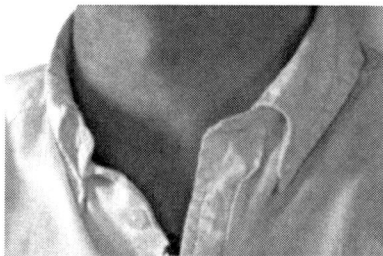

A key difference between a dress and a sport shirt is that the dress shirt has a stiffer collar.

Many men do not fasten the top shirt button, so they think it is irrelevant whether they wear a larger collar. As explained earlier, dress shirts often have a stiff collar. When the top button is unfastened, the collar tends to spring out. The larger the collar is, the farther it will spring out. A customer came to our store to buy dress shirts. I teased him that his collar puckered and looked like the one worn by Thomas Cech in the following photo. I told him that he could make all the dents and wrinkles in his collar disappear. He asked me how. I let him try on a shirt with a collar that was ½" smaller than what he had asked for. He was amazed to notice that his collar became perfectly smooth without any wrinkle or fold. Every time I showed customers the photo of Kobe Bryan, they just could not stop laughing.

Nobel Laureate Thomas Cech, Will Smith and Kobe Bryant's collar sprang out too much, indicating that the collar was too loose.

It is ridiculous to think that a 17" collar is more comfortable to wear than a 16" collar if the man only has a neck of 15". Many men do not even button the collar when wearing a dress shirt. Why do so many men want to wear a collar that is much bigger than their neck? This is incomprehensible.

Over a decade, I have met thousands of customers who came to the store to buy dress shirts. I asked them what size they had in mind. Many customers gave a vague answer, such as "16 or 16 ½ inch." This cannot be right. A half inch makes a big difference. Shirt experts believe that every other man needs a quarter size collars. The collars of readymade dress shirts in today's market are fitted to the half-inch instead of the quarter-inch. This means that many men are forced to wear a collar size that is imperfect. When a man says that he wears both 16" and 16 ½" collars, there is a fair chance that neither size is correct.

Women tend to have a smaller neck; therefore, they may have difficulty finding a closefitting collar. What is the excuse for most men who do not have a small neck?

The stunning beauty of a tall firm-fitting collar

8. Do I need a fitted shirt?

Frequently, I met customers, who wanted to buy fitted shirts. They said they did not like shirts that are too blousy. I wrote a book, entitled *The Stupid Things Men Do about Their Clothing.* One of the most foolish things men do is to buy an oversized dress shirt and ask for a fitted one. Dress shirts are sold by collar width and sleeve length. The body of a dress shirt is based on the collar size. For every inch increase in the collar, the body size increases about four inches. Many men wear a shirt collar that is much larger than their neck. It is no wonder that some of them wish to wear fitted shirts. If they buy the correct collar size, they may not need slim-cut shirts.

Fitted shirts are ideal for men with a relatively large neck, small torso, or both. The body difference between a regular and a fitted shirt of the same collar size is about two inches. For a normal man who is used to wear oversized collars, it is more effective and beneficial to reduce the body size by wearing a smaller shirt collar. The man can cut down the body size by two inches if he buys a collar size that is ½" smaller, or reduce the body size by four inches if he selects a collar that is 1" smaller. Fitted shirts are less common than regular shirts. They tend to have smaller shoulders, which are uncomfortable to wear for a built chest. They may also have a shorter tail, which is less likely to stay tucked in.

Some men have a built upper body. They tend to buy shirts with a larger collar just trying to acquire a larger body size. A better strategy is to buy shirts with a snug collar but with a fuller body cut.

No matter if you have a relatively small or large torso, it is always better to buy shirts with a close-fitting collar and use different cuts to accommodate your specific body shape.

Tom Selleck either wore an oversized shirt
or a correct-sized shirt with a full-cut.

Kevin Costner in a slim-fit (left) and a regular-fit shirt.

9. *Tall collars for long necks.*

Most men worry about the sleeve length and body size when they try on a dress shirt. Fewer men pay attention to the collar width as long as the collar is not tight. Hardly any man will notice that the collar height makes a difference. A man with a long neck needs a tall collar to cover his neck.

The former President (left) and Vice President of South Vietnam needed a tall collar to conceal their long neck.

At one time, it was considered inappropriate for men to expose their bare neck. They wrapped their necks with a variety of neckwear--including neck cloth, scarves, cravats, and modern neckties. George Brummell, the legendary dandy, was famous for wearing crisp neck cloth. His peers could not figure it out how he did it. So they spied on him and found that there was no secret. All he did was to spend half a day to wrap each piece of cloth around his neck one by one until he succeeded. He then walked out of his house. Today, it is no longer a taboo to show a man's neck. Nevertheless, it is not appealing to show a long neck. Any man with a long neck can use a tall collar to make his neck look normal.

In today's market, the normal back height of a shirt collar ranges from 1 $^3/_8$" to 2 ¼". Any man who needs a collar height that is taller than 2 ¼" probably

Collar Back Height

requires his collar be custom made. The contemporary shirt collar is called turned-down collar, in which the collar first stands up from the bottom edge of the neck and then falls down to rest on the garment. The shirt collar is one of the devices to keep a man's neck covered. The collar stand of the modern turned-down collar shirt cannot be cut too high; otherwise, the collar (fold) will be huge. A huge turned-down collar will diminish the size of the head and look unbecoming. If a man needs an extremely tall collar, he should consider

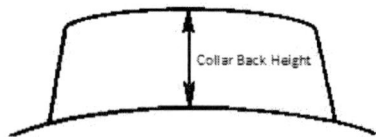

reducing the volume of the collar by wearing a collar with a small or no fold, such as a wing or Mandarin collar. Nevertheless, these types of collars are unpopular in contemporary western world.

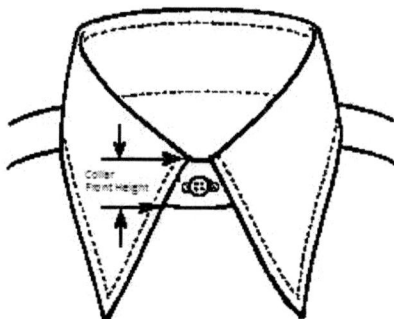

When a man grows older, his neck begins to show wrinkles. The man needs a taller collar front to conceal the wrinkles. The collar front height is usually shorter than the back height to help anchor the collar wings on shirt front. It is not easy to find a tall collar front in readymade shirts unless the man buys a shirt with a tall collar back or has his shirt custom made.

Whatever the situation is, a man should always wear a snug collar. The neck is somewhat like a cone, in which it gets smaller toward the head. A small collar will find a small circumference to settle. Hence, a close-fitting collar tends to rise up and cover more of the neck front. A common mistake with most men is that they wear a collar that is too large for their neck, causing the collar front to sink and expose more of their neck.

The collar height makes a big difference. A short collar makes a long neck look longer whereas a tall collar makes a long neck appear normal.

84

A huge turned-down collar diminishes the size of the head.

Screenshot, fair use.   By Georges Biard, CC-BY-SA 3.0.

A tall turned-down collar also appears large (top left). A man can have a tall collar without appearing huge by eliminating or reducing the size of the turned-down fold.

Top two photos: Karl Lagerfeld, fashion designer.
Bottom left: Viktor Grinard, Nobel Prize winning chemist.
Bottom right: Emilio Aguinaldo, President of the Philippines 1899-1901.

Clint Eastwood can use a tall collar front to conceal the wrinkles in his neck.

10.   *Trust but verify.*

The vast majority of men wear their shirt collars too large. I ended up arguing with almost every man who came to the store to buy dress shirts. After I had presented my case against a loose collar as described in previous chapter, most men were very impressed and changed their mind immediately. Some men still had doubts about my recommendation. They said that they wore shirts the same size or larger than what I recommended and the collars were too tight already. I teased the customers that they were imagining things. I gave them a shirt to try on and showed them how bad the collar looked. Most of them accepted my recommendation and made necessary change. Unless it is mismarked, the actual collar width is almost always larger than what the label indicates. Hence, it is pointless to argue that 'I wear a 17" collar and it is too tight.' When a man says he is wearing a collar size of 17", he probably is not.

The collar of a brand new shirt is ½" larger than the label indicates.

Many consumers buy shirts with a larger collar size for fear that the collar may shrink after washing. They are unaware that it is a custom in the garment industry to make the collar of a brand new shirt ⅜" to ½" larger than what its label indicates. The collar of a brand new shirt labeled 16" tends to be 16 ½". Manufacturers have already anticipated the percent of shrinkage and have made the collar larger than what it was designed to be. There are two kinds of shrinkage. Most of the shrinkage occurs after the garment has been washed or cleaned for the first time. This is called "relaxation shrinkage." The garment will continue to shrink little by little each time it is washed or cleaned. This is called "progressive shrinkage." The collars of better made dress shirts are top fused with one or more layers of interfacing to help keep collars staying crisp. The fused construction also helps prevent or reduce shrinkage. Hence, the collar of a quality dress shirt after repeated washes should not shrink more than ½" unless the collar has been heavily starched many times.

With the dramatic improvements of technology in shirt making, such as the non-iron treatment, many manufacturers have been able to offer shirt collars that guarantee no shrinkage. At the same time, manufacturers continue to give allowance to brand new shirts for shrinkage. This development has created a serious unintended consequence, which is that more men are wearing oversized collars. As fashion trend moves toward more casual and sporty setting, many manufacturers and vendors are offering shirt collars that are ¾" to 1" larger than the label indicates.

If you are measured, make sure that you are measured correctly.

Frequently, I was scolded by customers when I mentioned to them that they were looking for the wrong size dress shirts. They said they had just been measured at another clothing store. Some had their shirts custom made at reputed custom shirt companies. In previous chapter, I have mentioned that Mortimer Levitt once declared, "Salesmen in the country's best stores do not know how to take a measurement for collar size." Mr. Levitt was not exaggerating. Over a decade, I have hardly met a man who was measured correctly. A customer got so upset that he screamed in the store after I told him what size dress shirt he should wear. He said every time he entered a different store, he was told a different size. I taught the man how a shirt should fit and asked him to try on the right size shirt.

He came out of the dressing room with a smile and said to me, "I owe you a sincere apology."

Generally, salespersons in today's fashion industry are poorly trained or not trained at all. Most managers in clothing stores do not know much about men's clothing. They do not know how to tie a bow tie and have never heard about the Oriental knot. They are incapable of training their salespersons even if they want to. Some famous designers and large clothing companies may train their employees to some extent but they often give incorrect information. Ralph Lauren's training manual mistakes yarn size for thread count. Many clothing stores suggest a man should wear a long size jacket if the man is 6' or taller. One of my associates in the men's shoe department told me that he was taught by one of the major shoe companies in the nation that the color of socks should match the color of shoes or pants. He recognized the mistake after he spoke with me but he had sold the wrong socks to customers for decades. Many of my customers are salespersons. They envied my knowledge and mistakenly thought my employer taught me what I knew. Some of them told me that they sold men's clothing for more than 30 years but they had never heard what I taught them.

Once a while, you may meet a salesperson who is knowledgeable. But, he may be unwilling or may not be allowed to tell you all he knows. A retired policeman in the movie, *Double Wedding*, said that "A detective is like a doctor. He is not allowed to tell all he knows." This applies to salespersons. I have been threatened frequently by my superiors not to give certain information or opinions. The primary job of salesmen is to sell you products or services. No salesman will be able to sell you anything if he tells you his products or services are bad. John T. Malloy suggested that one of the main reasons that today's business men dress for failure is that they let their favorite salesclerks choose clothing for them. I am not suggesting that all sales persons are unreliable and you should not trust any of them. I am simply suggesting that you should be careful about the advice you have received. To learn the correct way to measure collar width and sleeve length, please refer to my book, *the Essentials of Dress Shirts*.

The collar is a good fit for a new shirt if the wearer can slip one or two fingers into the gap between the collar and the neck.

It is not always easy to attain the correct collar size by measuring a person's neck with a measuring tape. The neck is somewhat like a cone, in which it gets smaller toward the head. When you measure a person's neck, you may not measure at the same place where the shirt collar will sit. In addition, the slope of the collar can vary among different patterns, styles, brands or makers of the dress shirts. Still, the angle, at which the neck sits on the body, can also vary among different individuals. Since no one can tell how well the collar will rest on a person's neck until the person puts the shirt on, the best way of determining the collar size is to put the shirt on. The collar is a good fit for a new shirt if you can just slip one or two of your fingers (depending on the size of your fingers) into the gap between the collar and your neck. With no-shrinkage collars, you may want to choose a smaller collar size.

Although using a measuring tape may not be the best way, it is the most convenient way to estimate a man's neck size. Mortimer Levitt claimed that salesmen in the country's best stores do not know how to take a measurement for collar size. I doubt that salespeople are so incompetent that they do not know how to put a measuring tape around a person's neck and to take the reading from the tape. My guess is that sales clerks tend to exaggerate the neck size for the same reason that customers want a larger collar size. They all fear that a snug collar will prevent the wearer from breathing comfortably. If the measuring tape reads 16", the salesperson may tell the customer that he needs a 16 ½" or 17" collar. Salespeople in today's retailers are generally poorly trained or not trained at all. If you need to have your neck measured, you may want the measurement to be taken in front of a mirror so that you can see how the salesperson measures your neck. The neck should be measured the same way that you wear your collar. If you decide to follow my suggestion to wear the collar snuggly, it is pointless to have the measuring tape hung loose around your neck.

Many publications do suggest that the tape must be placed against the Adam's apple when taking the measurement for collar width. I doubt the accuracy of this assessment. Not every man has a prominent Adam's apple. Besides, the shirt collar may not sit at the same location as the Adam's apple. I am very sure that no man will enjoy wearing a stiff collar over the Adam's apple. Most authors also recommend that the collar width is half an inch bigger than the neck size. This is terribly wrong. Experts keep misleading readers. This may be the reason that men cannot wear their shirts correctly. They first tell readers to place the measuring tape at the wrong location, and then to add another half an inch to the measurement. Manufacturers already added half an inch or more allowance when they made the shirt. This reminds me of the story about an old man and his three daughters. The old men received a pair of pants that was too long. His first daughter got up at midnight to shorten his pants. His second daughter got up at 1:00 a.m. to shorten his pants again. His third daughter woke up at 2:00 a.m. to do the same. In the morning, the man discovered that his pants became too short to wear.

Some men want to buy shirts with a larger or smaller collar size because they expect or are experiencing weight changes. If you have problems maintaining a steady neck size, I suggest that you stock up with shirts in different collar sizes so that you will have correct size shirts to wear all the time. Life is too short. Why not dress well now? Experts suggest that you should have your neck measured at least once a year.

Some fashion consultants suggest that a fat neck person may wear an oversize collar to make the neck appear smaller. This is nonsense. Neither will look good when a collar is too tight or too loose.

Choose collar width according to the true size, not the label.

Because the true collar size is not the same as what the label indicates, it is useless to buy and wear dress shirts according to the label. Once you find a shirt collar that fits you perfectly, bring out a measuring tape and measure the collar from the center of the button at one end to the center of the buttonhole at the other end. This will give you the actual collar width regardless of what the label reads. Since not every shirt is made the same, you may end up buying shirts labeled in different sizes, especially when the shirts are from different makers.

I once encountered a customer, who came to the store to buy dress shirts with 34" sleeves. I informed the customer that the 36" sleeves would fit him better. He yelled at me and told me that he had one shirt of the same brand with 34" sleeves. The sleeves were perfect. He bought four shirts and brought them back in a few days. He was furious about the sleeves' being too short. He requested an exchange for new shirts with the same 34" sleeves. I told the customer respectfully that it was pointless to exchange for the same sleeve length. The man got angrier and told me that the shirt he was wearing had a sleeve length of 34". I asked him if he was so kind to allow me measuring the sleeve length of his shirt. The sleeve length he was wearing was actually 36" as I had suggested. The shirt was mislabeled for 34" sleeve length.

Many men came to the store to buy dress shirts without knowing their collar size or sleeve length. When I asked them what size they prefer, they requested me to look at the label inside their shirts. I wonder why so many men are careless about the size of their clothing. As explained repeatedly, the size indicated in the label was inaccurate from the start when the shirt was created. Many men use shrinkage as an excuse to buy new shirts with collars that are much larger than their neck. Different manufacturers give different amount of allowance to the collar and sleeves. A piece of cloth does not shrink only at certain areas. It shrinks throughout the entire piece of fabric by percentage. This means that a larger garment may shrink more inches than a smaller garment. It is doubtful, however, every manufacturer is so considerate that they give more shrinkage allowance to larger size garments.

Depending on the quality and the caring of the shirt, each shirt collar may experience different shrinking rate. It is easy to find out the actual shrinkage by measuring the collar width before and after washing. Most men exaggerate the shrinking rate. If a shirt collar shrinks more than half an inch, the shirt is not well made. You should not keep buying the same type of shirts. If you buy a shirt and the collar shrinks to a size that is smaller than what the label indicates, you may have the right to return the shirt to the vendor.

In short, you should be concerned about how each individual collar fits your neck rather than how your collar is labeled.

11. Dress well all the time, not sometime.

After I had explained the advantages of wearing a snug collar, most men agreed to my recommendation. Many men, however, expressed to me that their neck size fluctuates from time to time. They would rather buy shirts with a collar that is slightly larger than their normal size so that they will be able to wear the same shirts all the time. This is a legitimate concern. Many men experience slight weight changes from time to time. To say, a man normally has a neck size of 16" 90% of the time but his neck may grow a little larger the rest of the time. So, the man decides to buy shirts with a 16 ½" collar since a larger collar can fit a smaller neck whereas a smaller collar cannot fit a larger neck. The result is that the man will not look good 90% of the time.

A better approach is to stock shirts with different sizes so that the man will have the correct size shirts to wear all the time. The same strategy also works for other clothing items such as jackets and trousers.

I had a little difficulty to read small prints in front of me through progressive lenses. One of my eye doctors explained to me that my eyes might be unable to adjust quickly from long distance to short distance vision. The optometrist recommended me a Lasik eye surgery. She had her one eye corrected to see long distance while the other eye corrected for short distance so that she always has at least one eye that can see well at any distance. Whereas an eye surgery is a complex matter and requires serious considerations, wearing a dress shirt is a simple act. Unlike a belt, which is adjustable to some degree, most clothing items are nonadjustable in sizes. It is puzzling that few men would ever think about they should prepare themselves with different sizes of clothing. Most men would buy a different size of clothing when they experience significant weight changes. It is silly for a man to wear the same size of clothing when his body changes from time to time.

12.   *Why do some collars bend easily?*

Occasionally, I meet customers who refuse to buy dress shirts of certain brands because the corners of the collar wings bend easily. These are smart shoppers. Most consumers do not notice the problem even if they wear a bent collar.

Why do the two points of the collar wings curve or bend? Three explanations may be made. First, dress shirt collars are traditionally made stiff so that the collars will not bend or wrinkle as the neck moves around. To make the collar stiff, firm layers of interfacing are used to add thickness to the collar. The layers of interfacing are often glued to the top layer of the shirt fabric, called top fused. Collars of some sportier shirts may have a soft layer of interfacing or no interfacing at all. A thin or soft collar tends to curve or bend, especially when the collar wing is long.

Second, the layers of shirt fabric and interfacing are held together by stitching alongside the edge of the collar, called edge stitching, or by stitching at a quarter inch from the edge, called quarter topstitching. Some designers try to make a fashion statement by topstitching at ⅜" or more from the edge. Collar stays are unable to reach the corners of the collar wings. Consequently, the two points of the collar wings tend to curve or bent. Hence, you should avoid any collar with topstitching at more than ¼" unless the collar is made so stiff that it will not curve. On the other hand, some designers make their shirt collars without interfacing and without edge stitching or topstitching. These collars do not have the sharp edge of a decent shirt. They look swollen and puffy. Smart dressers should avoid this type of shirts.

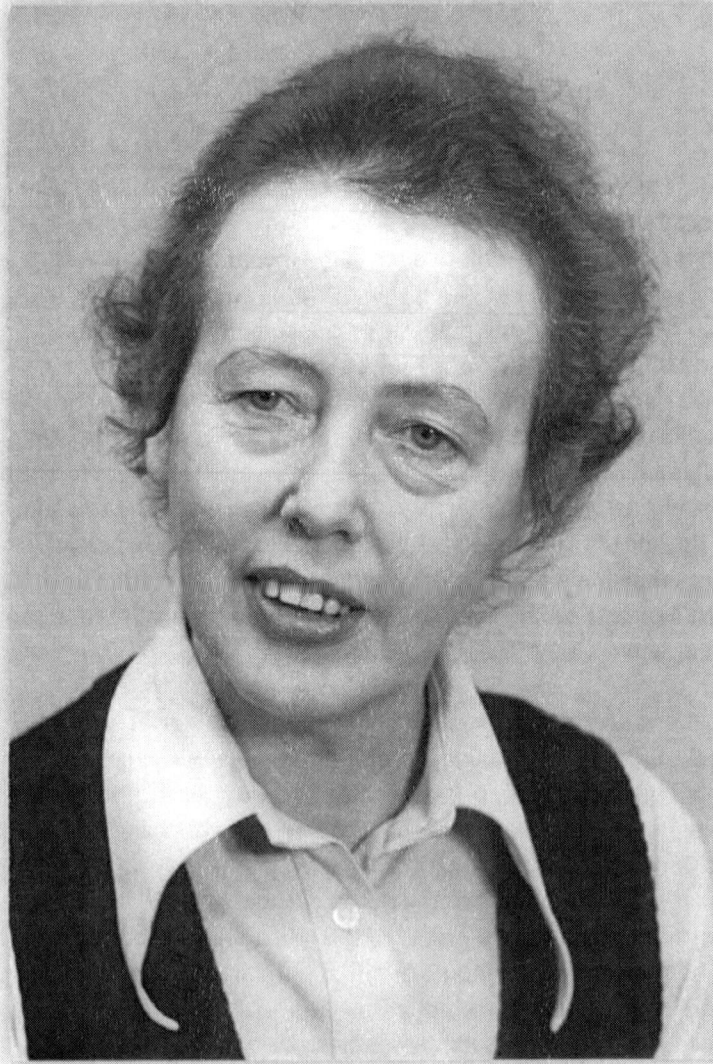

A soft, long collar wing tends to curve or bend easily.

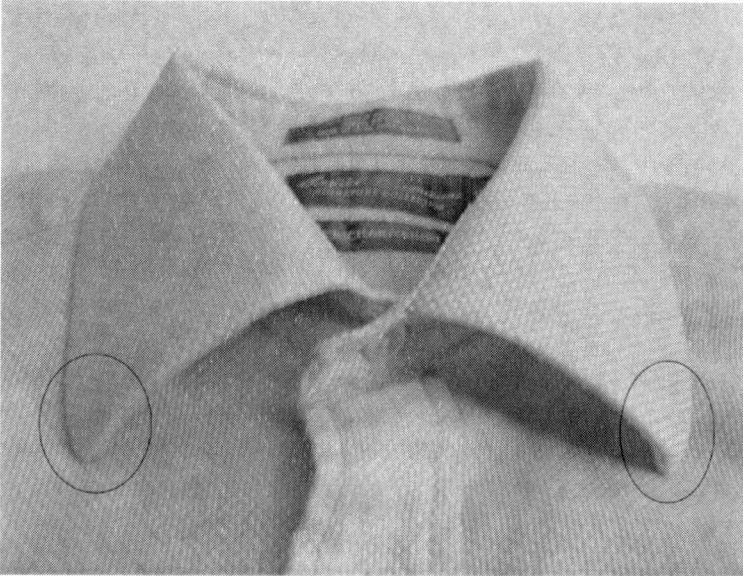

The topstitching is ⅜" away from the edge of the collar, preventing collar stays to reach the tips of the collar points. Consequently, the two points of the collar curve or bend.

The edge of the collar appears puffy or swollen without fused interfacing and topstitching.

Third, the collar is the most difficult part of the shirt to manufacture. Several layers of shell fabric and interlining are sewn together near the edge with the two layers of shell fabric being placed in the middle. The pile of stitched layers, (a), is then turned inside out to form a pointed corner, (b). The areas A and B, shown in figure (3), contain twice more whereas Area C contains four times more layers of fabric than those in the rest part of the collar. This makes Point f very vulnerable to bending, especially when the two lines of topstitching happen to intersect at Point f. Many shirt collars, including top-quality ones, bend easily because the collars are topstitched along the border of the double-thick area. A bent collar is a serious defect. Many shirt manufacturers, however, seem not to notice the problem and continue to produce defected collars. It is wise for consumers to pay attention to such a detail.

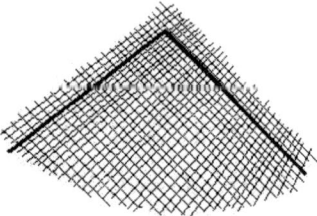

(1)

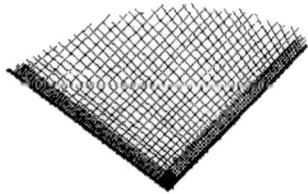

(2)

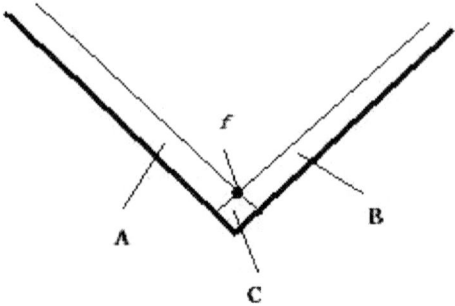

(3)

Button-down collars are usually made with light or no interfacing. They tend not to have a weak spot such as the Point f. In addition, the tip of a button-down collar is fixed to the shirt front by the collar button, reducing its chance to bend. Hence, it is rare to find a button-down collar that bends at the corner.

The corner of the quadruple-thick area is vulnerable to bending especially when it is the intersection of the two topstitching lines and the tip of the collar stay.

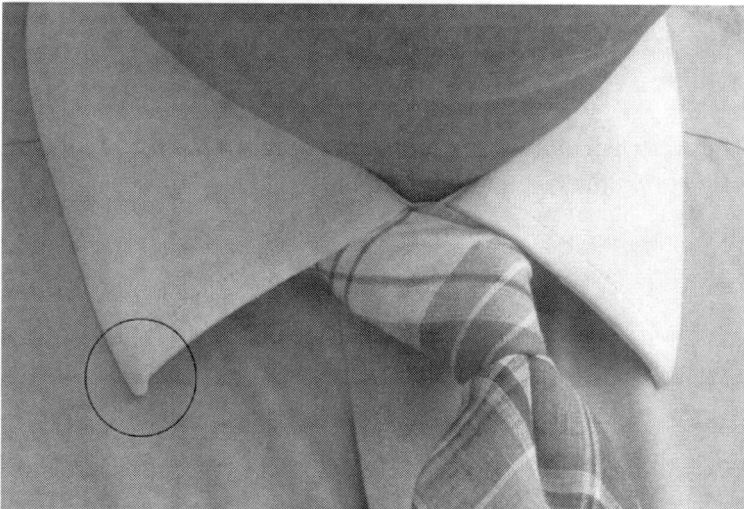

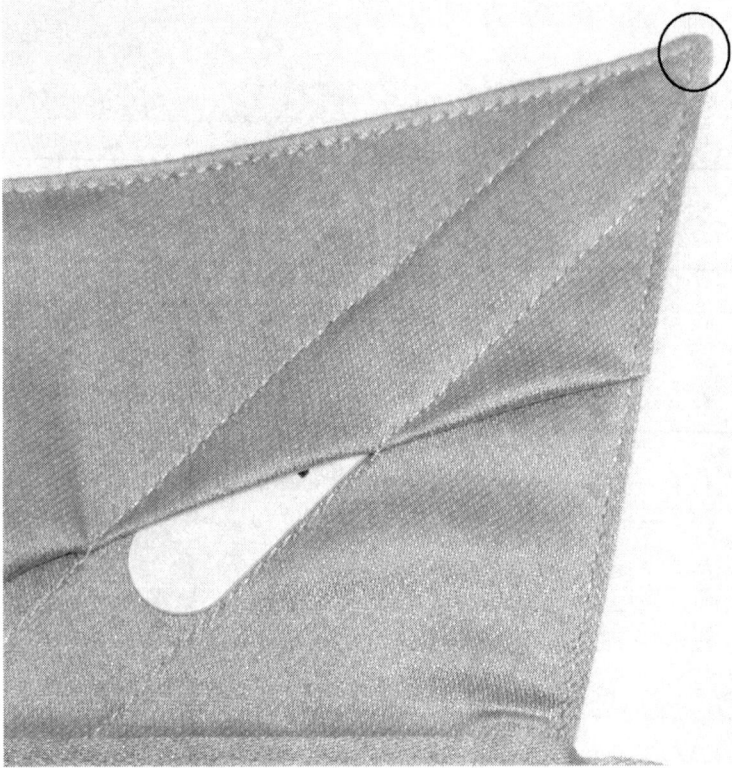

Edge stitching allows the collar stay to reach the tip of collar, preventing the corner from bending.

Journalist, John Stossel, wore a bent shirt collar.

A crisp collar with sharp edges and angles looks very becoming.

106

13. Collar stays—the necessary evil

Robert De Niro must have forgotten his collar stays.

The two points of a turned-down shirt collar should touch the chest front when the top shirt button is fastened. Collar stays are devised to help hold down the collar wings. Most point and spread collars are equipped with removable stays. They should be removed before the shirt is laundered and ironed. Pressing over the collar stays can cause damage to the shirt. Perhaps because of this reason, some manufacturers including famous designers often provide thin plastic stays to avoid or reduce the damage in case that the stays are left in the collar when laundered. Then again, thin collar stays are ineffective to hold down the collar. I suggest the thin stays be replaced with thick ones. Or, you may insert two instead of one thin stay for each collar wing.

Pressing over the collar stay can cause damage to the collar. The photo shows the imprint of the collar stay on a non-iron shirt. The damage could be much worse if the shirt is a regular cotton shirt.

I work in the men's department and frequently meet customers who come to the store to purchase replacement collar stays. It seems common that men lose their collar stays. Currently, there are no standards concerning the size of the stays. The length of the stay is determined by the length of the collar wing. The width and the thickness are subject to shirt manufacturer's interpretation. The most popular width is about $^3/_8$". Some designers may intentionally create stays of a different width just to render a fashion statement. In order to work with all different types of shirts, the universal collar stays tend to be narrower than $^3/_8$". The narrow stays may not work as well as the regular ones.

Different shirt makers often provide collar stays with different width. The same designer may give different widths for different shirts (middle three). The bottom two stays, one plastic and one brass, are universal stays, which tend to be narrow in order to fit most shirts.

Dressy shirts tend to have a stiff collar, which may be able to touch the shirt front without a collar stay if the collar fits the neck properly. Casual dress shirts, on the other hand, often have a soft collar, which may be unable to touch the chest front even with a collar stay. You may have to double the number of stays in order for them to work. Whatever you do, make sure that the stays are installed properly. Or, they may leave undesired marks on the collar.

Screenshot, fair use.

The tiny bump on Leonardo DiCaprio's collar is likely caused by a collar stay that is too long for the collar.

Collar wings bend at the location where the collar stay resides.

14. What is the proper length of a shirt sleeve?

A great number of American working class men do not know their proper sleeve length. Most men, especially the elders, like to wear their sleeves short. Consequently, the sleeves pull back whenever their arms stretch or bend.

From the beginning of ancient civilizations, shirtsleeves were cut straight with a wide opening at the end of the sleeves. Ancient men had to wear their sleeves short so that the fabric would not fall over the hands. Today, dress shirt sleeves are tapered and finished at the end with a band called barrel cuff or buttoned cuff, or finished with a fold called French cuff.

by Alan Light

The sleeve length of a barrel cuff shirt should be longer than the arm.

To wear a barrel cuff shirt correctly, the shirt cuff should fit snugly around the wrist to keep sleeve length from falling over the hand. Because the tight fit around the wrist will restrict arm movement, additional sleeve length must be added to the sleeve to allow the arm to stretch or bend without pulling the cuff. This additional sleeve length will hang above the wrist area and is called "drape". When the cuff fits snugly and the sleeve is long enough, the arm will be able to move in any direction without affecting how the cuff sits on top of the wrist. Thus, the shirt cuff and hand will move as a unit.

The proper sleeve length is affected by the width of the cuff. If you can find a barrel cuff that fits your wrist snugly, add one inch to your correct arm length for "drape." This will give you the sleeve length. If you have a built chest, you may want to add another ½" because the large chest will lift the shirt's armhole up into the armpit. If you wear a suit or sport coat, you may also consider wearing a slightly longer sleeve because the jacket may sometimes hold up the sleeve.

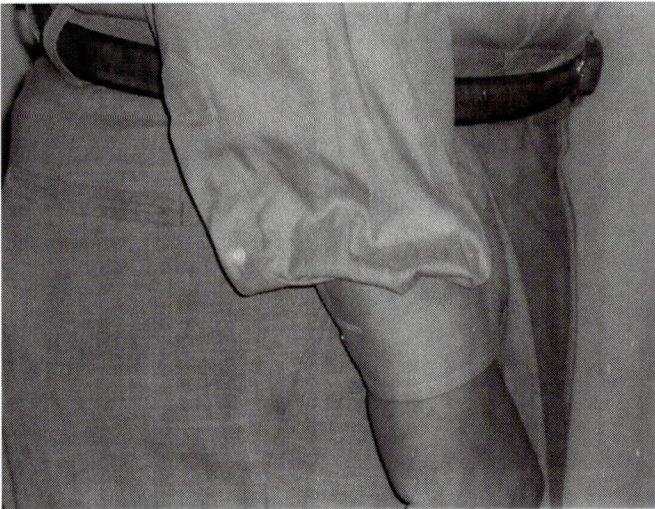

If worn correctly, a barrel cuff will not retreat with the jacket sleeve when the arm stretches or bends.

15. Control your sleeve cuffs!

Bill Gates' sleeves retreat because the cuffs are too large, the sleeves are too short or both.

by Mathieu Scroussi, CC-BY-SA 3.0

The shirtsleeve is designed to cover the arm, not the hand. In any condition, you should never allow the shirtsleeve to extend beyond the wrist--where the hand and arm meet.

In the past, dress shirts were made in the tailor shop. A tailor would measure a person's wrist width and determined how big the cuff should be. In today's market, shirts are made not to fit an average person but to fit most consumers. Hence, the width of the barrel cuff in most readymade dress shirts tends to be too large for an average person. I have observed that the barrel cuff in some fashion designers' brands is sometimes cut so large that it loses the purpose of having a cuff. A large cuff will cause the additional sleeve length to fall over the hand and hinder the hand movement if the sleeve is long.

Readymade dress shirts are sold in stores according to the collar size and sleeve length. Every man buys dress shirts according to his neck size and arm length. I have never met a man who will give any thought about the cuff width. Many men fear that the shirtsleeve will fall over the hand if the sleeve is longer than the arm length. Instead of dealing with the problem correctly by controlling the cuff width, they wear sleeves short without drape.

If you choose a barrel cuff, you should wear a sleeve length that is at least one inch longer than your arm length to allow your arm to stretch without pulling the cuff. The key is to fit the cuff snugly around your wrist to prevent the sleeve from falling over your hand. If you can slide your hand through the cuff opening without first unfastening the button, the cuff is too large and the additional sleeve length will definitely hang over your hand.

If you cannot find a shirt cuff that fits your wrist snugly, consider sending the shirt to a tailor to have the cuff altered. Or, you can simply move the button yourself to make the cuff fit. If you are unwilling to try either option, you may have to wear a shorter sleeve length.

If you wear a wristwatch or bracelet, consider the watch or the jewel a part of your wrist and adjust your cuff width accordingly. Some people wear the watch or bracelet outside the shirt cuff instead of hiding the jewel under the sleeve. It is showy and may damage the sleeve or jewel by friction.

16.   *You need only one button on your shirt sleeve.*

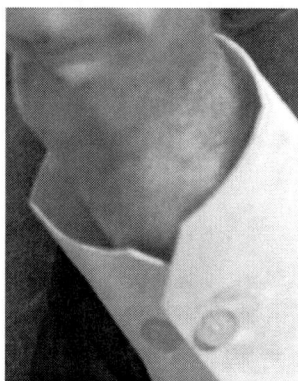

Prince Albert once said, "A gentleman will take care that his clothes are of the best quality, well-made and **suitable to his rank and position**." It is hard to believe that Prime Minister Blair wore a cheap shirt. What is worse is that he fastened the wrong button, leaving a large gap between the hand and the sleeve. President Reagan wore correctly a tight barrel cuff with one button showing.

Better made dress shirts are generally sold in exact sleeve length. Some dress shirts come with a so-called average sleeve length, such as 32-33", 34-35", and 36-37". The term, average sleeve length, is somehow misleading because the sleeve length 32-33" is actually a 33", sleeve length of 34-35" is a 35", and so forth. A 32-33" was designed to fit both a person with a 32" sleeve length and a person with a 33" sleeve length. You may think a 33" is going to be too long for a person who needs only a 32" sleeve. This is how it works. There are two horizontal buttons on the cuff of an average sleeve shirt. If a person needs a 32" sleeve and wears a 32-33" sleeve, he can button the second button. It is possible that some manufacturers may produce a true average sleeve length, to say, a 32 ½" for a 32-33" sleeve. Sport shirts that come with a small, medium, large or extra-large size are usually equipped with two horizontal buttons on the sleeve.

Many customers told me that they need a 35" sleeve length. The 34-35" sleeve is too short. It is a custom in the garment industry to give a brand new shirt ½" to ⅝" allowance in sleeve length to compensate for the shrinkage after the shirt is repeatedly washed or cleaned. Some manufacturers may not provide the allowance for an average sleeve length shirt since the allowance will make the sleeve be too long for persons who need a shorter length. Therefore, it is possible that a 34-35" sleeve is shorter than a 35" sleeve.

Many men prefer fancy dress shirts and have their shirts starched or pressed regularly. It is unconvincing to show how much you care about your shirt with two buttons on the sleeve, which is a mark of convenience and indolence. A man needs only one horizontal button on his shirt sleeve. If you occupy a high position in your workplace or community, or if you simply like to dress up, you may consider removing one of the two buttons. No one will notice that you wear an average sleeve length shirt when there is only one button on the cuff.

17. Why is the sleeve length of a French cuff shirt different from that of a barrel cuff shirt?

A French cuff is made differently from the barrel cuff. The French cuff usually has a large opening and requires a cufflink to close the opening. When you wear a barrel cuff sleeve, the extra sleeve length will drape right above the wrist area owing to the tight fit of the cuff. But if you wear a French cuff sleeve and if the sleeve is long, the extra sleeve length will fall over the hand because of the wide opening at the cuff. That is why you should always wear the French cuff sleeve shorter than the barrel cuff sleeve. Nevertheless, I have never met any customer who buys different sleeve lengths for these two different cuff shirts.

Most men prefer a barrel cuff to a French cuff shirt. A barrel cuff can be closed simply by fastening the button already sewn on the cuff, but a French cuff requires a cufflink to fasten it.

The French cuff looks elegant if it is worn with a suit or sport coat. The French cuff fills the gap between the coat sleeve and the hand with the wide and bulky cuff. On the other hand, the barrel cuff leaves a large gap between the coat sleeve and the shirtsleeve because of the narrow opening of the barrel cuff. When you wear a suit or sport coat, your shirtsleeve should extend beyond the end of the coat sleeve about ¼" to ½". As the arm stretches, the barrel cuff shirtsleeve stays at the

123

wrist but the coat sleeve retreats, exposing several inches of the shirtsleeve--which is unbecoming. If you wear a French cuff without drape and if you stretch your arm, the shirt cuff will retreat along with the coat sleeve and maintains its ¼" to ½" extension beyond the coat sleeve.

If you desire a French cuff shirt, wear the sleeves short without drape. Otherwise, the opening of the cuffs will soon wear out or get marked with sweat stain because the cuffs rub against hands constantly. Some manufacturers market average sleeve length French cuff shirts. Unlike an average sleeve length barrel cuff shirt that has two horizontal buttons, an average sleeve length French cuff shirt will have two vertical buttonholes on the inner layer of the cuff. The manufacturers expect the wearer to adjust sleeve length by using one of these two buttonholes. Nevertheless, the distance between the two holes hardly ever exceeds ½".

Many men wear both barrel and French cuff shirts. Few of them know that the proper sleeve length of a French cuff shirt is different from that of a barrel cuff shirt. Some men have a bizarre idea that the sleeve length of a French cuff should be longer than that of a barrel cuff. Alan Flusser claimed that 90% of all men wear their jacket sleeves too long. This makes it impossible or difficult for the barrel cuff sleeves to show. Some men believe that the French cuff shirt is dressier than the barrel cuff shirt; therefore, they wear longer French cuff sleeves so that the shirt sleeves can stick out under the jacket sleeves. They fail to realize that both barrel and French cuff sleeves should extend beyond the jacket sleeves and no shirt sleeve should fall beyond the wrist. The correct way is to cut short the jacket sleeves.

In order for the French cuff sleeve to function correctly, it should be worn short.

18.   *Wear double-sided cufflinks.*

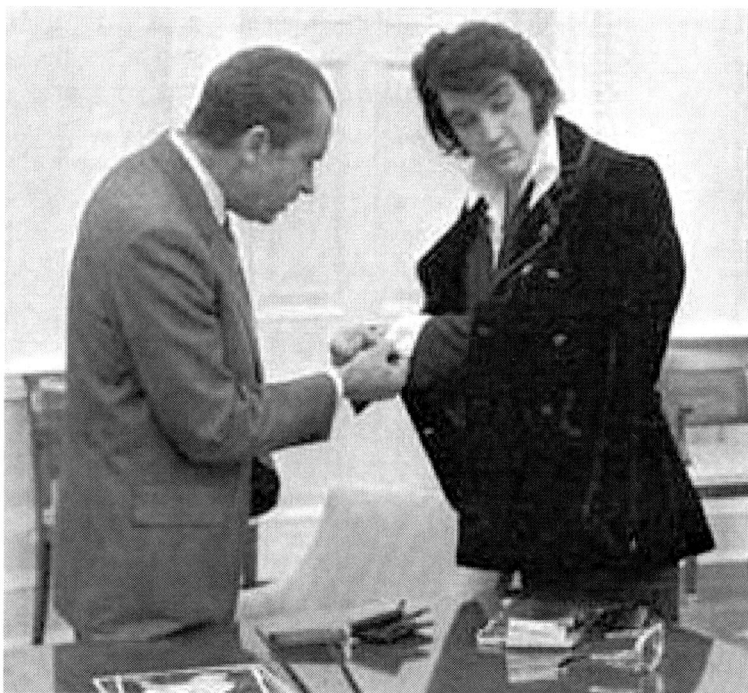

Present Nixon admired Elvis's cufflinks.

Frenglish cuff sleeves are fastened with a pair of cufflinks. Wikipedia describes the styles of cufflinks.

> Cufflink designs vary widely. The simplest design consists of a short post or chain connecting two disc-shaped parts. The part positioned on the most visible side is usually larger; a variety of designs can connect the smaller piece: It may be small enough to fit through the button hole like a button would; it may be separated and attached from the other side; or it may have a portion that swivels on the central post, aligning with the post while the link is threaded through the button-hole and swiveling into a position at right angles to the post when worn.

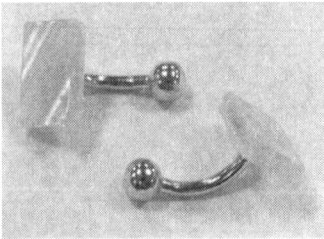

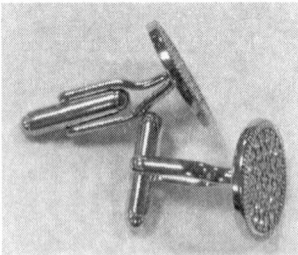

In general, cufflinks can be classified into two groups, the one-sided and the two-sided. If a man cannot afford both sides, suggest some fashion experts, he can forget wearing cufflinks. Nonetheless, most cufflinks sold in the market are one-sided.

One-sided links

two-sided links

Two-sided cufflinks are uncommon and costly. If you cannot find a pair at a price you are willing to pay, you can make one by yourself. All you have to do is to find two buttons and connect them with a few strings. So, what is the excuse not to wear a pair of two-faced links?

A prominent designer put the image of a two-faced cufflinks on one of his 7-fold ties perhaps because the double-sided link is a symbol of good taste.

I have worked at a reputed department store chain for more than a decade. I have seen only one style of double-sided cufflinks for one season. A customer returned a pair of this double-sided links, complaining about his being unable to thread the face of the link through the buttonhole. The customer preferred a pair of single-faced links for its being easy to use. I wonder why the customer did not simply enlarge the buttonholes to accommodate a pair of good cufflinks. It is rare to find a pair of double-faced links. Why give up so easily?

The main purpose of the cufflinks is to fasten the shirt cuffs. Hence, they should be simple and elegant, advised fashion experts. If you like gems, buy real ones. Some French cuff shirts come with a pair of cufflinks. They are generally not in good quality. You may want to replace them with a pair of good quality ones.

Screenshot, fair use.
Clark Gable wearing double-sided cufflinks.

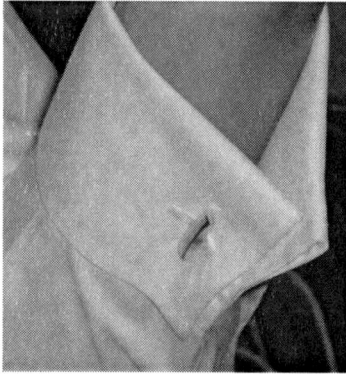

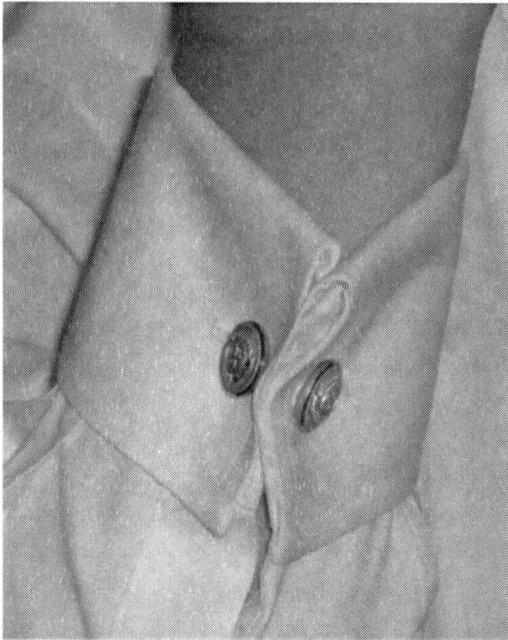

An overwhelming number of cufflinks in the market are single-sided (above photos). Don't you think it is a golden opportunity for you to dress differently and better than other men by wearing a pair of double-sided links (bottom photo)?

19.   Which is worse, a larger collar or shorter sleeve?

Frequently, I meet men with a small neck and long arms. These men should have their dress shirts custom made but most of them would rather buy readymade shirts because custom shirts are much more expensive and take time to produce. Most men do not know how precisely a dress shirt should fit. They often wear wrong size shirts without noticing the problem. It is common that a man with a 15" neck wears a 16 ½" or 17" collar because he is unable to find a 15" collar with a 36" or 37" sleeve length to cover his long arms.

Which is worse between a shirt with a larger collar, perfect sleeves and a shirt with a perfect collar, shorter sleeves? Fashion experts suggest that the collar is the most important part of a shirt. When the top button of the shirt is fastened, the collar frames the wearer's face. Despite this advice, almost every man and woman, whom I encountered, preferred a wrong collar with a correct sleeve length to a correct collar with a wrong sleeve length. It is understandable why they would rather err on the side of longer sleeves. It is noticeable when the sleeves are too short but it is not immediately obvious when the collar is too large.

As explained in previous chapters, the ideal length of a barrel cuff sleeve should be one or two inches longer than the length of the arm. The extra length is called "drape." The purpose of the drape is to prevent the sleeve cuff from retreating when the arm bends or stretches. Because a man does not bend or stretch his arms most of the time, the extra length can be forsaken. In other words, a man can wear his barrel cuff sleeves slightly short without drape, the same way he wears his French cuff sleeves. A man, who needs a 15" collar and 34" sleeves, may be better off to choose a shirt with a 15" collar and 33" sleeves instead of a shirt with a 15 ½" collar and 34" sleeves if the correct size is unavailable. Between the collar and sleeves, it may be wise to sacrifice the sleeves as long as the sleeves are not two inches or more too short.

Like Tiger Woods, many men never realize their collar is too large.

A risen shirt collar (top photos) brings the beauty of the jacket to the fore whereas a sunken shirt collar (bottom photos) does not. It may be better to have a perfect shirt collar, imperfect sleeves than to have an imperfect collar, perfect sleeves.

Most men worry about their shirt sleeves' being too short. In truth, a shorter sleeve may not look worse than a larger collar.

20. *What do these numbers mean?*

80's Non-Iron Pinpoint
100% COTTON

100's Dobby
100% Cotton

120's Twill
100% Egyptian Cotton
Made in China / RN 58909

STANEY SHIRT
170's Two-Ply Cotton

SUPER 120'S
ROYAL GABARDINE

Manufacturers spend millions of dollars each year to put yarn size information on the label of shirts, pants, and suits but they never bother to communicate with consumers about the meaning of the terms.

Consumers seem to know little about yarn size. When they see *"80's* 2-ply" in the label on a shirt, some of them will think "*80's*" means thread count per square inch is 80, whereas others will assume the shirt is made of 80% cotton despite the label also says "100% cotton." Shirt makers every so often provide yarn information on better quality dress and sport clothing, but they seldom explain what the term means. This gives consumers opportunities to speculate. Consumers often make wrong interpretations and buy the wrong items. Many famous fashion experts also misinterpret the yarn information and give consumers wrong advice.

What is 80's 2-ply?

Manufacturers of bed sheets put thread count information on each package of their products. The practice is so successful that most consumers know what thread count means. Consumers are obsessed with the thread count. They tend to relate any number found in the product labels to thread count. Even professionals in the fashion industry mistake yarn size for thread count. In several spring 2005 issues of Ralph Lauren's publication, *Polo Revue*, *80s/2-ply* was defined as "80 horizontal and 80 vertical threads per square inch and two plies of yarn twisted together before weaving." This definition is terribly inaccurate.

The designation, *80's,* is a measurement of yarn size, also known as yarn number or yarn count. Yarn is measured in terms of length per unit of weight: the higher the number, the finer is the actual yarn. In cotton, a *1*'s yarn has 840 yards per pound; a *10*'s yarn runs 8400 yards. The count is inversely proportionate to the size of the yarn. Hence, a *100*'s yarn is ten times finer than a *10*'s yarn. The term, *80's* 2-ply, means two single *80*'s yarns are twisted together to yield a *40*'s yarn.

A book presented by AskMen.com in 2007, *The Style Bible*, discusses the thread counts in shirts and suits.

[Shirt] Thread Count

> The higher, the better. Premium shirts can exceed 200 threads per square inch, but there's no need to go crazy here. Any count above 140 will put you into pretty nice territory.

Suit Thread Counts

> Thread counts are often attributed to linens, but many fail to realize that suits too benefit from a high thread count. The thread count of a suit not only determines its price (the higher the thread count, the more expensive it obviously is), but it also determines the quality and level of comfort of the fabric. First and foremost, it is important to note that in the world of suiting, thread count is referred to as the "Super" number. The finest "Supers" (in the range of 450) are extremely delicate and should be avoided by those who can't afford to replace their suits every year. For a more practical approach to suit-buying, men should stick to wool suits with a count in low hundreds. They're the most durable and provide quite a comfortable feel.

The author is the one who failed to realize that the "Super" number is a designation of yarn size, not thread count. The thread count information is not as important as yarn size in judging the quality of a fabric. The reason that a piece of fabric has a higher thread count is because the threads are finer. It is easier for a weaving machine to squeeze more threads into a fabric if the threads are thin. Today a piece of mediocre fabric has a thread count of 180 or more. Hence, it is ridiculous to suggest that consumers should buy a garment with a thread count around 140. A garment with a thread count of 140 will be terrible in quality. I doubt such a garment even exists unless the garment is made of extremely coarse yarns. Super 450 wool yarns do not exist under current technologies. It is absurd to claim that the finest "supers" are in the range of 450.

Some fabrics are made of yarns of different sizes to create textured surface. Oxford cloth, for instance, is woven in a basket weave by interlacing two thin warp yarns with every thicker weft yarn. Manufacturers often provide a set of yarn information only to indicate the size of the smallest yarns in the fabric, but not the size of other thicker yarns.

Is a higher yarn number always desirable?

Manufacturers often boast that their shirts are made of "fine", "finest" or "most luxurious" yarns. These adjective words are meaningless and may mislead consumers. You should judge the quality of a fabric or garment based on the industrial standards. A 50's single-ply yarn is finer than a 40's single. Consumers and fashion experts may consider that finer yarns are better in quality. I must caution readers to rethink the meaning of "quality." If a person claims that an *80*'s yarn is better in quality than a *50*'s yarn, he probably bases his judgment on the fact that an *80*'s yarn is more difficult to produce and therefore is more expensive. Consumers and fashion experts seldom realize that finer yarns are also weaker yarns.

A customer bought a designer's dress shirt made of *100*'s 2-ply yarns. A price tag was attached to the shirt through the buttonhole with a plastic string. The customer pulled the price tag, hoping to break the string without using a pair of scissors. He instead created a three-inch-long tear on the shirt. Interestingly, the shirt was not damaged at the buttonhole but was torn about an inch away from the buttonhole. Another customer returned a similar shirt with a five-inch-long tear near a buttonhole. Apparently, this customer also pulled the price tag string. Perhaps the tear would not occur if the two shirts were made of thicker yarns such as *40's* 2-ply.

There are extremely fine yarns available in the market, such as *200's* and above. Yarns in such a fine grade are very expensive and are therefore used only in custom tailored shirts. But what is the point to wear a cotton shirt in such a fine grade? The shirt will wrinkle as soon as it is put on. The shirt wears out easily and may have other complications. The store, where I work, once carried a line of dress shirts in the 1990s made of *140's* two-ply yarns. Few consumers know how to appreciate such extraordinary products, causing the company to discontinue the merchandise. I asked the store manager why the products were closed out. The manager replied that the dress shirts were poor in quality because they shrank too much.

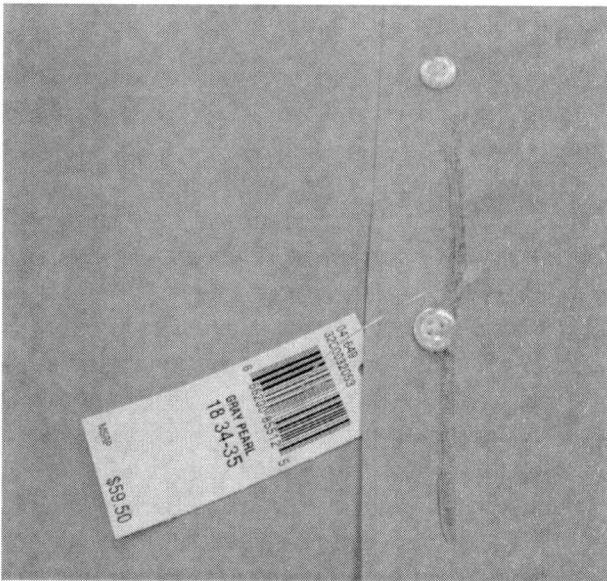

A customer pulled the price tag string and created a five-inch-long tear on a 100's 2-ply shirt.

SUPER 100'S
KING'S CLOTH

SUPER 140'S
EMPEROR'S TWILL

A manufacturer put humor into its labels, suggesting that super 100's is for the king and 140's for the emperor. Uninformed consumers probably can figure it out that 140's is better than 100's since emperors are greater than kings.

Jeans are made of 100% cotton. They do not wrinkle easily because they are made of thick *10*'s to *20*'s yarns. No manufacturer will make jeans with *80*'s 2-ply yarns only because *80*'s yarns are finer or better in quality. Garment producers choose yarns of different sizes to make various types of garments for specific purposes and functions. Industrial standards are therefore established. I once spotted a line of dress shirts made of *60*'s single yarns. This is a big world. There always are courageous and innovative shirt makers who will take risk to market dress shirts that go beyond the ordinary. Although their intention may be noble, their efforts are doomed to fail because they never educate consumers about the uniqueness of their products. How will consumers be able to distinguish the excellent from the mediocre? I would consider any cotton fabric that is made of yarns finer than 50's single or *80*'s double-ply a fine or luxurious fabric. Eventually, you may be lucky to find a shirt made of *100*'s or finer yarns. The shirt is like a piece of gold or diamond in jewelry. Give it a good consideration. It is a joy to be able to experience the best product that human technology can ever achieve. On the other hand, ultra fine yarns are very delicate. If a man is unwilling to give special cares, he has no business to complain about why expensive shirts lose shape or tear easily.

For fine wool, the S number is given a new meaning by representing the thickness of fiber instead of the thickness of yarn.

The yarn size in wool is calculated differently from the yarn size in cotton. The current yarn number system dates back to the 18th century in England, known as the worsted count system. In those days finished yarns were coiled into 560-yard-long loops called hanks. The yarn number indicated how many hanks could be drawn out of a pound of wool. The yarn count ran from *30's* to *100's*, which was the finest wool yarn available at the time. Contemporary fashion writings often give incorrect information. Esquire's *The Handbook of Style* mistakenly declares that the thinnest wool yarn is called Super 100's. Today a *100's* wool yarn is no more than an ordinary wool yarn.

The worsted count was originally devised as a rough and indirect measurement of yarn thickness. Today the S number system continues to be used as a measurement of fiber instead of yarn thickness. Nevertheless, there is a rough correspondence between the historical worsted count and the modern S number system. Fiber that yielded about 100 worsted hanks is roughly comparable to fiber designated as 100's using the S numbers.

The S number is now a direct measurement of average fiber diameter in microns and fiber distribution in standard deviations. The International Wool Textile Organization (IWTO) is the promulgator of the Fabric Labeling Code of Practice which governs the use of the "S" and "Super S" designations for fine wool and wool blend fabrics. Based on IWTO's specifications, President Bush signed into law in December 2006 *The Wool Suit Fabric Labeling Fairness and International Standards Conforming Act*, which amended *The Wool Products Labeling Act of 1939* to revise the requirements for labeling of certain wool and cashmere products. Under this Act, effective January 1, 2007, wool fabric claims must comply with a table matching a product's maximum average fiber diameter to particular quality claims involving the use of the descriptions "Super X" and "X" in advertising. Thus, a wool fabric labeled Super 100's must have an average fiber diameter of 18.75 microns or finer, or the product shall be "misbranded."

Does the Super S and S number mean much? A fashion writer, Nicholas Antongiavanni, wrote the following in an article in *The American* magazine.

The rise of the Supers was not without controversy. "Count" was never meant to be a precise measure of the fineness of individual fibers; it was merely a quick-and-dirty way for wool buyers to separate the good from the very good. Once the number became a selling point for consumers, problems of definition arose. What did "Super 120s" really signify, and did every suit claiming the honor actually deserve it? The more fundamental problem was that no one could say what cloth deserved any particular Super designation at all . . . But the larger controversy has never gone away. Are the Supers really that great? Is the width of fibers the most important thing one needs to know about wool? The weavers of Yorkshire and the cloth merchants of London don't think so. Talking to them, one hears over and over the contemptuous phrase "numbers game" used to belittle the Supers phenomenon. "There's more to wool than fiber diameter," says Graham of Smith Woolens. "There's the length of fibers [longer is better], crimp [i.e., waviness; more of it gives strength and resilience], consistency from one end of a strand to

144

the other, the amount and quality of lanolin and natural oils—and so much more. And that's before you even get to how the cloth is woven and finished, all of which has a huge impact on the quality of the final product."

Fibers are useless until they are drawn into yarns, from which fabrics and garments can be made. The quality of yarns is not less important than the quality of fibers. If the wool textile industry believes that the thickness of fibers is significant, why can the industry use the microns to indicate the diameter of fibers? The use of S numbers to describe fiber diameter is not only redundant, but also confusing.

Fabrics made of super fine yarns are irritatingly prone to become shiny or to wear through. They also tear and wrinkle more easily. According to *the Table of Maximum Fiber Diameters,* 17.75-micron wool fibers can be used to produce Super *120's* fabrics. Theoretically, the laws allow manufacturers to use the same fibers to produce coarser fabrics, or to produce the same fabrics but label the fabrics at a lower S number such as Super *100's* or *90's.* In such cases, the S numbers will not be an accurate indicator of yarn or fiber thickness. It is wise that consumers should not overly rely on the S numbers in judging the worth of any particular wool fabric or garment since the yarn or S numbers are barely the most important quality indicator.

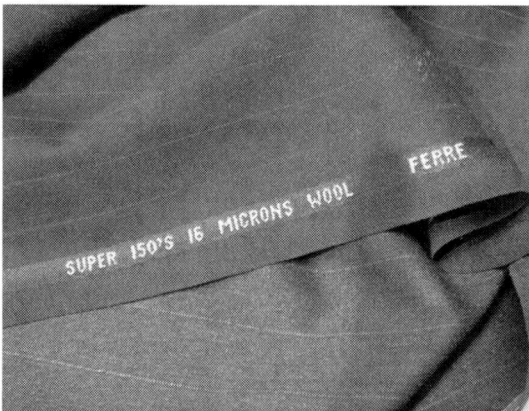

A Super 150's fabric made of 16-micron wool--a compliance with the Wool Products Labeling Act.

Photo by Teslar, GNU

Table of Maximum Fiber Diameters

Super S or S Number	Average Fiber Fineness
Super 80's	19.75 microns
Super 90's	19.25 microns
Super 100's	18.75 microns
Super 110's	18.25 microns
Super 120's	17.75 microns
Super 130's	17.25 microns
Super 140's	16.75 microns
Super 150's	16.25 microns
Super 160's	15.75 microns
Super 170's	15.25 microns
Super 180's	14.75 microns
Super 190's	14.25 microns
Super 200's	13.75 microns
Super 210's	13.25 microns
Super 220's	12.75 microns
Super 230's	12.25 microns
Super 240's	11.75 microns
Super 250's	11.25 microns

The fineness of wool is measured in microns.

The wool industry uses micron as a measurement of fiber diameter. A micron is one millionth of a meter. The average diameter of wool fibers is about 18 microns, whereas the average human hair is about 70 microns wide. Through careful selective breeding, diet and environment control, wool farmers in Australia and New Zealand now can produce superfine wool that is thinner than 12 microns. At an auction in Sydney in March 2004, a Chinese company purchased an 11.9-micron bale of wool for $675,000. Eight years earlier, a Japanese textile firm AOKI achieved international notoriety by purchasing a 13.3-micron bale for $1.2 million, a world record. The finest bale of wool ever auctioned sold for a quarter of a million during June 2008. The bale measured 11.6 microns.

Despite that wool producers are enthusiastic about what they can achieve, the number of microns may not mean much for consumers. A pile of 12-micron wool is unnecessarily better in quality than a pile of 18-micron wool. Diameter is just one quality component. Length, strength, color, crimp, and cleanliness are also important factors in judging the quality of wool. As the textile division president of Ermenegildo Zegna, Paola Zegna, pointed out, "You can have a good 15 micron wool or a bad 15 micron wool."

Manufacturers often use words, such as fine, extra fine, superfine, and ultra fine, to describe the wool fibers in their garments. These words mean little if you do not know the exact range of microns. In general, wool fibers smaller than 25 microns are made into clothing, whereas coarser grades are used for other textiles such as blankets, insulation, rugs and other furnishings.

The finest fibers are useless until they are drawn into yarns. Hence, the length and the strength of the fibers are crucial. Whereas the diameter of fiber may contribute to the softness of the fabric, it is the length and the strength of the fiber that make the super yarn possible. To make a super thin yarn, the fibers must be twisted very tightly. The longer and stronger the fiber, the finer the yarn that can be spun and twisted from it. Garment makers often provide information about the size of the yarns but not the fineness of the fibers. Theoretically, long or thin fibers can be drawn and twisted into coarse yarns. But manufacturers are unlikely to do so because fine quality fibers are pricey. Therefore, it is reasonable to assume that fine yarns are made of thin fibers.

The term, Super, has its specific definition.

The S number is often used in conjunction with the term, super. Some authors claim that the word "super" stands for merino wools. This definition is inaccurate even though most good quality wool garments are made of merino wools these days. The textile industry has the tendency of using the term super to describe something that is extraordinary. The word super originally meant the best wool. The trend started when a merchant, Joseph Lumb & Sons, decided that "the advent of 100s-count wool was an event worthy of note. Lumb bought an entire year's lot of the wool and, in partnership with the cloth merchant H. Lesser, brought to market suitings dubbed 'Lumb's Huddersfield Super 100s,'" wrote Nicholas Antongiavanni. The term is now widely used to describe the new breed of ultra-lightweight, high twisted wools, pioneered by Italian mills not a long time ago. The term loses its practical usefulness when almost everything becomes super these days.

In 2000, the International Wool Textile Organization (IWTO) finally reached agreement on the definition of the Super "X" claim. The agreement restricts the use of the term Super to be used only on pure new wool fabrics and on blends with natural fibers, namely rare hairs (such as mohair, cashmere wool, alpaca) and silk. The addition of elastane to give the fabric a stretch effect and the addition of up to 5% non-wool yarn for a decorative effect are permitted.

For wool blends, the use of word "Super" is prohibited. The S numbers, such as "100's Wool blended with polyester," is allowed, provided that there should be a minimum of 45% new wool in the blended fabric.

If you find the above information interesting and would like to learn more about fibers, yarns and fabrics, please read *What Fashion Experts Teach You Wrong or Did Not Teach You about Fabrics*, by Ivan M.C. Chen.

21. Are fabrics made of 2-ply yarns better than those made of single-ply yarns?

A woman asked for cashmere sweaters. I showed her some of the best sweaters in the market. The woman looked at the label and laughed, "It is not 2-ply." She then disappeared in a flash. I wonder why the woman wanted a woolen fabric that is made of 2-ply yarns and how she knew the sweater is not made of 2-ply yarns--the label does not indicate what type of yarns. In his book, *Style and the Man*, Alan Flusser wrote the following.

> Better dress shirts are made in two-ply cotton or two-fold yarns, less expensive ones in single-ply. Cotton-poly blends are never two-ply, therefore these fabrics tend to be found only in cheaper shirts . . . Since two-ply dress shirts are costlier, most manufacturers will include this designation on the label. If it is not so designated, it usually means the shirt is of a single-ply fabric and its cost should reflect this.

Both the woman and Flusser misunderstood the purpose of using a two-ply yarn. If the woman knew why the manufacturers use 2-ply or 3-ply yarns instead of 1-ply yarns, she would not have laughed. Fine fabrics are made of thin threads. But it is difficult to weave a thick fabric with thin threads. Manufacturers have a brilliant idea by twisting two or more thin threads together to form a thicker yarn known as a "cord", and weave these cords into a thick fabric. To say, a manufacturer wants to weave a piece of broadcloth. The producer can use *50*'s single-ply yarns or use *100*'s 2-ply yarns. Both fabrics will have about the same weight but the fabric made of *100*'s 2-ply yarns will be finer than the fabric made of *50*'s yarns. If the producer chooses *100*'s single instead of *100*'s 2-ply yarns, the producer will have to use twice the number of the 2-ply yarns in order to create a fabric of the same weight. It takes more work to produce the *100's 2-ply* yarns than the *50*'s single or the *100*'s single yarns. The fabrics made of *100*'s single yarns, however, is more difficult to manufacture than the same weight fabrics made of *100*'s 2-ply yarns because it is easier to twist two yarns into a bigger yarn than to weave twice the number of threads into a fabric. Weaving is the most time-consuming part of the fabric-making process. This is one of the reasons that the number of vertical warp yarns is usually higher than the number of the horizontal weft yarns in the thread count. A fabric of 220 thread count is not likely to contain 110 vertical yarns and 110 horizontal yarns per square inch. Instead, the fabric may have 120 or 130 warp yarns and 100 or 90 weft yarns per square inch. (The reduction of weft yarns also increases the internal mobility of the fabric, which improves the resistance to tear.) If warp yarns and weft yarns are in different sizes, the coarse ones are usually chosen for the weft yarns.

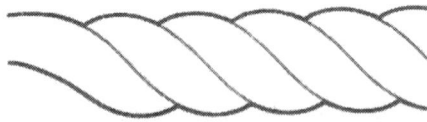

A single yarn

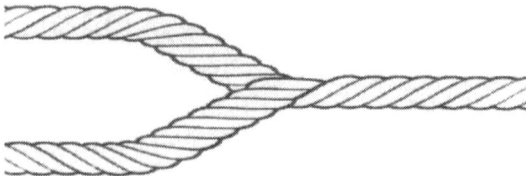

A two-plied yarn

A single-ply thread is finer than a double-ply thread if both threads have the same yarn size. A *40's* 1-ply yarn is thinner than a *40's* 2-ply yarn because the latter is actually a *20's* yarn. An *80's* 2-ply yarn has the same weight as a *40's* 1-ply yarn per length unit. No matter how fine the yarns are, the yarns are useless until they are woven into fabrics. Because it is time consuming--hence cost ineffective--to use fine yarns to weave any fabrics, manufacturers certainly will use double-ply or multi-ply yarns to produce fabrics with extra fine yarns. This is the reason that single-ply fine yarns are rare. It is absurd to generalize that 2-ply yarns are better than 1-ply yarns. The reason that an *80's* 2-ply yarn is finer than a *40's* 1-ply yarn is because of the *80's* yarn, not because of the 2-ply yarn. It is also ridiculous to assume that fabrics made of 2-ply yarns are more expensive than fabrics made of single-ply yarns.

You may think that a fabric made of *80's* 2-ply yarns with 200 thread count is better than a fabric made of *40's* single-ply yarns with 200 thread count, if all other factors are the same. You make the conclusion based on the fact that an *80's* 2-ply yarn has the same weight as a *40's* single-ply yarn, but the *80's* 2-ply yarn is finer. If you think this way, I am sorry that you are wrong. Woven fabrics are produced by the interlacing of warp and weft yarns. A fabric made of single-ply yarns with 200 thread count means that a total of 200 warp and weft threads per square inch are interlaced together, whereas a fabric made of 2-ply yarns with 200 thread count means that a total of 100 warp and weft threads are interlaced together in a square inch. When doing the thread count, a string of 2-ply yarns is considered two counts instead of one count. Hence, the fabric made of *40's* single-ply yarns with 200 thread count is actually a much stronger fabric than the fabric made of *80's* 2-ply yarns with the same thread count. High thread count fabrics are seldom made of single-ply yarns not because single-ply yarns are inferior to the double-ply or multi-ply yarns but because it is much more difficult to weave more single-ply yarns into a fabric of the same weight. Smart shoppers will pay more attentions on the yarn size, the thread count, and the weave than on the number of plies.

I once found a 100% cashmere sweater made of 4-ply yarns in a wholesale club. The sweater did not appear to be in good quality. Its price was about half of the price of a store brand or a quarter of the price of a designer's brand sold in a reputed department store. The vendor placed the designation, "4-ply," in giant print in the center of the box, but mentioned nowhere in the package about the yarn size. The manufacturer must think all consumers are fools, or they would not have put out such an irresponsible advertisement to mislead the consumers.

Many good quality dress shirts, especially famous brands, do not have the yarn size information in the label perhaps because famous designers rely on their reputation and name to sell their products. Flusser was wrong to assume that shirts without the designation of "2-ply" must be made of single-ply yarns. Shirt makers normally do not produce the fabrics that they use to make their shirts. They buy the fabrics in the market and tailor the fabrics into shirts. The shirt fabrics are usually standardized. Manufacturers tend to brag about the yarn size if it is above the industrial average. If the yarn size information is not provided, the fabrics are likely to be made of standard yarns. Standard broadcloth fabrics are made of *50's* single yarns and pinpoint oxford fabrics *80's* 2-ply yarns.

A customer was interested in buying a famous designer's dress shirt at $120.00, which is more than twice the price of a comparable store brand shirt in 2008. The customer asked me what the label, two ply, means. I told him that the labeling is troublesome, especially from a reputed designer. Most fine fabrics are made of 2-ply yarns. Hence, the designation, two ply, says little about the quality of the fabric. What is important is the yarn size information. Nevertheless, the designer chose to neglect the most important and put trivial and incomplete information in the label. I wonder how this type of meaningless labeling helps sell the products.

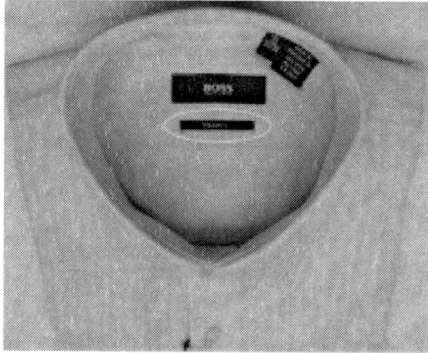

It is appalling that a famous designer includes only the number of plies without the yarn size information in the label of an expensive dress shirt.

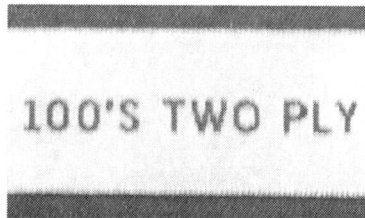

Another designer rightfully gives yarn size information in addition to the number of plies.

22.   *Why do oxford cloth dress shirts become less popular?*

Frequently, shoppers came to the store where I work to look for dress shirts made of oxford cloth. They were disappointed to find that the shirts were no longer popular. The company, which I work for, is the second largest department store chain in the United States. In 2009, it sold oxford cloth dress shirts only in white and blue with limited supplies. Consumers wonder why oxford cloth shirts have been disappearing from the market since late 1990s or early 2000s.

It has been said that a Scottish mill invented four fabrics named after the four universities, Harvard, Yale, Cambridge, and Oxford. The oxford cloth is currently the only surviving fabric of the four. Even so, oxford dress shirts are becoming less popular. The reason is obvious. In the past when technology was limited, the simplest way to keep cotton garments from wrinkling was to use thick fabrics. Oxford cloth was the ideal material owing to its bulkiness. Since the invention of non-iron fabrics in the 1990s, manufacturers have been able to produce wrinkle-free cotton shirts using chemicals instead of synthetic fibers or bulky cotton fabrics. Thus, oxford cloth has been replaced by pinpoint oxford cloth. Both regular and pinpoint oxford cloths have the same weave. The difference is that the yarn size in pinpoint oxford is twice finer than that in regular oxford cloth. This makes pinpoint oxford cloth a finer fabric and more comfortable to wear. The standard yarn size in pinpoint oxford is *80's 2-ply*.

Many consumers wonder why oxford dress shirts fray easily. Oxford cloth is a variation of basket weave, in which paired or multiple yarns are used in alternating pattern. The yarns are laid side by side without being intertwined together. This makes the oxford cloth looser, less stable, and often less durable than regular plain weave fabrics. Oxford cloth contains two, thin warp yarns woven to every thicker yarn in the filling direction. The two thin yarns expose on top of the thick yarn and absorb most of the friction. This unbalanced construction causes the thin yarns to break. At the same time, the coarse weft yarns are loose yarns and are subject to fray.

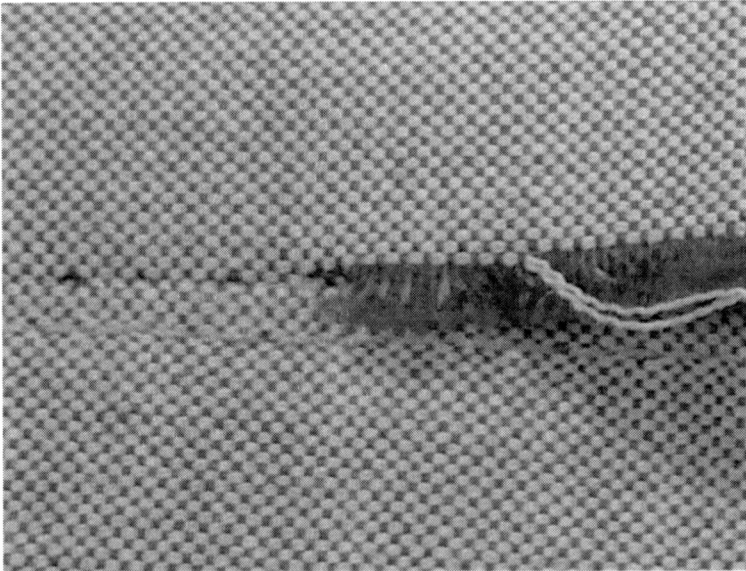

Both regular and pinpoint oxford cloth is an uneven basket weave, in which two thin yarns (white in the photo) woven to every thicker yarn (blue in the photo) in the other direction. In solid color oxford cloth, either the warp or weft yarns are often white. This gives the oxford cloth its distinct frosty look.

23.   Why are better made dress shirts top fused?

The collar of a dressier shirt is made stiff so that the collar will not bend or wrinkle as the neck moves around. To make the collar stiff, firm layers of interfacing are used to add thickness to the collar. Then, the surface of the collar puckers owing to shrinkage difference between the interfacing and shirt fabric. To prevent puckering, layers of interfacing are often glued to the top layer of the shirt fabric, called top fused. In the past, a fused collar may bubble owing to the breakdown of adhesive after repeated laundering and ironing. Nowadays, the adhesives used in the fusing process are reliable. Collars bonded with quality adhesive seldom come apart and bubble. You should feel comfortable to wear top fused shirts. The best dress shirts in today's market are made with top fused collar. Sleeve cuffs and placket front are usually made the same way the collar is made.

President Carter wore a bubbled shirt collar.

Occasionally, I met few consumers who complained about the collars of their dress shirts. The adhesive leaks out, or layers of fabric become loose, showing bubbles. This has been an unsettled debate between the industries. The garment

159

industry complains that the dry cleaning business ruins garments by using harsh chemicals and high heat. The dry cleaning industry fights back by suggesting that some manufacturers make faulty products because not every fused suit or shirt suffers from the same problem.

If you prefer to send your shirts to the cleaner, avoid dry cleaning your cotton shirts. Prefer hand ironing or soft press to hard press. If the cleaner cannot fulfill your wish, you should look for another cleaner. Or, you can always iron the shirts yourself. I have often spotted that many men wear shirts with unattractive impressions or unwanted creases in the collar and other places. Several of my customers own a dry cleaning business. They complained about how difficult it is to find competent workers.

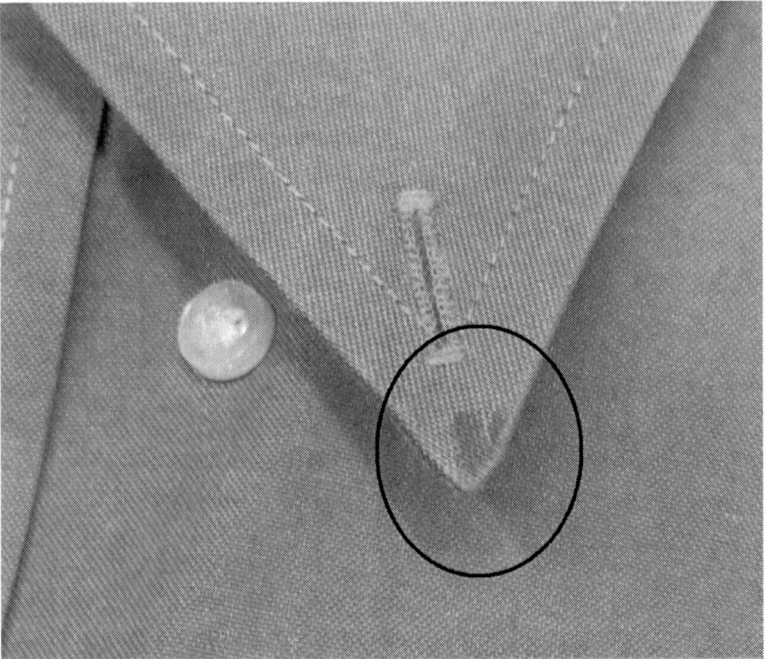

The adhesive in a fused collar leaks out through the tip of the collar wing and turns black under high heat during hard press.

160

24. A non-iron shirt is more than a wrinkle-free shirt.

Most good dress shirts are made of 100% cotton and they wrinkle easily. Many consumers do not wish to iron their shirts or send the shirts to the cleaner. They would rather wear wrinkle free, wrinkle resistant or permanent press shirts even if these shirts are less comfortable. For decades, the garment industry has used synthetic fibers such as polyester to make wrinkle resistant garments. Polyester products have earned bad reputation. Common complaints include pilling, being rough for the skin, and breathing poorly.

Many consumers think wrinkle free shirts are free of wrinkles because they contain polyester. There are different ways to make a fabric wrinkle resistant. One method is to weave coarse yarns into thick fabrics. Canvas and jeans, for examples, are made of 100% cotton but they do not wrinkle easily because the fabrics are too stiff. Any thin fabric made of yarns with a combined yarn size of 50 or higher, tends to wrinkle regardless of material. Cotton-polyester blend fabric does not work well in thin fabric such as common broadcloth or poplin. The fabric does not wrinkle as easily as a fabric made of pure cotton. But when it becomes wrinkled, the wrinkles are difficult to remove. You iron it; the polyester melts and shines. And if you accidentally iron it at the wrong place, you may create a permanent crease that is impossible to erase. If you have to iron a thin fabric, choose 100% cotton. Pure cotton fabrics are easy to iron. For tough wrinkles or creases, you simply dampen the wrinkled spot and iron it with ease. If you desire a permanent press or wrinkle free shirt, be sure that the fabric is thick enough and the weave is strong enough to resist wrinkles. The standard *80*'s 2-ply pinpoint oxford and regular oxford cloth are good choices.

Technology breakthroughs in recent years allow manufacturers to produce wrinkle resistant cotton fabric using chemical treatment instead of using synthetic fibers. Now you can enjoy a luxurious 100% cotton garment that is virtually wrinkle-free. Currently, this type of fabrics and garments are labeled "non-iron," "no-iron," or "iron-free" in the market. After being ironed, an ordinary pure cotton shirt will appear crisp but the crisp look may only last a few hours or a day depending on your body activities. The non-iron shirt will remain crisp 24 hours a day.

Many consumers prefer non-iron shirts because of their ability to resist wrinkles. Few consumers know that the chemicals used to produce the non-iron fabric often provide other important benefits such as color retention, shrinkage control and stain resistance.

It has been widely reported that the chemicals used to make permanent press and non-iron fabrics weaken the fibers and fabrics significantly. This is one of the reasons that some manufacturers blend in polyester to add strength to the fabric. Some manufacturers use chemicals such as high density polyethylene to restore some of the lost tear strength and abrasion resistance. Still, other manufacturers use mercerized cotton for it is stronger than ordinary cotton.

Despite this shortcoming, non-iron fabrics have other important advantages besides being wrinkle-free. The chemicals used to produce non-iron fabrics attract oil and may affect certain dyes or make the fabrics become stiffer. Manufacturers often have to give special treatments to make the fabrics stain-resistant, color-fast and soft touch. In addition, the chemicals and high heat involved in the non-iron process tend to eliminate or reduce the propensity to shrink. If you like

100% cotton non-iron shirts and slacks, you need not be panic about the weakening of the fabrics. The advantages far outweigh the shortcomings. Nevertheless, you should handle the non-iron garments with care, especially those garments made of yarns that are finer than *100's*. In one of the previous chapters, I mentioned two customers pulled the price tag string and created a long tear on their shirts. The two shirts were *100's* 2-ply non-iron shirts. If the customers knew about the problem, they probably would not have pulled the strings.

25.   *Not every non-iron shirt is made the same.*

Because of its wrinkle-free and wash-and-wear features, the new breed non-iron shirts become the most popular dress shirts in America. Most consumers, who shop for dress shirts, prefer non-iron cotton shirts. Nevertheless, few consumers know that not every non-iron shirt performs in the same way. Different manufacturers use different non-iron processes and tailoring methods, which affect the quality of the non-iron products.

A true wrinkle free shirt should be wrinkle-free throughout the shirt.

A great number of men wear ironed and starched dress shirts. Most parts of the shirt appear crisp, but the seams throughout the shirt are wrinkled and puckered. Many sports shirts are intentionally made puckered at the seams to provide a casual look. Some famous sportswear designers often make their dress shirts almost the same way they make their sport shirts. Many men wear a plain sport shirt in the place of a dress shirt perhaps because they cannot tell the difference between a dress shirt and a sport shirt, or because they prefer shirts made by famous sportswear designers. I wonder why people want to buy a dress shirt that is not dressy. If you happen to own a shirt that puckers at the seams, try not to iron or starch your shirt too much. A crisp look shirt with puckered seams appears pretentious and ridiculous.

To reduce the chance of puckering at the seams, you should choose a shirt that is tailored in single-needle stitching. Some areas of a shirt, such as armhole and side seam, require a double-seam construction. Manufacturers can sew two lines of stitching at the same time by using a twin set of needles, call double-needle stitching. They can also sew two lines of stitching one at a time, called single-needle stitching. Most experts prefer single-needle stitching because the double-needle method tends to cause the fabric to pucker between the two lines. The single-needle method may help reduce the puckering caused by sewing machine but may not help reduce the puckering caused by shrinkage after cleaning. Stitching affects the mobility of yarns within the fabric and therefore influences the shrinkage rate of the fabric near the stitching. This is the reason that puckering often occurs at the stitching, especially the double-seam areas. Some puckering can be smoothed out by ironing if the fabric is thin enough. It is difficult to flatten puckered seams by any mean if the fabric is thick or stiff such as an oxford or denim cloth.

It is difficult to smooth out puckered seams, especially those on thick fabrics.

A non-fused shirt tends to pucker at the seams.

The best way to prevent puckered seams is to fuse the seams with interfacing. Traditionally, a quality dress shirt is top fused at the collar, cuffs and placket front but not at the seams. Fused shirts are not the same as the wrinkle-free shirts. The ordinary shirts have to be ironed to maintain their crisp look. With increasing demand on wrinkle-resistant shirts, manufacturers are producing more permanent press shirts made of cotton-polyester blend or non-iron shirts made of 100% cotton. Nevertheless, a shirt that is made of wrinkle-free fabric does not mean that it is tailored in a wrinkle-free fashion. Many wrinkle-free shirts do not wrinkle except at the seams. My advice is that a true wrinkle-free shirt should be wrinkle-free throughout the entire shirt. Notice that fused seams are often sewn with a double-needle instead of the single-needle stitching. This may not be considered a deficiency because a fused seam does not pucker and therefore does not require a single-needle stitching, which is more time-consuming.

Good non-iron shirts should have fused seams.

Some manufacturers fuse every place where a double-layer or multi-layer construction is present. Other manufacturers fuse the interfacing at important areas such as the collar, the cuff, and the placket front, but not at the side seams. Cheap shirts may not have any fused part at all. If you shop for non-iron shirts, it is wise to buy those with fused seams.

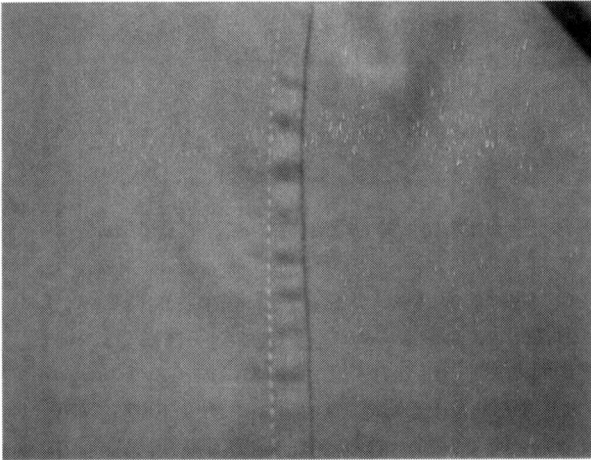

A bad non-iron shirt with non-fused seams that pucker.

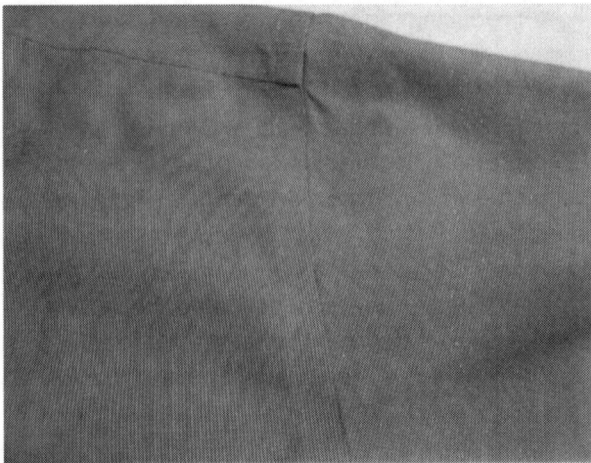

A good non-iron shirt with fused (flat) seams.

Good non-iron shirts should have sharp creases.

Many non-iron shirts do not have sharp creases at the arms, pleats, plackets, or pocket folds. The reason is that manufacturers dipped the shirts in the non-iron chemicals and cure the chemicals with high heat, known as the one-stage process. The cured chemicals make the fabrics resist creases the same way they resist wrinkles. A shirt without creases looks swollen and puffy, especially at the folds. The whole shirt looks like a cheap polyester shirt. Better made non-iron shirts use a two-stage process. The shirts are dipped in the chemicals and cured by heat. Before the chemicals are completely set, the shirts have to be pulled out and creased. After that, the shirts are returned to finish the curing process. Once the chemicals are cured, they secure the creases indefinitely and at the same time prevent the rest part of the shirt from wrinkling.

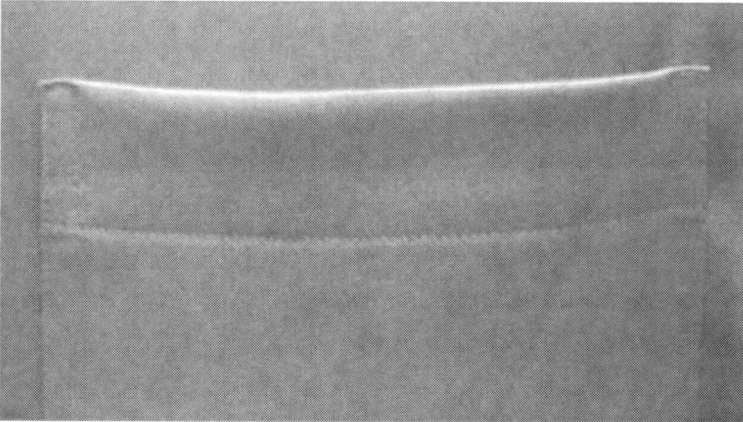

A swollen pocket fold tells you that something is wrong about the shirt.

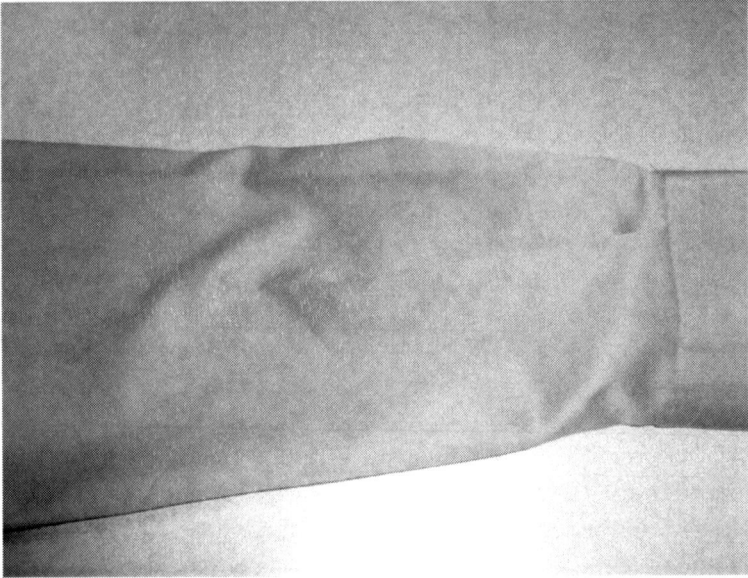

A bad non-iron shirt without creases.

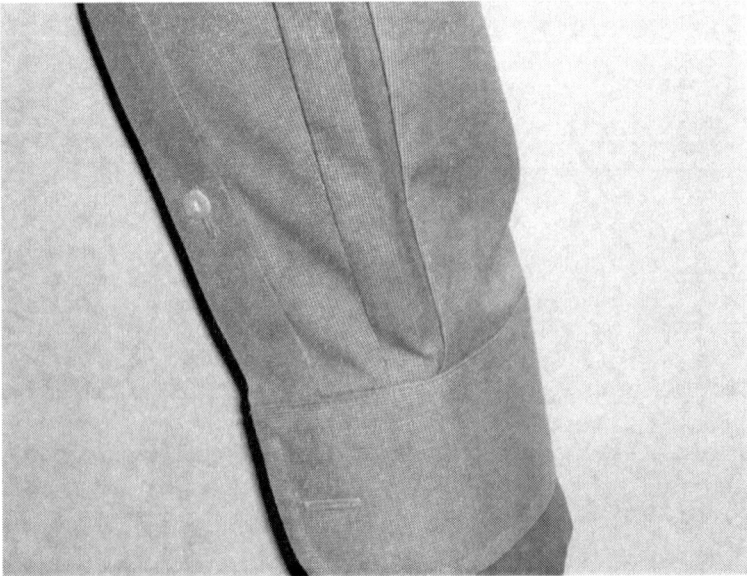

A good non-iron shirt with sharp creases.

One of the important factors that distinguish between the new non-iron shirts and the traditional poly-blend wrinkle-free shirts is that it is difficult to crease the polyester or poly-blend shirts. If you desire a wrinkle-free shirt, the 100% cotton non-iron shirt seems to be a better choice than the poly-blend permanent press shirt. Bad non-iron shirts cost no less than good non-iron shirts. If you shop for non-iron shirts, be sure that the shirts have sharp creases and are fused throughout the whole shirt. It is foolish to spend extra money to buy a shirt that you cannot even crease it when you want to.

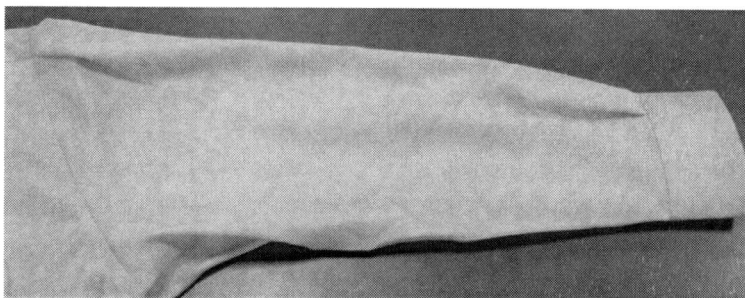

The pleated sleeve was once the trademark of Perry Ellis dress shirts. What makes the sleeve so attractive is actually not the pleat but the sharp crease that comes with the pleat. The one-stage non-iron process erases the sharp crease, making the pleat look redundant and unappealing.

Why do some non-iron shirts wrinkle?

Whereas the great majority of men who wear non-iron shirts are satisfied with the garments, a small number of men are dissatisfied with the performance of the shirts. They complained that the shirts are not 100% wrinkle-free and often need to be touched up with an iron. Manufacturers have the tendency to label every garment "non-iron" once the garment has received the non-iron chemical treatment. This is absolutely untrue.

I have constantly reminded customers that chemical treatments can only help resist wrinkling to some degree. Other factors (such as the type of fibers, yarn size of the threads, weave of the fabrics and thread count) also affect the ability of a garment to resist wrinkles. In general, fabrics made of long staple cottons (such as Sea Island, Egyptian and Pima) or made of thin yarns tend to wrinkle more easily. Under current technology, the 80's 2-ply pinpoint oxford cloth seems to work best with the non-iron treatment. The 100's 2-ply twill also performs satisfactorily. The 50's single-ply broadcloth tends to wrinkle slightly. A 100's 2-ply yarn is the same as a 50's single-ply yarn in fineness. Why does the shirt made of 50's 1-ply broadcloth wrinkle more easily? Textile experts explain that broadcloth has a plain weave structure, which restricts the mobility of yarns within the weave construction. Hence, fabrics made of plain weave such as broadcloth and poplin ten to wrinkle more easily than fabrics made of twill or satin weave. In truth, it is more likely that a piece of broadcloth or poplin wrinkles because the fabric is less dense than other types of fabrics. There is less material in the broadcloth to withstand the stress that causes wrinkling.

In short, not every non-iron shirt is iron-free. There are confounding factors that influence a fabric's ability to resist wrinkling. It is difficult for consumers to figure out all the factors. Most consumers like to examine the softness and the texture of the fabric by touching the garment. This may be a good shopping habit. A garment that has a soft hand or appears to be thin tends to wrinkle more easily. If you like to learn more about fabrics, please read my book, *what Fashion Experts Teach You Wrong or Did not Teach You about Fabrics.*

26. *Why should a non-iron shirt not be ironed or starched?*

Why does cotton wrinkle?

Cotton is composed of a material called cellulose. The molecules in cellulose contain many thousands of atoms and are shaped like long chains. The long, chainlike shape of the molecules makes cellulose a good fiber. The chainlike cellulose molecules are joined together with cross-linked hydrogen bonds, which make cotton fabrics wrinkle resistant. If you stress a dry cotton fabric slightly by folding it or sitting on it, these hydrogen bonds force the molecules back where it belongs, and no wrinkle will form. When the cotton fabric gets wet, water (including humidity and sweat) tends to interfere with those hydrogen bonds and prevent the fabric from returning to its wrinkle-free state when the fabric is stressed. This is the reason that natural fiber clothes coming out of the washer tend to wrinkle.

How does the non-iron treatment work?

In the early 1990s, the garment industry began to produce "non-iron" garments using advanced chemicals that provide strong cross-linking bonds between various fiber molecules. It was first thought that cross-linking strengthens cotton fibers and make the fabric wrinkle resistant. Scientists now believe it is the strengthening of the hydrogen bonds, which make cotton fabrics resistant to wrinkling.

While the industry continues to perfect the wrinkle-free technology, it seems that the non-iron treatment at this stage only works well with fabrics made of thicker yarns or stronger weaves. Chemicals can only assist in providing recovery from wrinkles to some degree. Many vendors exaggerate the effect of non-iron treatment. They tend to claim a garment to be wrinkle-free or non-iron as long as the garment has been treated with the non-iron process. For years, I have warned customers that non-iron dress shirts made with thin yarns and soft weaves, such as herringbone, tend to wrinkle more easily. Customers keep returning to the store and confirming what I said is correct.

Handle non-iron shirts with care.

Despite the effectiveness of the wrinkle-free treatment, you should launder your non-iron shirts carefully. Hand wash, line dry is always the best. If you prefer to use a laundry machine and a dryer, use the delicate cycle and dry the shirt in a small load with medium or low temperature. The advanced dryers these days are featured with a "de-wrinkling cycle", which magically reduces or eliminates wrinkles in the clothes. If for any reason your non-iron shirt appears slightly wrinkled, spray the shirts with water and the wrinkles will smooth out in no time. This method works because moisture such as cool water mist and hot steam can reset the cross-linked hydrogen bonds and smooth out the wrinkles. When spraying, avoid the creases as the moisture may smooth out the creases. Do not stress the damped area while the area is still wet, or the wrinkles will occur.

Avoid pressing the creases.

Many customers ask me what will happen if they iron a non-iron shirt. There is no reason that the non-iron shirts cannot be ironed. But why would any person want to iron a wrinkle-free shirt? As I have explained in the previous chapter, not every non-iron shirt is wrinkle-free. If you happen to own a bad non-iron shirt or if you mishandle a normal non-iron shirt, the shirt may become wrinkled and need a touch-up. You can remove the wrinkles by spraying the area with water.

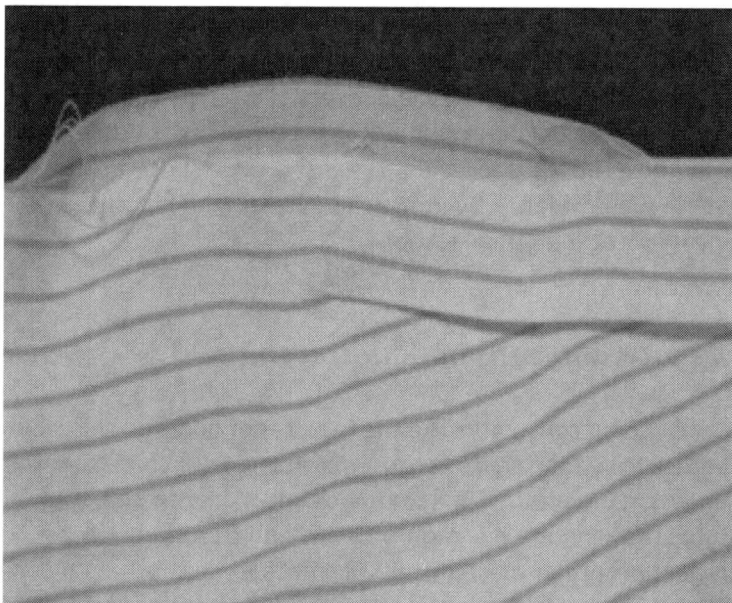

The permanent crease should be left alone. Repeated pressing often causes the crease to tear.

Creases are like wrinkles. The difference is that creases are designed while wrinkles tend to be random. It is difficult to crease a wrinkle-free shirt once the shirt left the factory because the chemicals or synthetic fibers that resist wrinkles also resist creases. As explained in the previous chapter, some, but not all, chemically treated non-iron and wrinkle-free shirts have permanent creases in all of the pleats and sleeve creases. The advanced chemicals used in the non-iron treatment are able to keep creases permanent. If you insist on pressing or ironing a non-iron shirt with permanent creases, you should

175

avoid touching the creases. If you have to re-shape the creases, be sure that you iron the creases at exactly the same place of the original creases. Otherwise, you will create another crease near the permanent crease. It is unsightly to have more than one crease at the same location. Try not to hard press the creases or the creases may break after repeated pressing.

Some customers refuse to buy non-iron shirts because the shirts tend to tear at the creases after repeated ironing. I tease customers by asking the question, "Why did you iron a shirt that tells you 'no-iron'?" Just as you can break a steel rod by bending the rod back and forth at the same spot, you can break a piece of fabric by ironing and pressing the fabric repeatedly at the same location.

The pros and cons of non-iron shirts

Some consumers like the features of non-iron shirts but hesitate to use the shirts because they send their shirts to the cleaners. Shirts returned from the cleaners are pressed. Why should they spend extra money to buy non-iron shirts? Most drycleaners prefer machine pressing because it is faster. Nevertheless, machine pressing tends to over press seams, vents, pocket flaps, double-thick layers, and other uneven surfaces, causing unsightly impressions. Machine pressing also flattens soft woolens and shines delicate fabrics, especially gabardine, acetate and satin. Machine pressing also create multiple creases at the same location.

If you prefer to send your non-iron shirts to the cleaner, remind your cleaner about the special features of your shirt. Avoid dry cleaning your cotton shirts. Prefer hand ironing or soft press to hard press. The best way is to have your non-iron shirts laundered without hand ironing or machine pressing. If the cleaner cannot fulfill your wish, you should look for another cleaner.

A huge difference between a pressed or starched regular cotton shirt and a non-iron cotton shirt is that the non-iron shirt are 24 hours wrinkle-free whereas a pressed regular cotton shirt may stay pressed for a few hours.

As mentioned before, the non-iron treatment weakens the strength of cotton fabrics significantly. Starch is not recommended for non-iron shirts. The application of starch involves high heat, which further damages the cotton fabrics. Repeated pressing and starching also increases the shrinkage rate. Non-iron shirts are not a good choice for those people who like to have their cotton shirts starched.

As the new breed of non-iron fabrics are gaining popularity in the garment industry, many consumers are wondering what makes a cotton shirt or a pair of cotton pants wrinkle-resistant or wrinkle-free. There are different methods to produce wrinkle-free garments. A popular approach is to strengthen the weak hydrogen bonds between adjacent cellulose molecular chains in the cotton fibers. Currently the most common cross-linking agent, DMDHEU, releases a chemical called formaldehyde, which is toxic and can pose health hazards. Hence, additional treatments or alternatives are required to replace, remove or reduce the toxic chemicals. While manufacturers assure that the amount of toxicant in non-iron products will not affect health, the products may be avoided for those people who have a sensitive skin. The various chemicals used in the non-iron process may cause irritation or allergic reaction.

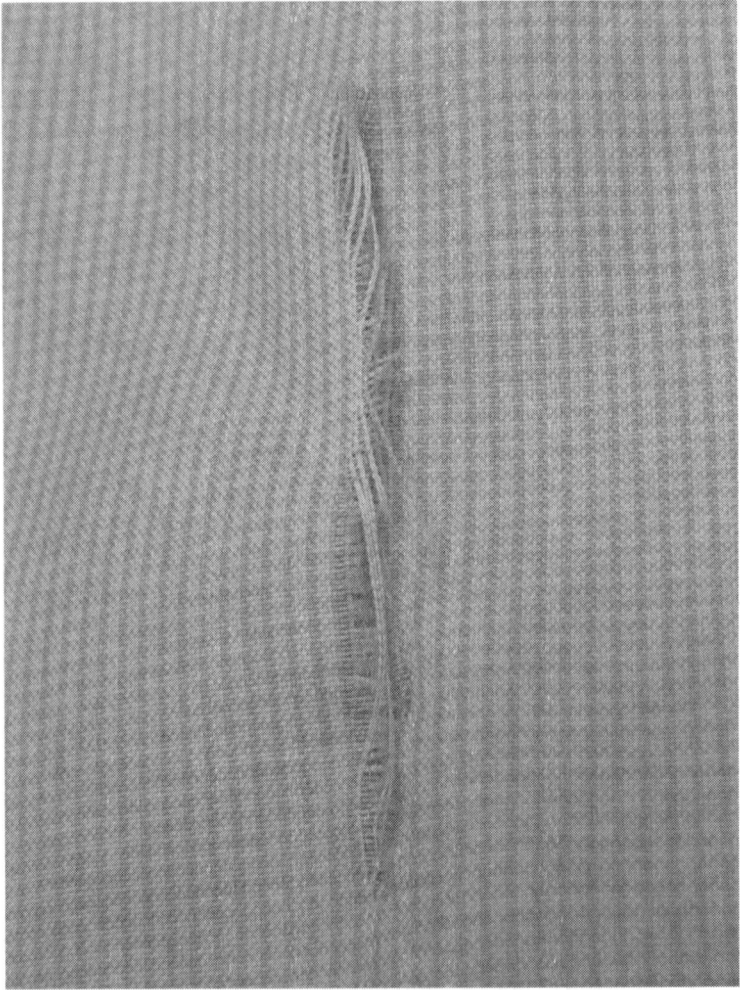

Non-iron treatment weakens the strength of the fabric, reducing the fabric's ability to resist tearing, especially at the seams.

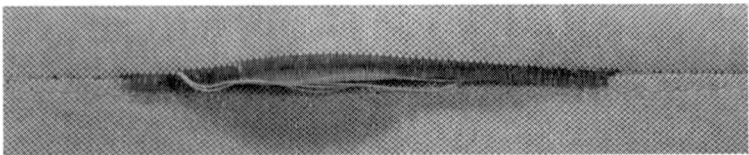

27. A pocket or no pocket?

At one time, men did not leave home without a jacket. They put most of their accessories such as a wallet inside the pockets of the jacket. It was unnecessary then to have a pocket on the shirt. As suit jackets and sport coats are less popular these days, shirt pockets become convenient or necessary to many people. The great majority of men prefer dress shirts with pockets. Some men even demand a pocket on their polo shirts.

Frequently, I met customers who wanted to buy dress shirts without a chest pocket. This can be a problem because the majority of dress shirts sold in clothing stores have a pocket. Some designers do produce dress shirts without a pocket, but the selections are often limited.

One solution is to rip the pocket off the shirt. This can be done easily because most shirt pockets are patch pockets, which are pieces of fabric sewn directly onto an already completed garment. As the color of the shirt may begin to fade after the shirt have been worn a while, the removal of the pocket should be done when the shirt is new. Or, the area once covered by the pocket may show a different shade of color. Most shirting fabrics are made with some types of plain weave, which are prone to tearing. Hence, you should be careful when ripping the pocket.

In previous two chapters, I have mentioned that some good non-iron shirts are made with a two-stage process. The shirts are pressed, creased and then secured with special chemicals. When the pocket was machine pressed during the manufacturing process, an impression was created under the pocket. The impression has been secured by the non-iron treatment and is very difficult to be removed. Hence, you may not try to remove the pocket of a non-iron shirt.

28. Why should a man not wear too long a jacket?

An old tailor's saying goes, "Compromise on quality if you must, never proportion." A jacket changes the proportion of a man's head and body dramatically. President Reagan's long legs disappeared once he put on a jacket. A well-dressed man should never neglect the effect of his jacket length.

A man should wear a jacket length according to the inches he needs, not the size manufacturer gives.

Frequently I encountered tall men who were looking for a long size jacket. When I mentioned to them the coat they were trying on is too long, most of them were offended. They yelled at me and said that they had worn long size jackets all their lives. Readymade jackets are usually sold in short, regular, long, and extra long size. Every designer or manufacturer uses the same system but interprets the size differently. Most consumers understand that a 42-long jacket made by one manufacturer can be longer or shorter than another same size jacket made by a different maker. Consumers seldom realize that the same designer or manufacturer also interprets the size differently each season. During early 2000s, slim fit became fashionable. Most designers or manufacturers made their jackets much longer than those they made a decade or a few decades ago. Most men never noticed the difference and continued to wear the same size jacket they wore many years ago.

Fashion trend changes frequently but a grown man's height does not. For this reason, a man should stick to the inches he needs instead of the size manufacturer gives. If a man needs a 32- inch-long jacket, measuring from the bottom of the collar to the base of the buttocks, why should he care about how the coat makers label the jacket?

Do not cup the fingers to judge the length of a suit or sport coat.

I often hear customers comment that men look their best in a jacket. A suit or sport jacket has definite shape. It hides the bad parts and showcases the good parts of a man's body. No other men's clothing item requires more precision in fitting than the suit and sport jacket. A man ought to know how a jacket should fit his body. Even so, I have not met any man who really knows how a jacket should fit, especially the coat length. Almost every man cups his fingers to determine the length of a jacket. When I told the customers it had been wrong perhaps for hundreds of years to measure the length of the coat by cupping the fingers, they were stunned and did not know what else they should do.

The length of a jacket has more to do with the length of a man's torso and rise than the length of his arms. Men of the same height and size often have a different arm length. Manufacturers do not make jacket length according to the length of arms. Why should a man buy a jacket based on his arm length?

Choose the correct jacket length according to the length of torso, not the length of arm.

Most men wear their jacket too long because they have no idea about how long a jacket should be and what the consequences of wearing a wrong size jacket are. Some men have long arms. They would rather buy a longer coat to satisfy the need of their arms even if the long jacket will shorten their leg line and make them look ridiculous. As I have often suggested, manufacturers have a bad habit of making garments that fit most of the target population instead of an average person. Because a longer sleeve can be shortened whereas a shorter sleeve cannot be lengthened beyond a certain length, manufacturers have the tendency of making the jacket sleeves longer than an average man needs. This is the reason that most men need to shorten their new jacket sleeves. Unless a man has extremely long arms, a jacket that fits his body usually has enough sleeve length to cover his arms. Between a jacket that fits the body perfectly but is slightly too short for the arms and a jacket that fits the arms perfectly but is too long for the body, a man should choose the jacket that fits his body. It is just as easy to lengthen as to shorten a sleeve of a brand new jacket. Most jacket sleeves can be lengthened up to 1 ½".

If a tall man is tall because of his long legs, the man may not need a long size jacket.

Men's clothing stores nationwide are training their salespersons to recommend long size jackets to any man who is six feet or taller. Some stores even give out brochures to promote this erroneous belief. Their recommendation is as follows.

Short:	under 5' 8"
Regular:	5' 8" to 6'
Long:	6' to 6' 4"
Extra Long:	over 6' 4"

A man is tall mostly because his legs are long. But, the jacket does not cover the legs. The legs of an ideal body are about one half to one head length longer than the combination of the torso and pelvis. Unless a man has a long upper body, or his legs exceed this perfect proportion, a man should not ruin his asset by wearing a long coat. John Wayne and James Stewart were tall men. They look marvelous in the movies with a short coat.

Manufacturers proportion the length of a jacket to the chest size of the jacket. A 44-Regular jacket is likely to be longer than a 42-Regular jacket. For this reason a tall man with a small chest may need a long size jacket, whereas a man of the same height with a larger chest may not need a long size jacket.

Why should a man avoid a long jacket?

Most men these days wear too long their jacket. There are five reasons that a man should not wear a long jacket.

First, a jacket will be sat on if it is too long. Although it seems obvious, few men ever notice the problem.

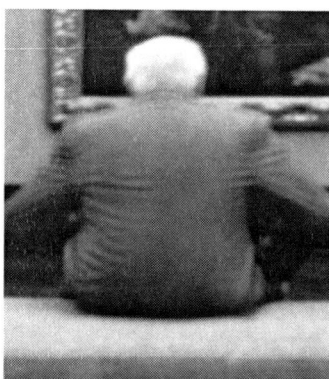

A long jacket not only runs the risk of being sat on, but also creates more lines of wrinkles when the wearer is seated.

(Screenshots, fair use)

Second, a jacket that is too long may distort the proportion of the head and torso. The ideal human body has a torso of two head lengths, a pelvis of one head length, and a pair of lower limbs of three and half to four head lengths. A long jacket diminishes the head and shortens the leg line.

President Bush and Prof. Joachim Sauer, husband of German Chancellor Merkel, appeared having short legs because their jackets were too long.

Third, a jacket that is too long creates excessive lines of wrinkles when the wearer sits or places his hand in the trouser pocket. For some reasons, many men prefer a jacket length and sleeve length that is longer than what they should wear. To show them the consequence of wearing a long jacket length and sleeve length, I often asked the customers to button the jacket and place both hands inside the trouser pockets. The extra length of fabric bunched up at the elbows and above the pockets, which looked very unbecoming. Many customers changed their mind and wanted a shorter jacket or sleeve length.

Fourth, the long jacket tail tends to flap against the rear of the wearer, especially when the jacket is vented.

Last, a longer jacket may create a larger gap between the jacket and the pants as the legs become smaller toward the ground. The larger the gap, the less attractive the outfit.

Because pant legs are tapered toward the ground, a longer jacket tends to create a larger gap between the jacket and the trousers.

It looks unbecoming to have a large gap between the jacket and the trousers. A pair of full-cut pants not only provides a better transition from the upper- to the lower-body, but also provides a better balance between the volume of the upper- and the volume of the lower body.

189

The tailor's method

To determine the length of a jacket, most men line up the bottom of the jacket with their thumb knuckle. When a man bends his fingers, the tips of his four fingers are in line with the thumb knuckle. This is why men all over the country cup their fingers when they try on a new jacket. Using this method, a man with a short or average torso but long arms can end up with too long a jacket.

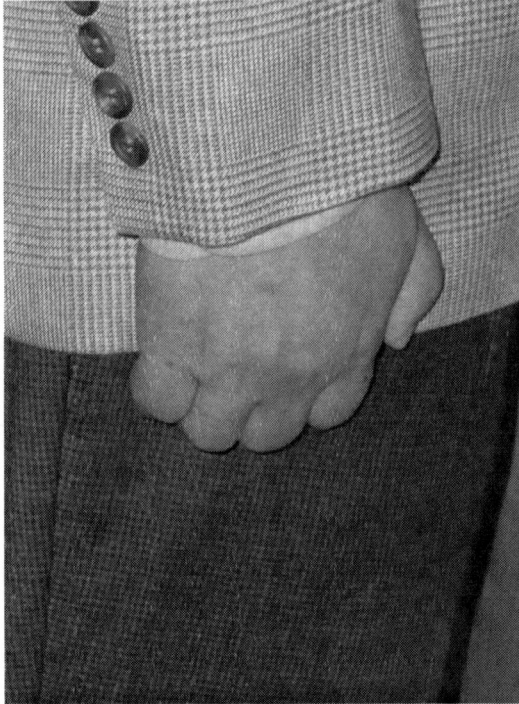

Another method is less known by the general public but is popular with tailors since the method is taught in most formal tailoring schools. The method measures the length from under the jacket's back collar down to the floor and divides by two. This method never works for a short man or tall man. The method also contradicts the perfect proportion of an ideal body.

What is the proper length of a jacket?

I am amazed by the fact that our current knowledge allows us to send men out of space and to alter our gene but does not enable us to find a simple method that can determine the proper length of a jacket. Isn't it so obvious to find the correct length just by considering the following two factors? One factor is that the coat has to cover the curvature of a man's buttocks. The other factor involves the components of an ideal human body. As mentioned previously, the ideal human body has a torso of two head lengths, a pelvis of one head length, and a pair of lower limbs of three and half to four head lengths. A suit or sport coat should be short enough just to cover a man's torso and pelvis. This will help elongate the leg line and achieve the esthetic proportion of an ideal human body. Putting these two factors together, the only conclusion is that the jacket should end at the joint where a man's buttocks and legs meet. If a jacket extends too much beyond the buttocks, the jacket length will shorten the leg line when the man is standing and the jacket tail may be sat on when the man is seated.

Over the years, I have devised a few guidelines to determine the proper length of a jacket. Customers call my guidelines scientific. I would consider these guidelines simply "common sense."

1)   The jacket must cover a man's seat. Hence, the bottom of the jacket should line up with the base of the buttocks.

2)   If a man has a built lower body in relation to his upper body, the man should exaggerate his upper body by wearing a slightly larger or longer coat. If he chooses a longer one, the man can wear a jacket length up to one inch longer.

3)   A tall man can wear slightly longer jacket and still looks all right. But in no time, should the jacket length exceed

the length from the bottom of the coat to the ground.

4)   A short man should wear a short jacket length but not
        shorter than one inch above the base of the buttocks.
        According to my experience, a short size jacket is still
        too long for most short men. A short man can have his
        jacket shortened but the jacket should cover most of his
        buttocks. Women's suit jackets are often made so short
        that the bottom of the jacket cuts across middle of the
        pelvis, inviting eyes to focus on the center of the
        buttocks and genital area, which is extremely
        unbecoming. A jacket should either cover the seat or
        end at the waist such as in the case of a waistcoat.

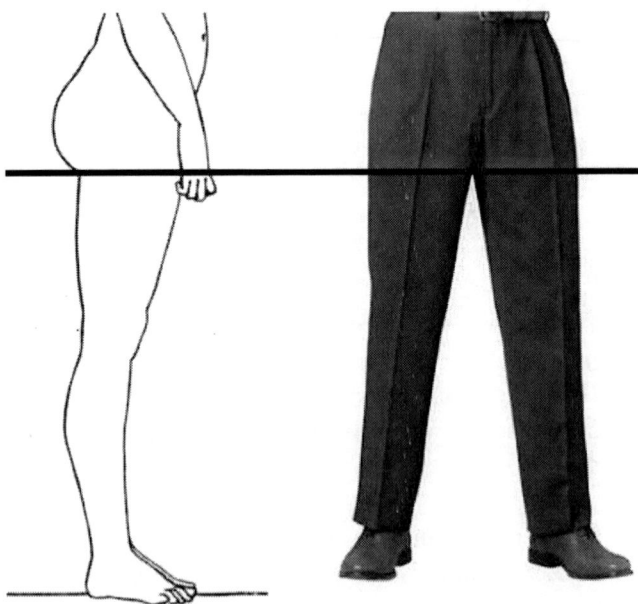

While the best jacket length depends on individual's height and body proportion, the proper jacket length for an average man should end at the base of the buttocks, or where the pant legs part, providing that the man wears his pants correctly.

193

Better to be short than to be long

Fashion experts suggest that a jacket should be ½ the length from under the back collar to the ground. This may be undesirable because it contradicts the figure of an ideal man. For a tall man, I am inclined to recommend a jacket length that is slightly shorter than ½ of the total length unless the man has a relative large lower body, which may make a short jacket appear insignificant.

Bob Hope wore a jacket that is less than ½ of the total length.

One of the biggest fashion mistakes that today's men commit is wearing too long their jackets. Among the leaders in the G-7 Economic Summit of 1983, President Reagan wore the shortest jacket in proportion to body height. He looked marvelous.

194

*Between a long coat, short legs and a short coat, long legs,
which is more attractive?*

29. Why do so many men wear too long their jacket sleeves?

Jacket sleeves should extend to the end or the middle of the wrist bone.

Throughout my career in men's clothing business, nothing is more frustrated than to discuss the jacket sleeve length with a customer. It is funny that the great majority of men want to wear too short their shirtsleeves but want to wear too long their jacket sleeves. Alan Flusser believes 90% of all men wear their coat sleeves too long. Indeed, most men do not even know how long the coat sleeves should be. Many men have heard that dress shirt sleeves should extend half inch beyond the jacket sleeves. But, few men are willing to wear a jacket sleeves short enough to allow this to happen. When I told customers that the jacket sleeves should rest somewhere on the wrist bone, most of them gave me a look of disbelieving. They argued that the sleeves retreat too much when the arms bend.

Most men wear extra jacket sleeve length to prevent the sleeves from becoming too short when the arms bend. They have such a bizarre idea because they do not understand how different types of sleeves function. The jacket sleeves and shirt sleeves are cut differently.

A barrel cuff dress shirtsleeve is tapered and has a narrow opening at the wrist. The purpose of a narrow opening is to prevent the sleeve end from falling over the hand. Then again, the narrow opening will make it more difficult for the arm to stretch. Consequently, a barrel cuff sleeve requires additional sleeve length, called "drape," to absorb the stretch when the arm moves. In contrast, a suit or sport coat sleeve is only slightly tapered and has a wide opening at the wrist area. The sleeve must be short to prevent it from falling over the hand. Because there is no extra sleeve length, the sleeve will be pulled back when the arm moves. If the jacket sleeve does not retreat, it may be torn somewhere along the sleeve length. A man stretches his arm only once a while for a very short period of time. It is ridiculous that a man wears extra jacket sleeve length for fear that the sleeve may be pulled back by the arm. A jacket sleeve that moves freely with the arm actually gives "life" to that jacket. Most men never realize that the extra jacket sleeve length bunches up when the hand is in the trouser pocket, creating excessive wrinkles.

To determine the proper length of the jacket sleeve, some authors suggest that for an average man the tip of the jacket sleeve should come about five inches off the tip of the thumb. Other experts recommend 5 ¼" or 5 ½". Because different men have a different size of hands and because the sleeves do not cover the hands, it is silly to measure the sleeve length according to the hand size instead of the arm length. Since the dress shirtsleeve should extend to where the wrist breaks with the hand, the jacket sleeve should end at ¼" to ½" above where the arm and hand separate. This will allow a ¼" to ½" band of linen to show below the jacket cuff. If you are unsure about the exact place where your arm and hand separate, you may allow the sleeve extend to somewhere on the wrist bone. Because the jacket sleeve may retreat after the new jacket is "broken in", it is a good idea to have the new jacket sleeve finished at the end of the wrist bone.

One of the serious problems of having a sleeve that is too long is that the sleeve wrinkles terribly when the arm bends. The extra length of fabric bunches at the elbow and appears very unbecoming.

Use the three lines on the wrist to guide the proper sleeve length of your shirt, jacket, and overcoat.

If you bend your hand outward, you may notice the three lines on your wrist. These lines are perhaps the best guides to help you determine the proper length of your sleeves. Place the end of your jacket sleeve on the first line (away from your hand), shirt sleeve on the second line, and the overcoat on the third.

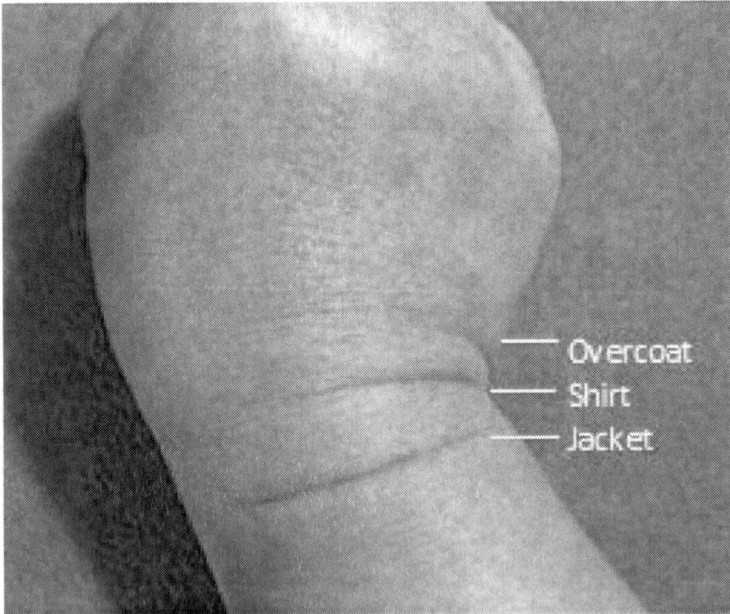

When properly dressed, a suit or sport jacket should never touch any part of the skin of the wearer.

Reading so far, if you are still confused with what the correct jacket length and proper sleeve length are, remember this: a properly fitted jacket should never touch any part of your skin. It is a custom that a sophisticated dresser will have his regular shirt collar show ½" and his wing collar show ¾" above the jacket, and also have his shirt sleeves peek out ¼" to ½" from under the jacket sleeves.

Most men are unable to show the ¼" to ½" shirt cuff because they wear their shirtsleeves too short, because they wear their jacket sleeves too long, or because both. Some men wear a short sleeve dress shirt with a jacket. Some men like to wear a jacket without a dress shirt. They wear a T-shirt, a polo shirt, or a sweater under a jacket, causing the jacket collar and sleeve cuff to touch the bare neck and hands. When the jacket rubs against the skin, it picks up the oil and sweat from the skin. Additional cleaning to remove the stains can reduce the longevity of the jacket.

To protect his investment, a man should not allow his jacket to touch any part of his skin. If the jacket touches any part of a man's skin, he definitely is not well dressed.

How do we know that Congressman Skelton's jacket sleeves were too long? The jacket sleeve did not retreat when the arm bent and the sleeve touched the hand.

Photo courtesy of www.kremlin.ru.

Russian President Putin's jacket was too long and the sleeve almost covered the entire hand.

30.   What are the disadvantages of pant cuffs?

The great majority of American men prefer cuffed pants to non-cuffed pants. If you ask those men what the advantages of cuffed pants are, no one will be able to name even one benefit. Some fashion experts claim that the cuff adds weight to the bottom of the pants and pulls to anchor the pants. In truth, a cuff can help anchor the pants only when the pair of pants is worn short without a break. When the pair of pants is long enough to produce a break, the weight of the cuffs rests on the top of the shoes, canceling the effect of adding weight to pull the pant bottom. Non-cuffed pants have a much wider hem than cuffed pants. The wide hem can do the same trick without the many problems of the cuffs, as explained below.

First, a cuffed bottom cannot be slanted and therefore can create more unwanted break that ruins the long vertical crease line in the front of pants.

Second, cuffs add bulkiness to the bottom of the pants. Hence, pants that are made of thick fabrics should not be finished with cuffs. Bulky cuffs draw unwelcome attention and cease the continuation of the leg lines.

Third, creases on both the top and the bottom of the cuffs should be sharp and stay sharp all the time. Pants made of synthetic or thick fabrics are difficult to be creased. They also tend to lose the creases after being cleaned.

Fourth, cuffs produce uneven surfaces, where unsightly shining and impressions often occur when the pair of pants is ironed or pressed. Uneven surfaces also lead to crocking, which is the color of fabric being rubbed off.

Fifth, cuffs add stiffness to the bottom of the pants because of the multi-folds. They often affect the drape of the pant bottoms.

Sixth, cuffs are the best places to collect dust, dirt and other objects. A real estate agent once told me that he could never wear cuffed slacks because the cuffs collected grass every time he showed clients around the house he was selling.

Last, cuffs on modern pants are seldom made correctly. In the past, pant legs were tapered to the knees and then straight down to the bottom. Today, pant legs are tapered all the way to the bottom, making it more challenging to construct hems or cuffs. The dressmakers or tailors have to stitch a smaller circumference of fabric to a larger one. It takes 3 ½" length of fabric to make a 1 ½" cuff. This means that the difference between the two circumferences can be close to half an inch or more. Ordinary dressmakers and tailors will not take time to open the side seams to compensate for such a big difference. Hence, cuffs on modern pants are usually imperfect and tend to have one or more of the following signs.

1)   The cuff has a tendency to stay open.

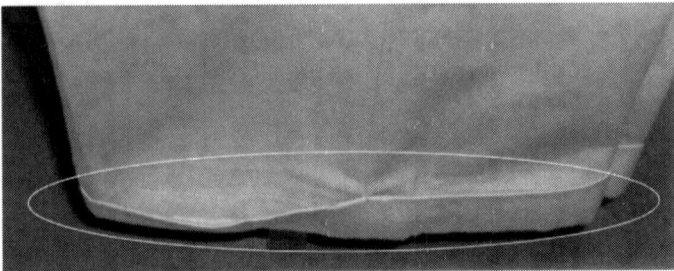

2)   The cuff has a pucker, dent or fold inside the cuff near the crease.

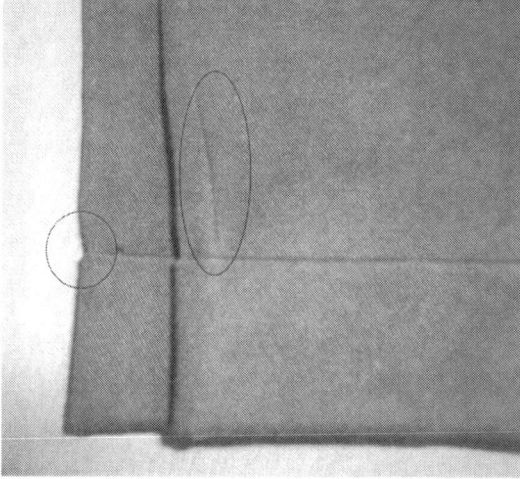

3)   The top of the cuff looks like the roof of a house, having two slopes.

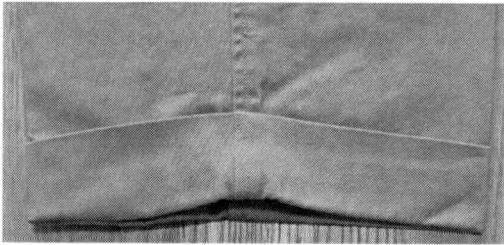

4)   Most manufacturers and tailors take the easy way out by making short cuffs.

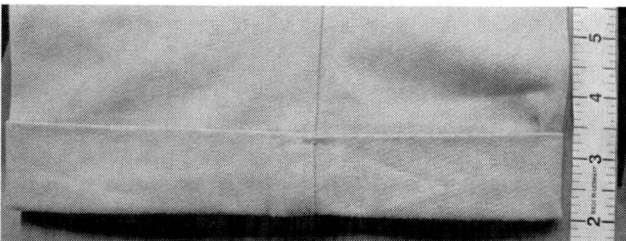

*American singer
and songwriter,
Arthur Fields, wore
a pair of puckered
and dented cuffs.*

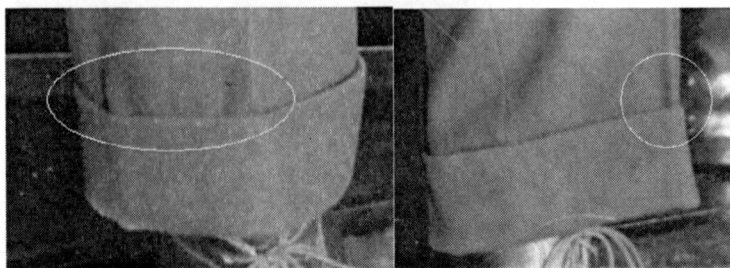

31. To cuff or not to cuff – that may not be a personal choice.

The cuffs on President Obama's pants look very unattractive.

To cuff or not to cuff is an important decision for most men when they buy a suit or a pair of dress pants. The majority of men in the U.S. prefer cuffed pants, whereas a smaller number of men like non-cuffed pants. Some men have no preference. Whatever the choices are, few men know the significant difference between the two options. Even the experts are unsure about which finishing is preferred. Most experts claim that it is a personal choice. Some authors suggest that cuffed pants are dressier than the non-cuffed pants up to a point. This is a silly suggestion. How can one style of pants be dressier up to a point and then become less dressy? Those authors have to say so because their recommendation contradicts the fact that the dressiest slacks in formalwear never have cuffs.

Whether a pair of pants should be cuffed or not, in my humble opinion, should be based on one single important consideration that is how the bottom of the pant legs is cut. In the past, non-cuffed pants are finished with a slanted bottom. Cuffed pants can only be cut horizontally straight across the pant legs. As the workmanship declines along with the rise of the mass production methods, the readymade non-cuffed dress pants are seldom slanted these days. Therefore, it makes little difference now whether a pair of readymade pants is cuffed or not.

John T. Molloy recommends cuffed pants simply because most business executives in the country wear them. Cuffed pants offer none or few advantages but many problems. Why should a man wear cuffed pants because other men wear them?

Egon Von Fürstenberg, a fashion designer, suggested that cuffed pants originated some time ago from men rolling up their pant legs while crossing a muddy street. Hence, any serious business suit pants should not have cuffs. When he was a child, Fürstenberg had the opportunities to observe many of the world's most influential people who came to visit his father, the Prince of Austria. Fürstenberg noticed that the most important men wore non-cuffed pants.

It is my opinion that a man has the liberty of choosing cuffed pants if he is sure that the cuffs are done right. It is extremely rude to wear a pair of pants with sloppy cuffs.

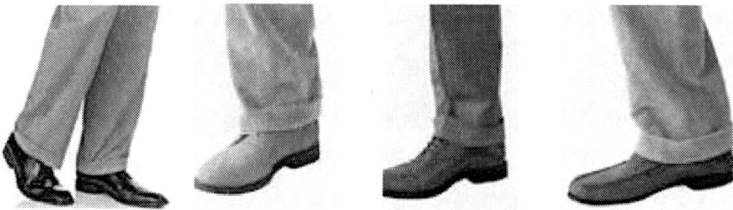

Cuffed pants originate some time ago from men folding the bottom of their pants when they crossed muddy streets; therefore, cuffed pants tend to be short. Many men these days like to wear their pants too long. They have no business to wear cuffed pants as the multi-folds in the cuff are difficult to rest gracefully on top of the shoes.

32. What is the proper width of pant cuffs?

Source: private archive of Monteforti family, GNU.

*Pant cuffs should be wide enough to make
an impact and render a statement.*

The majority of American men prefer cuffed pants because they mistakenly think cuffed pants are dressier. Cuffs serve no real purpose. In addition, they have more disadvantages than advantages. If a man insists on wearing a pair of cuffed pants for whatever reason, do you not think the man ought to wear the cuffs correctly? As explained previously, cuffs on modern pants are seldom made correctly because the pant bottom tapers too much. To make the job easier, most manufacturers, including many famous designer brands, would rather construct cuffs that are 1 ¼" or shorter.

Kenneth Karpinski, an image consultant, claimed that the width of the cuff is not a serious issue. Then, what is the reason for wearing cuffed pants if the width of the cuff does not matter? May a man wear 0" cuffs? The gentleman's rule is that the width of the cuff should be 1 $^5/_8$" if the wearer is shorter than 5'10" and 1 ¾" if the wearer is 5'10" or taller.

Most American men desire cuffed pants, yet few men wear a correct cuff width because the majority of the readymade cuffed slacks have the wrong cuff width. Many men wear tailored slacks but they do not know that cuff width matters. Few tailors or dressmakers will finish a pair of pants with a cuff width of 1 $^5/_8$" or 1 ¾" unless the customer asks for it.

Everybody knows that the devil is in the detail. How wonderful will it be if you are the only person around wearing the correct cuff width? It is a rare opportunity to distinguish you from the rest of the crowd. For those men who desire cuffed pants, I recommend them to have the cuffs of their pants altered properly.

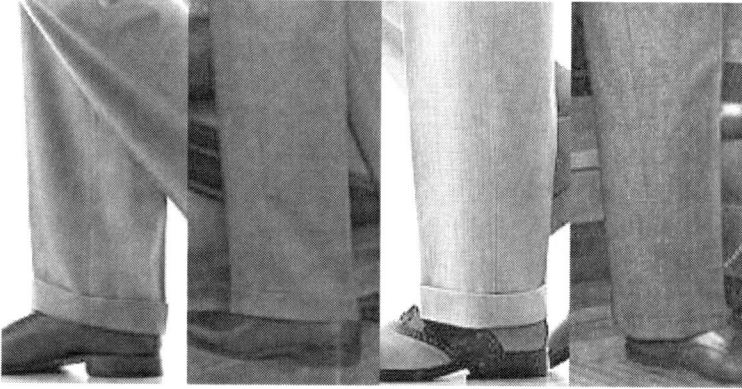

Insufficient cuff width makes the cuffs look insignificant and make the pair of pants look cheap.

33.   *Plain front pants should never have cuffs.*

A customer bought a pair of plain-front pants and wanted the pants to be shortened. The salesperson asked the customer whether he wanted his pants to be cuffed. The customer said, "Yes." When the customer returned a week later to pick up his pants, I happened to be around and noticed the problem. I mentioned to the customer that he probably would be the only person in the city who wore a pair of plain-front pants with cuffs. The customer felt embarrassed and asked me to change the bottom finish of the pants. (The left photo shows Francis Quimet, the 1913 U.S. Open golf champion, wore a pair of plain front pants with cuffs.)

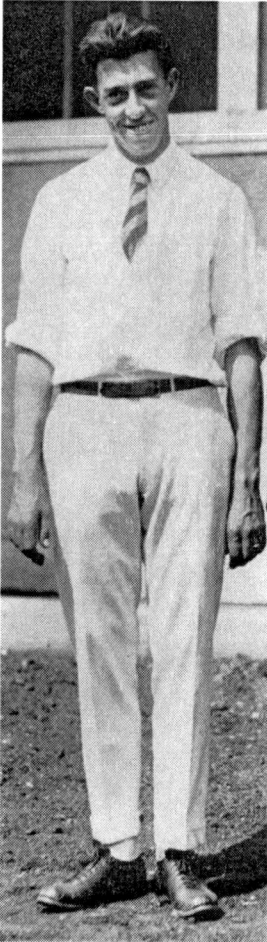

Another customer brought back to the store a pair of tailored pants and complained that the cuffs were not done right. There were unwanted creases on one of the cuffs. A salesclerk at the suit department accepted the return. Another associate smoothed out the wrinkles with a steamer. I looked at the pants and found that the pair had a plain front. It amazed me that so many people had handled the same pair of trousers and no one ever told the customer that flat front pants should not be cuffed.

Although making flat front pants with cuffs is an easy task, traditionally men do not wear cuffs with a pair of plain-front pants. Manufacturers make readymade plain-front pants with cuffs for women's slacks but not for men's slacks. Some men do express to me their desire to buy a pair of plain-front pants with cuffs. They will be disappointed for being unable to find any in the market. When a man buys a pair of tailored slacks or wants to alter the bottom of a pair of readymade slacks, he has the opportunity to request the pants to be finished with or without cuffs. If a man is uninformed and if the fitter and the tailor are ignorant about this sartorial blunder, the man may have a rare chance to make such an awkward mistake. I hope someone in the street or in his workplace will stop him immediately.

The Duke of Windsor sometimes dressed himself in unconventional ways, such as inserting his tie between two buttons on the shirtfront. Fashion critics often comment that the master understood the rules and therefore knew how to break the rules. There are a few customs in men's clothing, such as unfastening the last button of the vest and wearing non-matched set of tie and pocket square. I do not believe it is a big deal if a man disobeys the tradition by fastening the last button of a vest or wearing a matching tie and pocket square set. But, it is intolerable to wear a pair of plain front pants with cuffs. Connoisseurs consider the act a sartorial terrorism. It is extremely rare that a gentleman would intentionally commit such a mistake.

It is unclear whether Lester B. Pearson, former Prime Minister of Canada and Nobel Peace Prize winner, wore a pair of plain front pants with cuffs or rolled up the bottom of his pants.

34. Why is it better to have the pant legs finished with a slanted bottom?

Booker T. Washington lectured in front of Mark Twain at Carnegie Hall. I wonder how Twain would think about the manner of Washington, who wore an awful long pair of trousers. Twain once wrote, "Clothes make the man. Naked people have little or no influence on society."

A common mistake in wearing a pair of pants is to wear the pants too long. Although it is also a mistake to wear a pair of pants too short, most men recognize the problem right away. After serving tens of thousands of customers, I have found it disturbing that most men do not know the proper length of a pair of pants. Most men can tolerate pants that are too long but not ones that are too short. Current readymade pants have a much smaller leg opening than those pants made in the good old days. Even though a pair of pants is three or four inches too long, the pants are unlikely to fall under the shoes. The extra length will fold and bulge on top of shoes. You may think this is unattractive. Yet, many men wear their pants this way; some even enjoy this style.

What is the proper length of a pair of pants?

The answer is more complex than what an average man thinks. To make it simple, a pair of pants is too short if the bottom front of the pant leg does not touch the top of the shoe. Similarly, a pair of pants is too long if the bottom back of the pant leg touches the ground or has any wrinkle or break.

Many fashion experts commend that all pants should have a little break because they believe every pair of pants should be long enough to cover the socks. This is unintelligent thinking. Whether or not the socks will be seen has something to do with the type of shoes, the bottom width of pants and the length of pants. You can cover your socks without a break if the bottoms of your pants touch the shoes. Although it is proper to cover the socks while a man is standing straight, it has never been a shame for a man to show his socks when he is moving around or sitting down.

It is disturbing that all ten leaders from the G-8 nations in 2001 wore too long their trousers. Compare the sloppiness of their trousers with the neatness of those worn by the Queen's Guard at Buckingham Palace.

None of the five living U.S. presidents in 2009 wore a proper length of trousers.

The amount of break not only has something to do with the length of the pants, but also has something to do with how a person wears his pants and how the bottom of the pants is finished. Hence, it is ridiculous to determine the length of a pair of pants by the break. Do you know you can have your pants cut long without any break?

The break is the result of the pants being too long. Why would a man wear a pant length that is longer than he needs?

Think of the creases as the soul of the pants. Nothing looks more magnificent than a pair of razor-sharp creases. To keep the creases uninterrupted, a man ought to minimize the amount of break. Owing to the shape of our foot, breaks in the bottom front of the pants may be unavoidable. Breaks in the back of the pants are inexcusable.

A pair of properly fitted slacks should have sharp creases with little or no break.

223

What a difference between a pair of lively pants that has sharp creases and a pair of dull pants that has no creases!

The pant legs are better off finished with a slanted bottom than with a straight bottom.

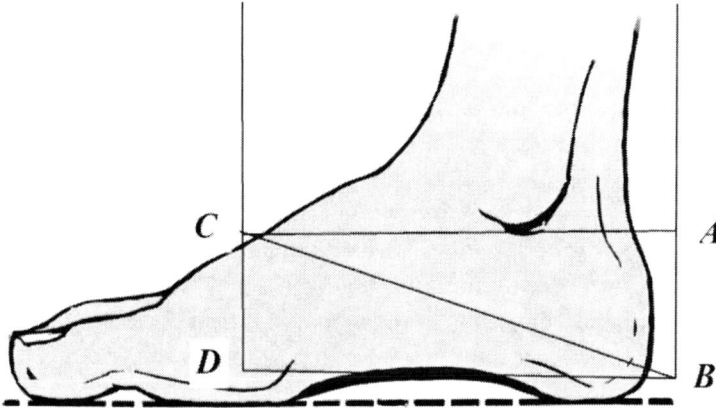

Because of the human foot shape, a man can avoid a break if he wears his pants short (AC). If he wears a pair of long pants (BD), the excess length (CD) will fold on top of the foot or shoe, known as the "break." To avoid a break with a pair of long pants, the man can tilt his foot by wearing high heel shoes. Since men do not usually wear high heel shoes, the only way to avoid a break is to slant his pants (BC).

Experts cannot agree on the proper length of a pair of pants. Some authors suggest that a pair of pants should barely touch the top of the shoes. When a pair of pants is cut this short, several problems emerge.

First, much of the socks will be seen when the wearer moves around.

Second, the bottom of the pants keeps falling inside the shoes, especially when the man wears a pair of loafers instead of oxford shoes.

Third, a pair of shorter pants makes the legs look shorter. Some image consultants suggest that a short man should wear a shorter length of pants to make the legs appear relatively longer. This is dreaming. To help lengthen the leg line, it is more effective to include the foot as part of the leg. To achieve this, the pair of pants should be long enough to stay in contact with the top of shoes without excessive break. The proper length of pants will extend the leg line, whereas a pair of pants that is too short will cut off the leg line above the foot.

Last, uneven pant legs will show through a pair of shorter pants. Some men have an uneven waist or a pair of uneven legs. Other men may have a normal body but they pull their pants up unevenly at the waist. It is also possible that both pant legs are cut unevenly. Regardless of the reasons, the uneven pant legs will be exposed when they are suspended in the air.

Theoretically a pair of pants can reach anywhere on the back of the shoes; however, the ideal position for a pair of pants to end is where the back and the heel of the shoe meet. When a pair of pants is cut this long, the pants will have a break a few inches long in the front. To eliminate the unnecessary break, a man either tilts his feet by wearing high heel shoes or by wearing a pair of pants with a slanted bottom. Because men do not usually wear high heel shoes, the only remedy is to slant the bottom of the pant legs. The amount of break determines how sharp the slant should be. A few factors influence the amount of break.

1) If everything else is held the same, the length of the pants is the most important factor that determines the amount of break.

2) If a man wears his pant waist lower in the front or if a man has bad posture and leans the body forward, additional break will occur.

3) High heel shoes reduce the amount of break. Many women look marvelous wearing a pair of pants with high heel shoes. The pair of pants drapes gracefully without any break, producing two sharp crease lines.

4) The larger the opening of the pant legs, the less the amount of break.

5) The bulkier the top of the shoes, the more the amount of break.

Some experts suggest that a man should wear a pant length that is ¾ inch shorter in the front. Because each individual is affected by a combination of different factors as mentioned above, I urge each man to weigh the factors that apply to him. A man can slant the bottom of his pants up to 1 ¼ inches. A pant bottom that is slanted more than 1 ¼ inches may draw unwanted attention. Keep in mind that the sole purpose of slanting the pant bottom is to eliminate the unnecessary break. If a man prefers to wear his pants short without a break, he needs not to have his pant bottom slanted.

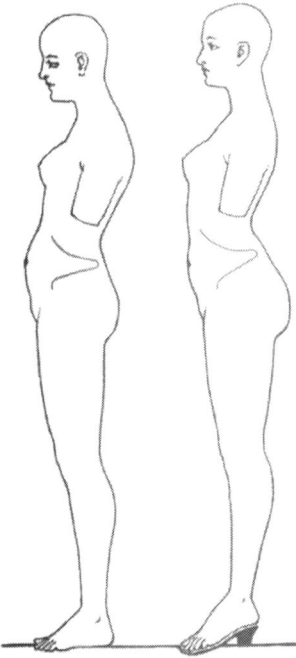

The heels of shoes help keep the body standing erect. A high heel helps eliminate unnecessary break and drape the pants freely.

(a)   (b)

A pair of short length pants, photo (a), shortens the leg line, exposes much of the socks, and may get caught inside the shoes. A pair of long length pants (b), on the other hand, creates too much break in the front. The break disrupts the sharp crease and leg line. The only way to have a long length without unnecessary break is to finish the pair of pants with a slanted bottom.

The perfect pant length

The back of the pants: reaches the joint where the back and the heel of the shoe meet.
The front of the pants: barely touches the top of the shoe with very little or no break.

A pair of properly slanted pants has little or no break even if the pant legs are cut long.

Readymade pants these days are seldom slanted. If you prefer a slanted pant bottom, you may have the pants altered in a tailor shop. Be cautious that many tailors cut the bottom of the pants slightly shorter in the front, but they hem the pants using the wrong method, which produces a straight instead of a slanted bottom finish. To test whether your pant bottom is slanted, flatten your pant leg with the front crease in the center. If you notice that the front crease is shorter than the back crease and the opening of the pant leg looks like a lip or flat diamond shape, then you know your pant bottom is slanted.

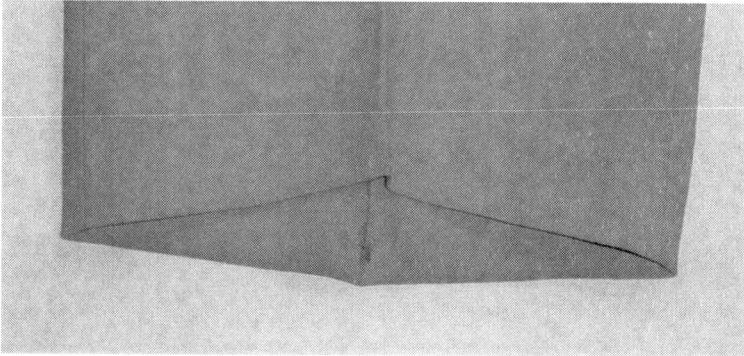

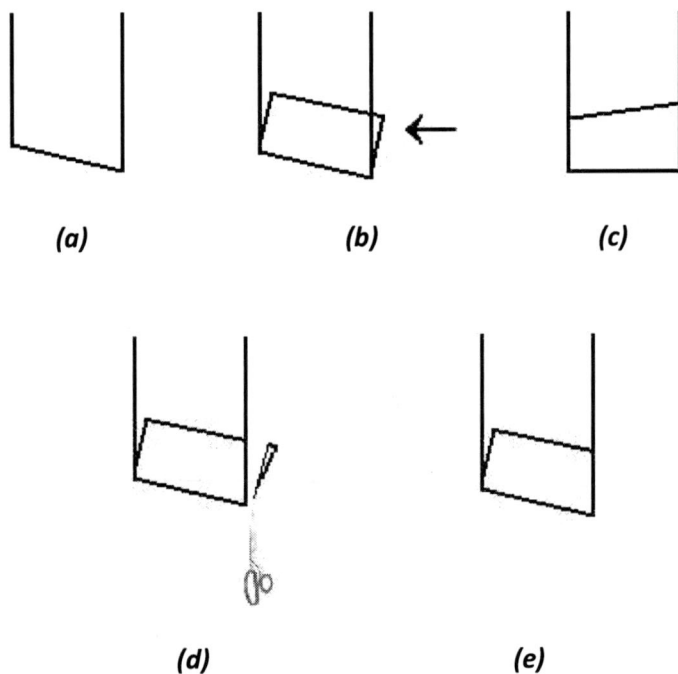

(a) (b) (c)

(d) (e)

When a pant leg is cut slanted (a), the hem will stick out (b). Most tailors use an easy way to finish the pant leg by pushing the hem inward. The result is a flat (c) instead of a slanted bottom. A better way to finish the pant leg with a slanted bottom (e) is to trim off the excessive fabric that sticks out (d) before hemming.

35.   Should you give your trousers a break?

Trousers: Give Yourself A Break

Cuff - No Break   Cuff - Half Break   Cuff - Full Break

Plain - No Break   Plain - Half Break   Plain - Full Break

Proper break (the amount of fabric that rests on your shoe tops) is an important consideration when you're having trousers altered. The type of break also determines where the bottom of the trouser will fall on the back of your shoe or heel.

Alteration and tailor shops use the "break" to determine the length of pants. The concept is somehow flawed. Many men look at the poster and tell their fitter or tailor what type of break they prefer without considering various factors that cause a break.

Many clothing stores and tailor shops use the concept of break to help consumers determine the length of their pants. The concept is misleading. All the salesperson or tailor does is to cut the pants shorter if the customer wants "no break" and to cut the pants longer if the customer wants "full break." The break is the result of the pants' being too long. Why would any man want to wear a pair of pants that is too long? If a man prefers a pair of long pants, why can he just say so? It is silly that many men use the term to justify their wearing a pair of sloppy long pants. They think they wear their pants appropriately because the pair of pants has a half or full break. They do not realize there is no criterion to determine how long the pants is considered having a full or half break. Many men wear their pants so long that the pants have multiple breaks in the back, which is inexcusable. They also do not realize that they can have a pair of long pants with little or no break if they finish the bottom of the pants properly.

Pants with excessive break look ridiculous no matter how you call it, a half or full break.

Pants that fall straight down from the waist without any break look marvelous.

Breaks interrupt the crease and leg line. They should be avoided. As explained in previous chapters, dress pants are better off to be finished with a slanted bottom, which helps eliminate or reduce the amount of fabric resting on the shoe tops. Cuffed bottom cannot be slanted using conventional hemming methods. Hence, break may be unavoidable with cuffed bottom unless you cut your pants short or use other methods. There are confounding factors that influence the amount of break. You should consider these factors before you tell your fitter or tailor what type of break you prefer. To reduce the amount of unnecessary break, you should keep your waistband horizontal to the ground all the way around. You may also choose pants with a wider leg opening and avoid bulky shoes.

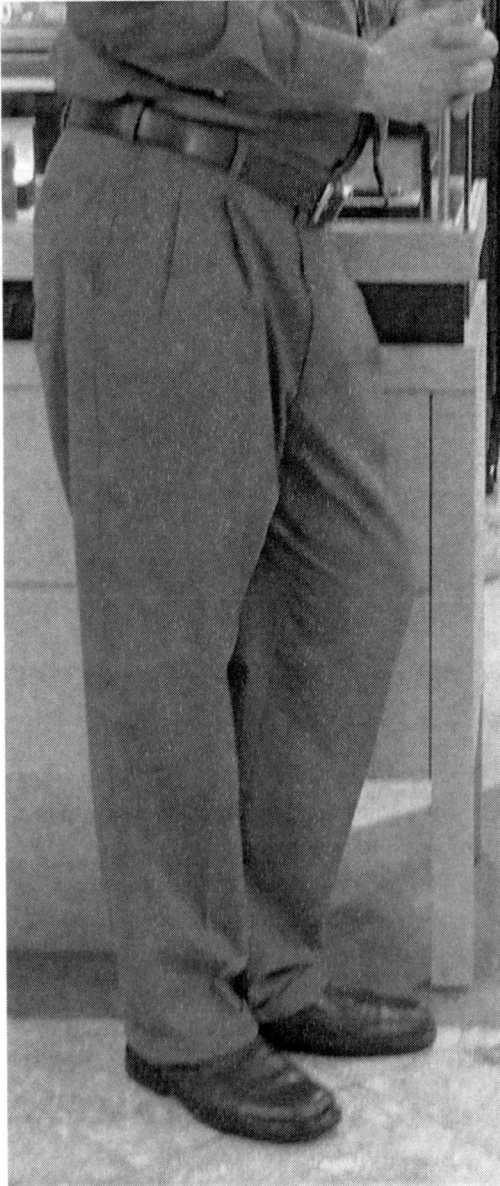

The way you wear your pants will affect the break on top of your shoe.

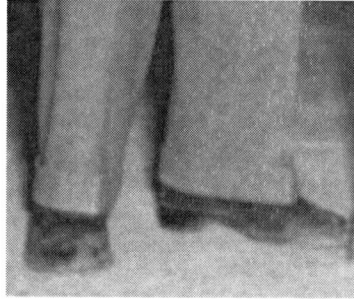

The bottom width of the pant legs and the type of shoes also affect the amount of break.

36. Why does the bottom width of the pant legs matter?

I sold a customer a pair of ready-to-wear slacks and recommended him to have the pants shortened since the pants were too long. I was stunned by the price he paid--three times the price of a simple hemming. The customer told me that his tailor insisted on tapering the bottom of the pant legs because the legs were shortened too much. In the past, pant legs are tapered from the waist to the knee and then cut straight down to the leg opening. Today, readymade pants are tapered from the waist to the leg opening. It was a waste of money to taper pant legs that were already narrow.

Like this customer, most men prefer a trimmer cut for pant legs but they never realize the consequences. If you do not know the problems with a pair of slim pant legs, just look the left leg of Secretary of Navy, Dan Thomas's pants. When pants are cut too short or too narrow, it is easy for the pant legs to be caught inside the shoe or on top of the shoe.

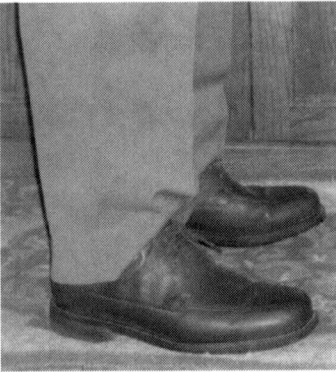

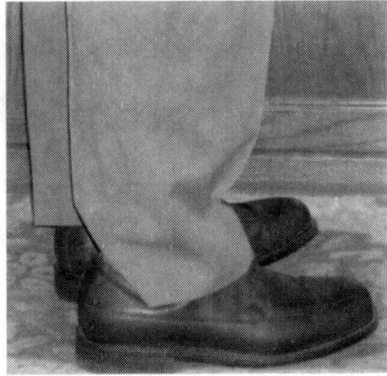

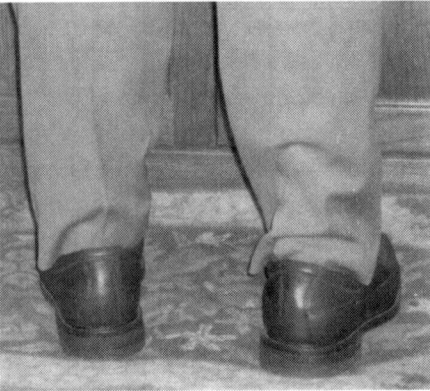

Different fashion experts suggest different bottom widths of the pant leg to cover from ½ to ¾ of the shoe. In truth, it is difficult to determine the proper width of the pant leg solely on the size of the shoe. Foot size varies greatly among different men. I believe the width of the pant legs should correspond to the wearer's body figure and the rest of his ensemble. How large a portion of the shoe should be covered by the pant legs is less important. If everything else is the same, I recommend slacks with a larger leg opening. Slacks with a small leg opening are problematic. They keep falling inside the shoes, create more unwanted break above the shoes, and expose more of the socks especially with loafer shoes. Ideally, the bottom width of the pant leg is to cover about $^2/_3$ of the shoe.

If you prefer and cannot find readymade pants with a wider leg opening, you may intentionally buy longer pants and have them shortened to the proper length.

37.   It is inexcusable to wear a pair of uneven pants.

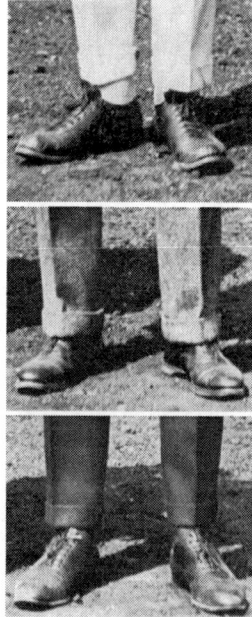

How was it possible that the three of the five amateur golfers who ever won the U.S. Open happened to wear a pair of uneven pants at the same time?

A man can justify his wearing a pair of wrong color, pattern or style of pants by claiming individual taste or preference. But, it is difficult to declare innocence for wearing a pair of uneven pants. Why do many men, including the presidents of the United States, walk around with such a pair of pants?

Many suit departments, alteration shops, or tailors use an upside down "Y" bar to assist in the measurement of pant length. The customer stands on a level platform. The fitter places the one-foot long Y bar upside down on the platform against the back of each leg and makes a mark on the pants at the top of the upside down Y bar. Whoever alters the pair of pants will cut the bottom of pants by lining up the marks on both legs instead of lining up both sides of the pants from the waistband. It is my belief that the Y bar method is responsible for most of the uneven pant legs.

Why do merchants use the Y bar? They use the Y bar to make their alteration jobs easier. Because a pair of pants is hung from the waistband down, it is logic to assume that the pair of pants should be aligned from the top of the waistband. But this will require the tailor to spread out and to line up the entire pants from the waist to the bottom on a large tabletop. It is no wonder that alteration and tailor shops prefer to line up both pant legs at a place near the bottom of the pants. To save a few minutes for each pair of pants can mean a large reduction on the overall work load for a busy shop. In our alteration department, it takes only four minutes to hem a pair of cuffed or non-cuffed pants with a sewing machine.

What is wrong with the Y bar method? How a pair of pants hangs at the waistband will affect the look of the pant bottom. If a man hangs his pants one side higher than the other at the waistband, the two pant legs will appear uneven at the bottom. This happens quite often because every man does not necessarily hang the pair of pants correctly each time they put on one, even if the pair of pants fits perfectly. When a man finds a suit jacket that fits, the suit trousers are often too tight or too loose and require alteration. It is difficult to try on a pair of trousers horizontal to the ground if the waist is either too tight or too loose. The Y bar method works only if a man wears his pants correctly at the waistband, but there is no guarantee that the man will do so during the fitting.

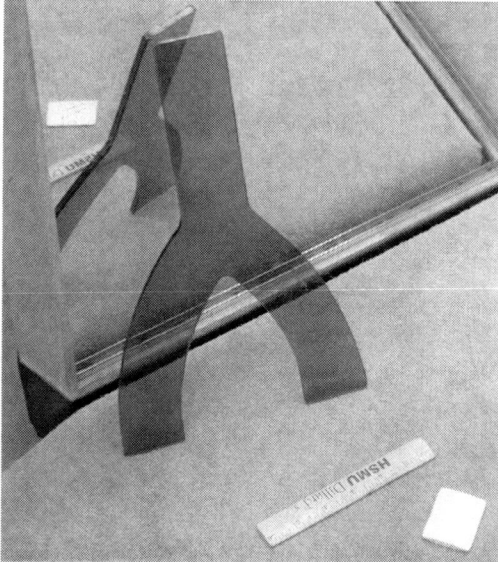

The supporters of the Y bar method claim that a garment should be tailored according to the way a person wears his clothes. If the wearer hangs his pants higher on one side of his waist, the length of the pant leg should be adjusted accordingly. This is a fallacious thinking because not every man wears his pants at the same location each time he puts on a pair of pants. In truth, most men do not even notice it if they hang their pants uneven on both sides of their waist. If a man cannot show his pant legs even to the ground by wearing a pair of equal length pants, do you think he can do better with a pair of unequal length pants?

The supporters of the Y bar method also claim that the Y bar marks can correct the length difference if a man has a pair of uneven legs. When a man has a pair of uneven legs, he is not going to hang his shorter leg in the air when standing. The uneven legs will result in an uneven waistline. The man is better off to wear a high heel shoe to compensate for the shortage of leg length. Or, the man may wear a pair of specially tailored pants with one side higher on the waistband to conceal the uneven waist. After all, the purpose of a garment is to hide the bad parts and showcase the good parts of the body. If a man has an uneven pair of legs and is unwilling to adopt either remedy, he may have the reason to cut his two pant legs differently. It is inexcusable for a man with a pair of even legs to wear a pair of uneven pant legs.

The photo of the three amateur golfers reflects how common it was some time ago for men to wear a pair of uneven dress pants. It is less common these days to see a man wear a pair of uneven dress pants for two reasons. One is that most men wear readymade instead of tailored slacks. Readymade pants are cut evenly for both pant legs. The other reason is that many men wear their pants too long. It is difficult to tell whether the two pant legs are even if the extra length of pant legs bulges on top of the shoes. No matter if your pants are cut evenly or unevenly, you should make sure that both of your pant legs are equal to the ground when wearing.

244

38. Does it make a difference between a two-button and a three-button jacket?

I am surprised by the number of men, who refuse to wear a three-button jacket. They think that the two-button is the norm and one extra button makes the jacket look weird. They do not realize that the three-button was invented before the two-button jacket. In the past, jacket front opening was cut high to protect the wearer from the harsh elements. As modern living settings become climate-controlled, men have less need for a warm jacket indoors. Over the years, the jacket front V opening has been cut lower and lower to the current popular two-button style.

Both two-button and three-button jackets are acceptable in business. The one-button jackets are common in women's clothing but are rare in menswear these days. Any single breasted jacket with four buttons or more is considered a costume rather than a dress.

Most men have two balance points.

Scholars studied the portraits of great artists and found that the head in the portraits often appears in balance with the upper body. They discovered an important concept of balance and proportion, called balance points. Most people have two balance points. The first balance point on the upper body can be determined by measuring the length of a man's face from hairline to chin with a tape or string and by letting the tape or string fall from the chin down the man's chest. Where the tape or string ends is the man's first balance point. The second balance point can be decided in the same manner except that the length is taken from the widest part of the face to the chin.

Frans Hals's Gipsy Girl

Eva Gozal's Portrait of
a Woman in White

Portrait of John Ruskin (author
unknown)

Charles Bird King's Portrait
of David Vann

*Portraits showing that the chest front opening
corresponds to the first balance point.*

Van Gogh's self-portrait shows that the vest opening corresponds to the second balance point.

The length of the jacket V opening should be one or 1.6 times the head length of the wearer.

When a jacket is buttoned, the jacket front forms a V opening and becomes the focus of attention beneath the face. It is wise to have the V opening correspond to the face according to the balance points.

One of the advantages of the three-button jacket is that the V opening of the jacket corresponds to a man's face because both the V opening and the face are about the same length. In other words, the sharp angle of the V opening is at or near the first balance point of the upper body. This makes the jacket very attractive when the head and the upper body are the focus of attention.

Suit designers lower the positions of gorge, chest pocket, and waist, to balance the body line of a tall man. The gorge is the seam that joins the jacket's collar to its lapel. None of these details, however, are as effective as the V opening of a buttoned jacket in playing down the height of a tall man. A short V opening escorts the viewer's eyes upward, whereas a long V opening invites the eyes downward. A small V opening will appear disproportionate to a long or large jacket. For this reason, I would recommend a three-button jacket to a man, who is short or sits a lot. For those men, who are tall or stand up frequently, a two-button jacket may be a better choice.

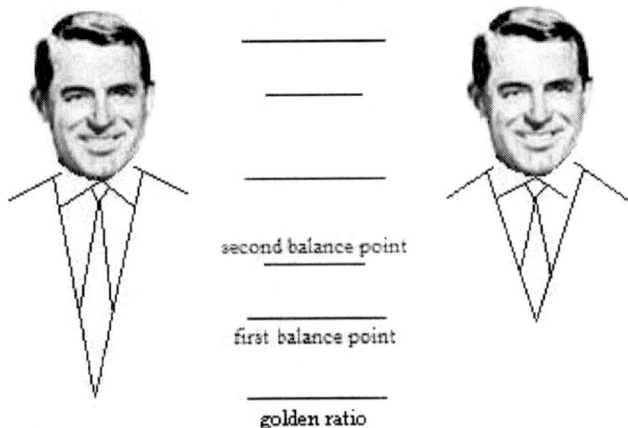

second balance point

first balance point

golden ratio

Ideal V opening of a 2-button jacket

Ideal V opening of a 3-button jacket

The best length of the V opening on a two-button jacket is about 1.6 times the length of the head based on the golden section. The great masters of art have found that the relation of one part to another is very pleasing to the human eye if the ratio is about 5 to 3, or 1.6 to 1. This visual proportion is known as the Golden Section, Golden Mean, or Golden Ratio. Any V opening that approximates or exceeds two times the length of the face will diminish the proper balance of the head.

Place the triangle of the vest V opening at the first or second balance point.

If a man wears a three-piece rather than a two-piece suit, or if a man wears a non-matching vest under a suit or sport jacket, the position of the vest V opening becomes an important consideration. Because no other place can achieve a more harmonious relation to a person's face than the first and the second balance point, I sincerely recommend that a man ought to place the triangle of the jacket V opening at the first balance point and the triangle of the vest V opening at the second balance point if the man wears a three-button jacket. If a man wears a two-button jacket, he ought to place the triangle of the vest V opening at the first balance point.

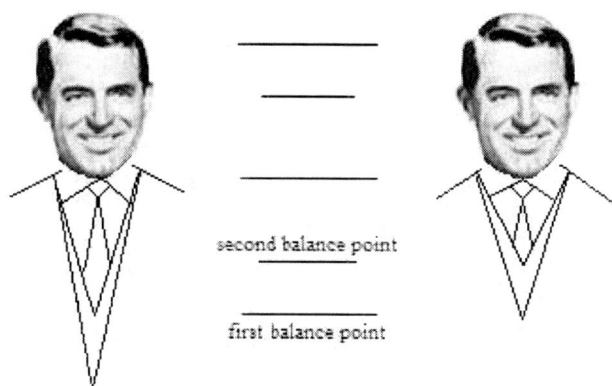

second balance point

first balance point

Young Harry Truman, Gandhi, and President Wilson's jacket front opening land at second balance point.

250

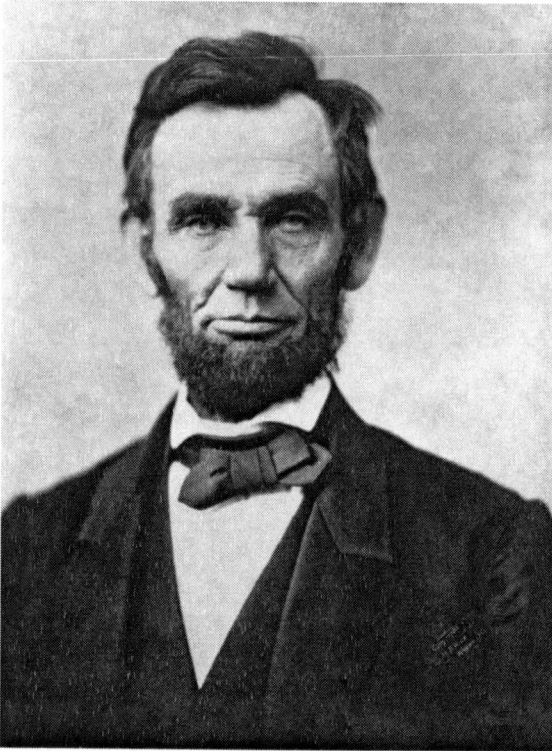

General Petraeus's jacket V opening, Gary Cooper and
Lincoln's vest V opening correspond perfectly
to their first balance point.

Douglas Fairbanks, Jr. and President Bush's jacket opening are in the golden ratio whereas President Kennedy's equals two head lengths.

JFK, Jr.'s coat opening exceeds two head lengths, diminishing the significance of the head.

Avoid a V opening that approximates or exceeds two times the length of the face.

The V opening invites viewer's eyes downward. When the V approximates or exceeds two head lengths, it diminishes the significance of the face. An ideal man has a torso of about two head lengths. It is esthetically unbalanced to wear a jacket V opening that falls beyond the waistline or two times the length of the head.

39. Wear a cardigan instead of a high-cut V or crew neck sweater with a jacket.

Sweaters are designed to keep the body warm. Hence, most sweaters have a high-cut neckline. The problem with a high-cut sweater is that it covers a large portion of the shirt collar and the tie. Furthermore, a high-cut neckline does not respond to any balance point.

Many men enjoy wearing a sweater or sweater vest under a jacket. It is my recommendation to wear a low-cut cardigan or V-neck instead of a high-cut V or crew neck sweater because a cardigan sweater tends to have a larger chest opening that balances the head or face of the wearer.

(a)

(b)

The chest opening of a low-cut cardigan (c) or V-neck (b) allows the shirt collar and the tie to be shown and tends to correspond to the balance point while the chest opening of a high-cut crew or V neck (a) sweater does not.

(c)

40. Where to place a tie tack, clip or chain

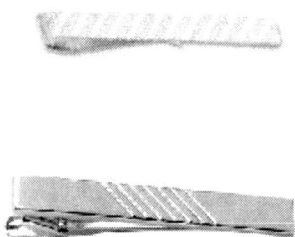

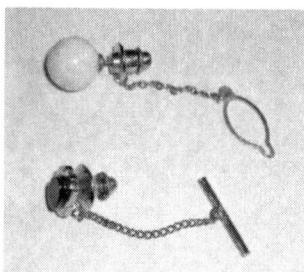

When a man bends his upper body, his tie tends to swing around. A tie bar, clip, tack or chain is used to secure the tie. Nevertheless, few men know the proper location to put on these accessories.

Like President Reagan, most men put on their tie tack, clip or chain at random without thinking there may be a better location for the jewelry. Consequently, the tie tack or bar often lands at a different place each time the man wears the accessory.

Some time ago, men wore high-cut vests and jackets. There was no need to hold down the tie with a tie tack or clip. Most men wore tie accessories for decoration purpose. Tie tacks, clips or chains were placed high near the tie knot for visibility.

Today, most men wear low-cut jackets without the vests.
Consequently, men are moving down their tie accessories.

It is mind blowing that President Johnson placed his tie tack right on the triangle point of the jacket V opening. The top button has the same effect of securing the tie as the tie tack does. President Johnson should raise the position of his tie tack, making it more visible. Or, he could just forget wearing one.

To prevent the tie from swinging around, it is more effective to place the tie tack or clip near the bottom of the tie. Nonetheless, the placement lures eyes downward and looks unattractive.

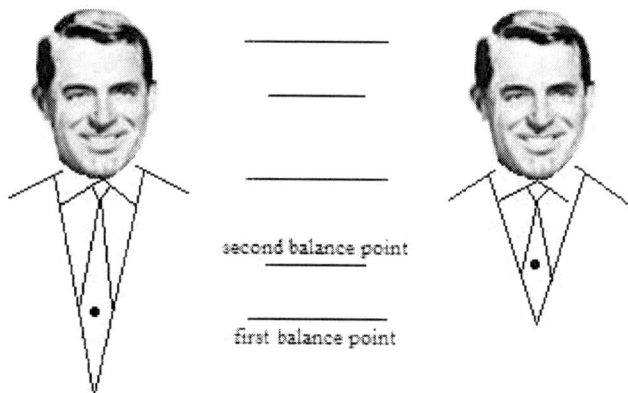

second balance point

first balance point

The best place for a tie accessory is the first balance point. The next place is the second balance point if the first point has been taken. The concepts of balance points will be discussed later in this book.

Because a flat tie that falls straight from under the collar is lifeless, it is wise to use the tie tack or clip to help suspend the tie for a lively arch. It is a custom that a well-attired man should not match his pocket square with his tie. Fashion experts believe that the matching set invites eyes to look sideways instead of looking vertically. For the same reason, the tie bar should tilt a little.

Edward and Robert Kennedy placed their tie clips too low and did not tip the clips. Edward contradicted the effect of his diagonally striped tie by wearing the tie clip horizontally.

It is smart to tilt the tie bar or clip to lure the eyes from looking sideways. A tilted bar is in harmony with the long narrow tie.

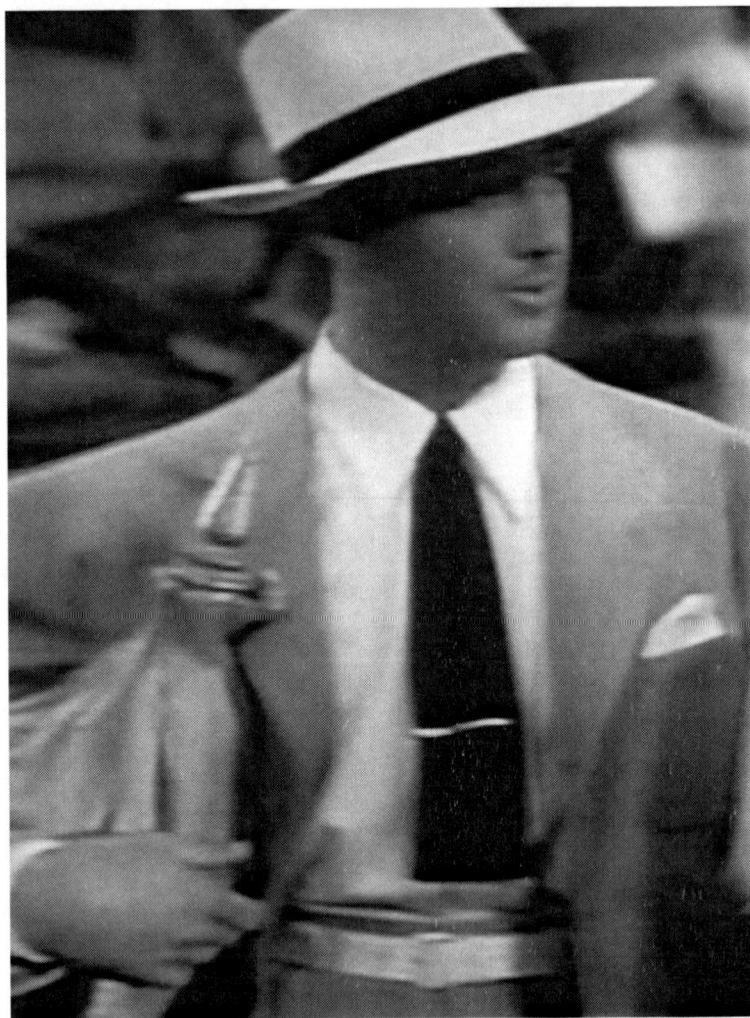

One exception is to have the tie bar go across the tie horizontally when wearing it with a square-ended tie.

Isn't it redundant to wear a tie clip to hold down a tie when the tie is already tucked inside the pants?

41. Should a pocket square match the tie?

During my long career in men's clothing business, I have encountered countless customers, who wished to purchase a pocket square that exactly matches his tie or vice versa. I told each customer that the pocket square does not have to match the tie. Some customers appreciated the advice. Others gave me a suspicious look. They probably doubted my words, thinking what a sales clerk would know.

While fashion experts unanimously suggest that the pocket square should not match the tie, most consumers do not know this advice and continue to look for a perfect match between these two items. It is hard to blame consumers for being naïve about this issue. Merchants all over the country, including many famous designers and tie houses, sell matching tie and pocket square sets in fancy boxes. How could you not expect that consumers will think the tie and pocket square should come in a pair? Manufacturers make the matching set perhaps because modern neckties are cut on the bias at an angle of 45 degrees to the weave. What should manufacturers do with the corner piece? They might use the piece to make a pocket square and sell it together with the tie.

Fashion experts explain that what a man wears should encourage the viewers to look vertically instead of sideways. Hence, a pocket square should relate to the tie as little as possible. To ensure that a pocket square will not overtly relate to the tie, Alan Flusser came out with an idea. He proposed that the texture s of the tie and pocket square should differ. "If the tie has a silken luster, the pocket square should be of a dry material such as linen. If the tie is of a dulled material such as wool, linen or cotton, the pocket square can be shiny, such as a printed solid or foulard." The proposal may be too strict to be practical. Most ties and pocket squares are made of fine silk. It is unreasonable to ask a man not to wear a tie or pocket square made of the best material. Fashion experts often suggest that the texture of the tie should somewhat conform to the texture of the suit or sport jacket, such as a coarse wool tie with a textured jacket. It makes absolutely no sense to wear a shiny satin handkerchief on a nubby tweed jacket only because the smooth surface of the silk square will contradict the rough texture of a wool tie.

The expert's explanation does not sound convincing. It is unclear that a matching tie and pocket square set is more distracting than a non-matching set. If a pocket square will distract the view from the tie, should it be better not to wear one at all?

Men's clothing lacks variety and looks uniform. A man only wears few decorative items. Why forsake the opportunity of adding interest and versatility to the ensemble by wearing different tie and pocket square? A matching pair looks pretty much the same and suggests that both items come from the same package.

The shirt serves as the background for the tie whereas the jacket is the backdrop of the pocket handkerchief. Most men wear contrast shirt and jacket, such as a light shirt and a dark jacket. This makes it more difficult to choose a matching tie and square set that goes well with both the shirt and the jacket.

There is no sound reason that a pocket square should not match the tie. At the same time, there is no sound reason that a pocket square should match the tie either. If a man insist on a matching tie and pocket square set, I find no reason to object the practice. What is silly is that many men mistakenly think a pocket square must match the tie. They will not wear one unless it is perfectly matched.

The pocket square and the tie are separate items. It is absolutely unnecessary to relate one to the other. If you enjoy wearing pocket squares, choose those that coordinate well with your jackets. If you bought a tie and a pocket square in a set, this does not mean that you are obligated to wear both in the same outfit. If you insist on matching, match between the minor colors in the tie and pocket handkerchief.

Although the reason for wearing a non-matching tie and pocket square set may be unpersuasive to many men, it is my opinion that a well-attired man is better off to follow the tradition, the same reason that a well dressed man will unfasten the last button of a vest. There are different stories about the last button of the vest. One story suggests that King George IV forgot to fasten the last button of his vest. His friend, George Brummell, the legendary dandy, noticed the mistake and immediately followed suit. Another story claims that King Edward VII was so heavy that he could not get the bottom button fastened on his vest, or he simply forgot. The act became a gentlemanly tradition. If you decide to correct the past mistake by fastening the last button of the vest, no one will consider you a smart person. If you leave the last button open, some sophisticate dressers may think you know the history and follow the custom. If you insist on matching your tie and pocket square, you are taking the risk that someone may regard you as an ignorant person. What do you have to lose if you follow the conventional wisdom? "Overtly coordinating, or even worse, matching the tie and handkerchief, is a sure sign of an unsure dresser," observed Alan Flusser.

It is unclear that a matching tie and pocket square set (top two photos) is more distracting than a non-matching set (bottom two photos). Fashion experts recommend that the pocket square should not match the tie.

Cheaper ties sold with a matching pocket square at $49.50 each in 2009.

More expensive ties sold with a non-matching square at $95.00 each in 2009.

George Foreman wore a matching tie and pocket square set, made from the same fabric. The practice has been considered a sartorial blunder.

42.   How to buy and wear pocket squares

273

As explained in previous chapter, most consumers have difficulty finding a pocket square because they mistakenly think a pocket handkerchief must match the tie. Once they realize the mistake, the task becomes quite simple.

To choose a pocket square, you should first know how you will fold it. Most customers worried too much about the color of the fabric. When I asked them which form they intended to use, most of them were stunned. Some of them did not even know how to fold any style. I showed customers the photo in previous page. They were excited to learn that there are many interesting ways to fold a pocket square. Some forms can be presented more effectively with a stiff piece of cloth while other forms are better to be displayed with a piece of soft material.

Most pocket squares are made in a single solid color. If you wish to create multi colors, you can use a handkerchief with patterns or trims in different colors, or combine more than one solid color handkerchief. Some handkerchiefs have a different color on the reverse side. Some have different color arrangements in different sections of the square. This is like several handkerchiefs in one.

In recent years, fake squares are gaining popularity. I have been asked by many customers about where to buy them. Fake ones are made by gluing small pieces of fabric on the top of a cardboard. The cardboard can be inserted into the jacket's chest pocket, showing only the fabric arrangement. I discourage the use of any fake pocket square since it suggests the wearer is either lazy or unintelligent to learn how to fold a simple piece of cloth.

Fashion experts suggest that the pocket square should not peek out of the pocket more than an inch or so. In truth, the height of the handkerchief should base on the style of the fold. For a traditional TV fold, one half inch is sufficient. For fancy patterns, such as the "three points" or "peak," they may require more than an inch.

Because the handkerchief is folded to reveal its points, the edges need the graceful roll and stitch to convey its refinement. It is preferred that the hand-rolled edges are shown when you fold and place your handkerchief in the pocket.

The pocket handkerchief should not be too large that it bulges. Nor should it be too small that the cloth shifts around inside the pocket. The ideal size for a handkerchief is the twelve-to-fourteen-inch square for thick fabrics and sixteen-to-eighteen-inch square for thin materials. Alan Flusser wrote the following.

Wearing a handkerchief that looks neither affected nor sloppy is akin to developing a discerning palate for good wine or food; it takes some practice. Douglas Fairbanks, Jr. often reminded me that if you want to dress well, it takes time to look as if it took no time at all.

There are no golden rules concerning how to fold a pocket square. In this chapter, I am to provide a few samples of popular forms. You can create your own styles. It is just as simple as you fold your napkins on a table top. Some folds, such as the Peaks, the Three Points and the Four Points, appear more studied while some forms, such as the Puff and the Flop, produce a random shape every time you fold it. The choice of the fold should not only accommodate your outfit and the atmosphere of the event, but also reflect your personality and your mood.

I do not believe that any man in his right mind would intentionally fold the handkerchief so small that it falls out of sight. My guess is that the folded hank does not fit the pocket securely. It shifts and falls inside the pocket after the man has moved around a while.

Fashion experts suggest that a pocket square should be displayed in a modest manner (top photo). It is ridiculous to wear a pocket square so high that it falls and flutters around (bottom photos).

Fashion authorities advise that a pocket square and flower should not be worn together for the combination is distracting. It has been well known that Fred Astaire (top photo) was insecure about the look of his face. He often wore both to distract viewers from looking at his face.

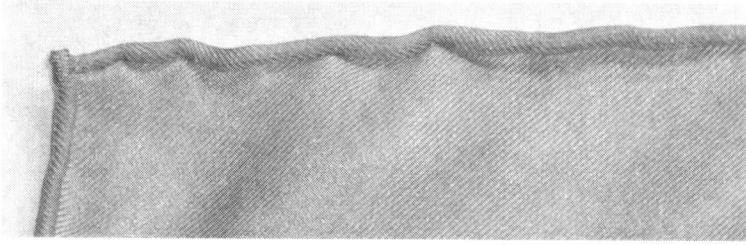

The edges of a fine handkerchief are always hand rolled and stitched.

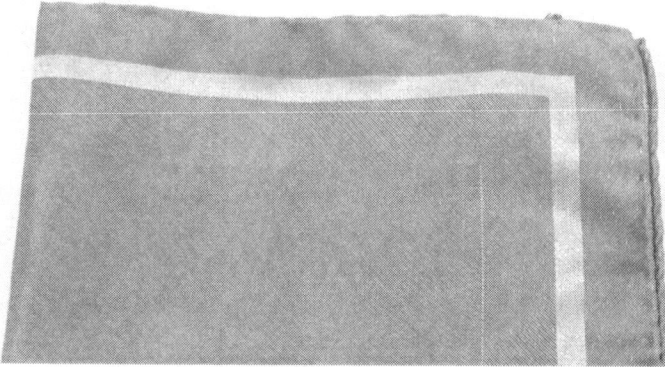

Handkerchiefs with trims or borders can create interesting patterns when folded.

Some pocket squares have a different color on the reverse side. Some have different color arrangements on different sections of the cloth. This is like having two or more handkerchiefs in one.

How to Fold the TV Fold

The TV fold originated in the 1940s and became very popular during the 50s. It is one of the simplest forms and is usually done with a solid stiff handkerchief.

There is no certain way to fold a TV fold. As you fold the hank to about one-eighth its full size, slip the hank into your pocket with the most edges showing about one-half to one inch above the pocket line. Make sure it is razor straight. The fold may be unfeasible for a slanted chest pocket. If you insist on wearing one with a slanted pocket, you may tip the handkerchief so that the edge of the hank parallels the line of the pocket opening.

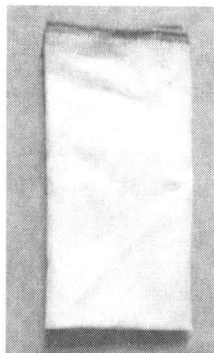

Keep the TV Fold thin and razor straight.

How to Fold the Puff

The Puff was allegedly invented by Fred Astaire. It is one of the few folds that do not show the edges. Hence, it is best done with a soft silk foulard.

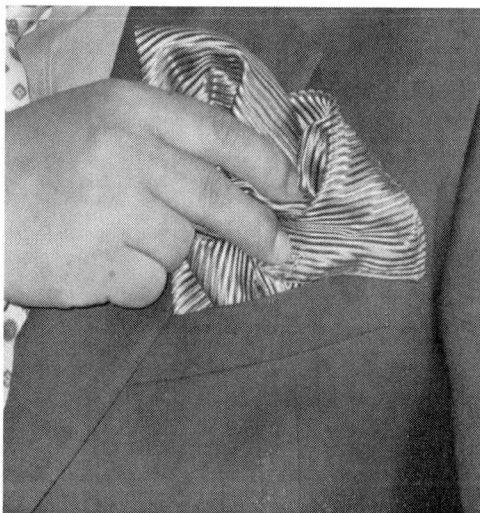

To execute the fold, you grasp the hank by its center and insert the entire hank into the pocket with the points hanging straight down first. You then pull and spread the fabric so it fills the pocket opening with only a "puff" of fabric showing.

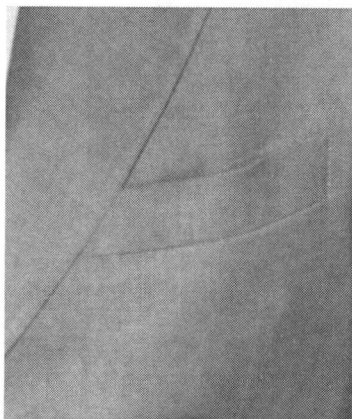

Prince Charles wearing a Puff.

How to Fold the Three Points

Fold the square into a triangle with the points matched perfectly. Have the flat side toward you, the top facing away.

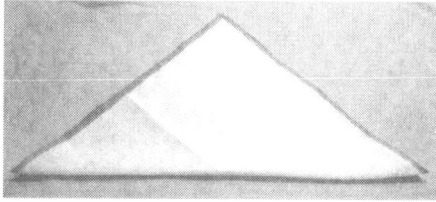

Move the lower right corner to the left of the top by a couple of inches. Then, move the left corner to the right of the top.

Adjust the points so that they are even in height and spacing. Fold the bottom up. Flip the hank and insert it into the pocket.

No matter how many points a hank has, keep all points sharp. It is pointless to showcase multi-points while none of the points is pointed.

How to Fold the Four Points

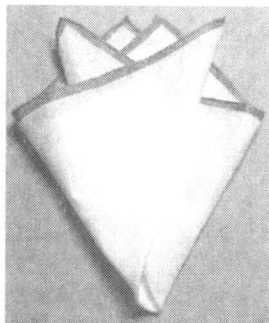

Star by folding the square into an imperfect triangle, showing twin points instead of one point at the top. Follow the same procedure that you fold the Three Points.

TV screenshot, fair use.

I have had difficulty finding a photo showing a man wears a handkerchief with multi-points. The style is less common perhaps because it is more methodical than other folds.

Chris Wallace, Fox News anchor, wore one version of the Four Points.

How to Fold the Peaks

To highlight the sharp points of the Peaks, this fold is best done with a stiff hank such as a piece of starched linen.

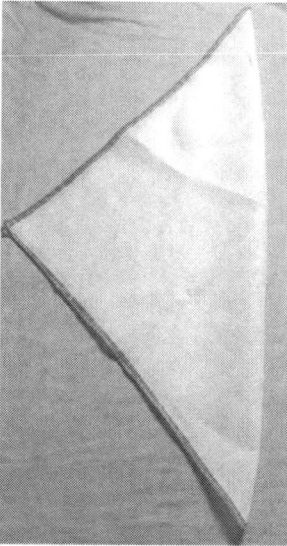

Fold the square into a perfect triangle with the flat side to your right. Move the bottom edge up to the right of the top. Then, move the left hand corner to the right of the two peaks just created. Fold the base up and insert the hank into the pocket.

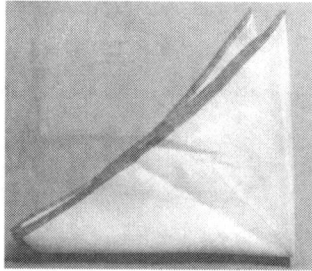

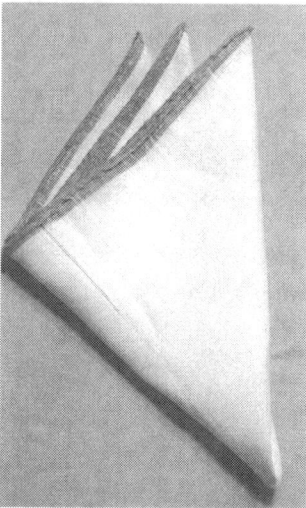

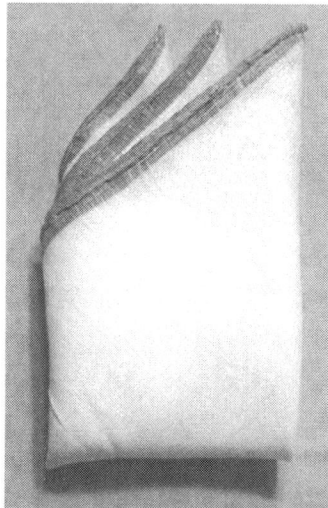

Charles Rangel wore his Peaks backward. It is preferred that the slope of the peaks parallels the slant of the jacket lapel.

How to Fold the Flop

To create the effect of a flop, this fold is best done with a soft hank. First, you hold the fabric by its center. Use the thumb and forefinger of your other hand to circle the hank as it hangs straight down. Slide your circling thumb and finger down more than half way and insert the center into the pocket, allowing the points to fall freely with a "flop."

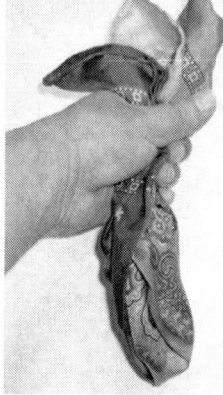

You can also knot the center of the cloth and insert the knot into the pocket. You may angle the points toward the shoulder. "This positioning helps in fostering a degage air, while emphasizing the lapel's diagonal slant and shoulders' breadth," wrote Alan Flusser.

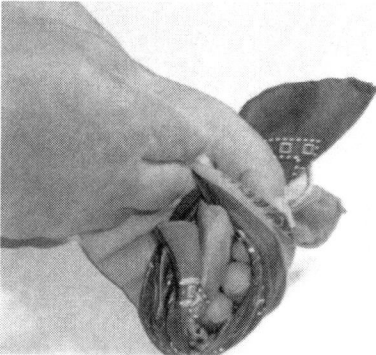
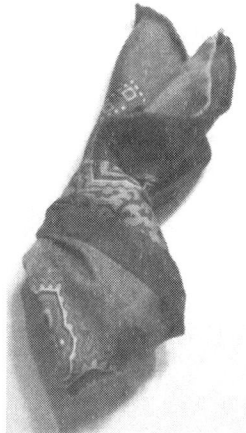

A common problem with the Flop is that it tends to collapse if the hank is pulled up too high.

Photo by Alan Light

The "flop" can be spread out symmetrically or slanted to one side. It the latter is chosen, the points should angle toward the shoulder.

293

How to Fold the Angle

This fold is a simple design, recommended by Alan Flusser for a stiff handkerchief. There is no name for it. I call it the Angle because the point of the fold is angled toward the shoulder to emphasize the slant of the jacket lapel and the breadth of the shoulder.

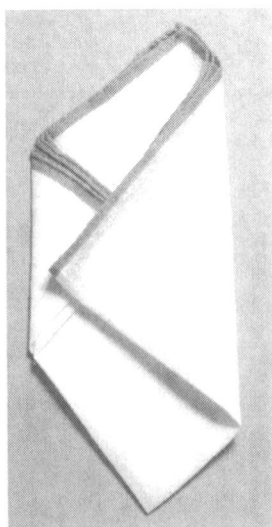

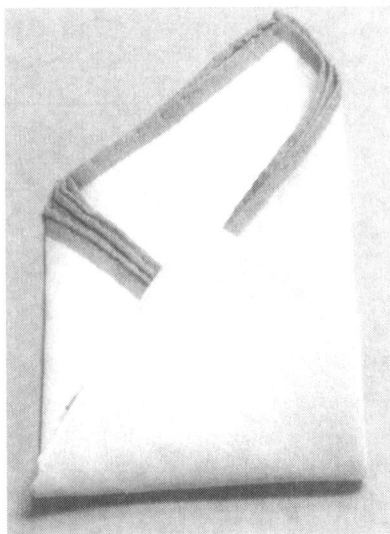

Whenever there are asymmetrical points, they are always angled toward the shoulder. It would be better if President Reagan tilted his handkerchief the same way Nelson Rockefeller tipped his.

How to Fold the Plop

This is my least favored style because the fold tends to be too narrow to fill the pocket opening.

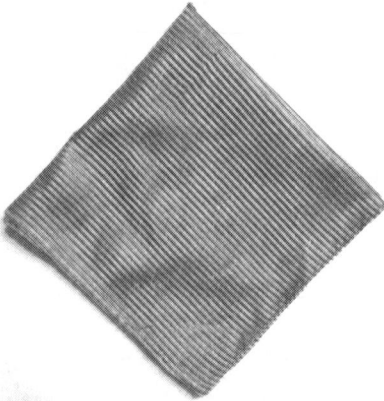

Fold the hank to a smaller square, one-fourth its full size. Pick up this smaller square by its center. Use the other hand to roll all of the loose corners together to form a cone. Insert the hank into the pocket and arrange the pointed top so that a dimple shows in the center.

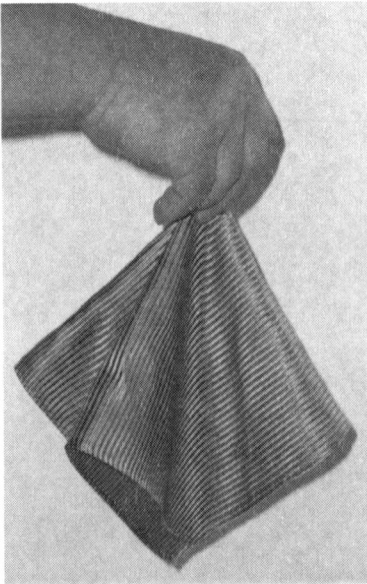

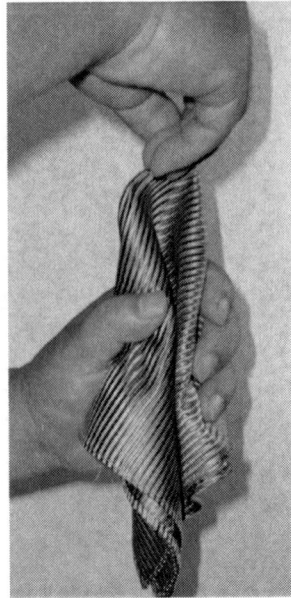

Did Cary Grant and Gary Cooper wear a Plop, or did the hank simply fall down inside the pocket? It is redundant to wear a handkerchief that is too small to be noticed.

Sharron Angle appeared on O'Reilly Factor wearing a well-executed Plop with a nice dimple.

43. *The health benefit of wearing garments of different colors*

Fabrics serve as a color filter. The reason a shirt looks yellow is that the shirt absorbs all the colored lights except the yellow one. When you wear a yellow shirt, the unabsorbed yellow light will pass through the weave of your shirt and reach your skin. Each time the light strikes your skin, it triggers chemical reactions that generate different types of substances such as vitamin D and other hormones. Sunlight can change the color of your skin. Don't you think sunlight can also do something else to your body?

For thousands of years, practitioners of medicine have used colored lights for healing and health maintenance. Solar ray therapy, Chakras, chromatherapy, color acupuncture, color-energized water treatments, and crystal and gem healing are examples. The painting on the right shows a yogin with seven chakras. Modern physicians suggest that walking under sunlight twenty minutes a day will help a person sleep better. Since ancient time, men have been warned not to wear other people's clothing because doing so will pick up other people's spirits left in the clothing. Ancient people believed the existence of spirits. They

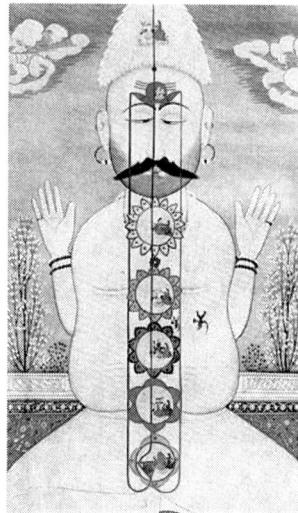

also believed that spirits exit from the feet. Thus, men were advised to take their shoes off when entering a temple. Moses was told by God to take off his sandals because he was on holy ground (Exodus 3:5). The word, spirit, may be equivalent or similar to energy vibration in today's physics. Silk is considered the best material in permitting the lights to vibrate through. Vitamin D is generated by ultra-lights, which human eyes cannot see. Whatever the colors of the shirt that you wear may not affect the production of vitamin D, but the material of the shirt may. Hence, it always pays to wear better quality shirts made of fine natural fibers.

President Obama couldn't stop taking his shoes off when he visited Middle-east countries.

We use clothing or umbrellas to protect ourselves from over exposure to the sun. On the other hand, we should not allow poor quality garments to block proper amount of sunlight that is essential to our health. The colors of our garments will also affect the ranges of light energy that reaches our skin. When a man wears a white broadcloth shirt, we can see through his shirt and know what he is wearing under the shirt. When the man is wearing a blue broadcloth shirt, however, we can no longer see through his shirt. A white shirt permits white light to pass through, whereas a blue shirt allows only blue light to go through. Because the white light contains the seven colors of light in a rainbow, it has a higher energy level than that of the blue light alone. Hence, we can see through a white shirt but not a blue shirt. The effect of the colors of a garment is evident.

Just as different color food contains different types of nutrients, different color light generates different types of substances. Whereas it is wise to eat different color food to receive a variety of nutrients, it is also wise to wear different color garments to benefit from the full spectrum of light energy. The author of the Complete Book of Color, Suzy Chiazzari suggested that "Wearing black too often, attracts negative energy and can have a detrimental effect on our health because the body requires light energy in order to function normally as a living organism."

Every time I mentioned the benefits of wearing different color shirts. Customers stared at me and gave me an incredible look of admiration. They thought I am a genius of some kind. Some customers considered me the greatest salesperson. All their lives, they had never met anyone who was able to tell them such a fantastic theory in order to sell more shirts. There is little scientific research done on this subject. I am unsure about the magnitude of the benefits associated with wearing a variety of colors. First, do no harm. What can be worse if a man wears garments of a few different colors? At lease, we know that varying the colors of our clothing can be a boost for the mental state or morale.

44. *The advantages of mercerized cotton*

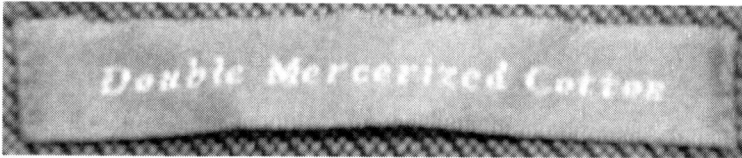

The best quality knit shirts these days tend to be made of mercerized or double mercerized cotton.

As non-iron fabrics become increasingly popular, some manufacturers begin to produce knit shirts with the non-iron feature. The main reason for using non-iron fabrics is to prevent the garments from wrinkling. Because knit shirts do not usually wrinkle, it is unnecessary to wear a knit shirt treated with non-iron chemicals. The non-iron treatment adds unnecessary cost to the knit shirts. The chemicals also affect the properties and performance of the cotton fabrics such as the strength and feel of the fabrics. The chemicals, such as formaldehyde, are hazardous to human bodies although manufacturers assure that the little amount of substances will not harm consumers. Moreover, manufacturers often apply the non-iron treatment to ordinary knit shirts. Why should you pay extra money for an ordinary knit shirt that has been treated for wrinkle resistance while you can put the extra money toward a better knit shirt that is naturally wrinkle-free without the treatment? If you are looking for cotton knit shirts, the best products are made of mercerized cotton.

The fiber of unmercerized cotton is flat and ribbon like with alternating left and right spiral twist every two or three turns. Because the twists reflect the light in different directions and cancel one another out, cotton fabrics usually look dull. In 1851, John Mercer was granted a British patent for work he had done on cotton and other vegetable fibrous materials. He found that caustic soda caused cotton fibers to swell, become round and straighten out. At that time, the British cotton trade was not interested in his finding. In 1890, Horace Lowe was granted a British patent by applying Mercer's caustic soda process to cotton yarn or fabric under tension, imparting a resultant high luster to the fiber. His discovery revolutionized the cotton industry. Today the mercerizing treatment refers to Lowe's process.

To picture the effect of mercerization, you may imagine that an untreated cotton fiber is as flat and twisted as a section of fire hose before it is filled with water. After mercerization, the cotton fiber goes straight and becomes perfectly round just as the fire hose does when it is filled with water.

Although the primary goal of mercerizing is to attain the permanent silken luster, the process also makes cotton fibers become stronger, more absorbent, more susceptible to dyes, and softer to touch. Vendors often brag about their cotton products are made of extra-long-staple (ELS) cotton. Garments made of ELS cotton are unnecessarily made of mercerized cotton. On the other hand, mercerized cotton tends to be ELS cotton, such as Sea Island, Egyptian or Pima. This is because fine, long stapled fibers generally have the lowest twist, which is required for treating under tension to gain luster. Hence, if you buy mercerized cotton, you are also getting the best types of cotton.

Because of the significant benefits of mercerizing, many manufacturers use cotton materials that have been mercerized twice, called double mercerized, one treatment during the yarn stage and the other during the fabric stage. Manufacturers and retailers put the term, "mercerized cotton" or "double mercerized cotton" on the label of the shirts, but few consumers know the meaning or the significance of mercerization.

Some consumers dislike mercerized cotton polo shirts because they have been used to the traditional bulky polo shirts made of 40's 2-ply yarns. Owing to the superior quality and strength of mercerized yarns, mercerized cotton polo shirts are usually made of fine 60's or 80's 2-ply yarns. These fine yarns make the shirts appear thinner and lighter than regular polo shirts. In the past when technologies were limited, manufacturers used thick fabrics to help keep garments in shape. With today's advanced technologies, garments are made of thinner and lighter materials with stronger and superior performance. I watched 2008 Summer Olympic Game. Many news reporters wondered why many world records were broken. Sports experts explained that today's athletes are better trained and better equipped, especially the lightweight clothing they wear. One reporter asked an expert whether a lightweight jersey would affect the scores in a basketball game. The expert replied, "Every ounce counts!" It is fair to say that Michael Phelps owed some of his success to his lightweight Speedo suit. Ironically, he lost his world record to a barely known German swimmer in the 200-meter freestyle at the world championships on July 28, 2009. It is believed that the German's polyurethane swimsuit gave him an edge over Phelps's once-revolutionary LZR Racer. If you do not prefer high tech garments such as lightweight polo shirts, heavyweight mercerized cotton knit shirts are available in today's market.

Medical professionals often suggest that silk is the best clothing material because it allows the greatest amount of light energy vibrating through. Silk fibers have a triangular cross section with rounded corners. This reflects light at many different angles, giving silk a natural sheen. Mercerized cotton fibers are straight with little twist and have a circular cross section. These also give the fiber a natural luster. Garments made of regular cotton with vegetable or pigment dyes often fade and garments made of silk tend to breed. Unlike ordinary cotton and silk, mercerized cotton takes dyes beautifully and retains colors definitely. Because mercerized cotton holds colors better and allow more light energy vibrating through, garments made of mercerized cotton may provide more health benefits than garments made of ordinary cotton or other fibers. Furthermore, mercerized cotton garments reduce the workload of your heart owing to their lightweight.

Because the primary reason for mercerizing cotton is to gain luster, mercerized cotton is more often used in knit shirts than in woven shirts. If you happen to spot a woven shirt made of mercerized cotton, you can be sure that the shirt will not be in poor quality. Mercerized cotton is used in better quality garments due to its superior properties. You may wonder how much more you have to pay for a mercerized cotton shirt. Surprisingly, the average price difference between a mercerized and a regular cotton shirt by a same designer or brand is only a few dollars. The reason is that designers or vendors tend to mark up the prices of inferior quality merchandise to keep up with their reputation. No designers or vendors will admit that they make or sell inferior products by selling these products at low prices. Hence, it usually pays to spend a few dollars more to buy a much better quality product.

Although mercerized cotton was developed more than one hundred years ago, the product has not become widely used until recent years. Mercerized cotton was first used to make expensive golf shirts. As the product becomes popular these days, more manufacturers are using mercerized cotton to make T-shirts, underwear and socks. If you buy cotton knit products and none of them is made of mercerized cotton, you are not wearing some of the best clothing items indeed.

Dr. Isadore Rosenfeld suggested that too little sunlight may be a cancer risk. He wrote in an issue of *Parade* magazine.

Fair-skinned Scandinavians who spend the most time in the sun are least likely to develop several forms of cancer, especially malignant lymphoma and leukemia. Also, the farther north you live in the U.S., the greater your chances of developing all kinds of cancer. Too little sunlight is said to result in a risk of death from cancer of the colon, prostate, breast or digestive tract 30 times greater than from sun-induced skin cancer.

So, some doctors are now recommending that we spend 15 minutes in the sun--without any sunscreen--three or four times a week. This amount permits the absorption of enough vitamin D to decrease the risk of cancer . . .

If you decide to follow the advice and spend an hour or more in the sun each week, what is the point to wear garments made of poor quality fabrics so that they can block most or much of the sunlight, which you try to catch? It is beneficial to wear clothing made of good quality natural fibers, such as mercerized cotton.

The best cotton socks are made of mercerized cotton. The photo shows that the only information that is singled out by the manufacturers is the designation, "mercerized cotton." Manufacturers will be disappointed, however, if they realize that few consumers know what mercerized cotton is.

45.   *The advantages of stretch underwear?*

In the movie, *The Hot Chick*, a teenage girl switched her body with a man. She, the man, went into the man's room for the first time and did not know how to take a leak. The waiter in the room said to her, "Sir, if you shake more than twice, you are playing." Many women who buy underwear for their loved ones asked me how men do when they go to the restroom. They asked such a question because many contemporary underpants do not have any slip opening. Traditional underpants have a side opening or a fly in the middle. Nevertheless, the openings are often too small, in the wrong places, or difficult to operate such as unfastening the button with one hand. The great majority of men place their reproduction organ on the left side of the pants, known as "dress left."

Manufacturers, however, place the side slip on the right because the fly of the pants faces to the right. For the above reasons, most men find it more convenient to pull up the pants from the bottom leg opening or to pull down the pants from the waistband. The underpants tend to lose shape quickly after repeated pulling. It is no wonder that advanced undergarments these days often contain stretch fibers to help keep the garments in shape. Elastic yarns are made with a core of either natural rubber or synthetic fibers, such as spandex, with cotton or other fibers wrapped around it.

Many manufacturers now add elastic materials such as spandex into everything from socks to suits. The rationale behind this movement is that spandex adds stretch and holding power to fabric. Spandex can stretch five times its length without breaking; hence, a few percents in the fabric are sufficient.

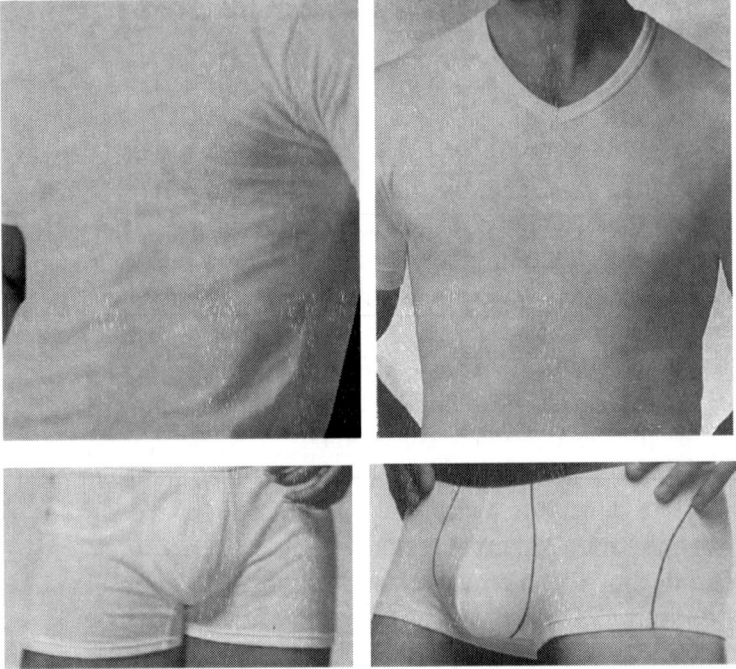

Ordinary cotton undershirts and underpants (left) tend to leave puckered lines. Stretch undergarments (right) contour to the body for a smoother fit.

Spandex is a polyurethane-polyurea copolymer. It is lighter, yet stronger and more durable than natural rubber. Spandex does not deteriorate from oxidation like rubber thread and will not be damaged by body oils, perspiration, lotions, soaps and detergents. Good quality stretch undergarments tend to contain spandex or other advanced synthetic fibers instead of rubber latex threads, which make a heavier garment and cannot be woven into a fine texture that characterizes spandex products.

Spandex was invented in the late 1950s at DuPont. The material was patented by the Spanjian brothers and was used in the products of their company. The name, spandex, was given to Spanjian family for their contributions. Whereas spandex is the preferred name in North America, it is often referred to as "elastane" in many European countries. Lycra is a popular trade name of spandex own by Invista, formerly DuPont.

Designers and manufacturers claim that the addition of spandex or Lycra improves the ability of a garment to give and therefore adds comfort to the wearer when he moves. Just a little bit of elastane will double or triple the life of the garment. There are shortcomings of spandex. One is that they cannot survive the high heat and chemical process required to make a non-iron fabric. They tend to lose stretch after repeated tumble drying.

A new stretch fiber, XLA, marketed by the Dow Chemical Company, has been granted a new generic classification, "lastol," by the Federal Trade Commission in the United States. Manufacturer of this new fiber claims that XLA fiber provides a soft stretch for ultimate mobility and comfort without the shortcomings of other stretch fibers such as spandex or Lycra. XLA is inherently resistant to high heat and specialty treatments, including the chemical process for making a non-iron fabric.

Whether they are elastic or non-elastic, most woven or knit underpants have an elastic waistband. Some underpants also have an elastic band in the leg openings. Elastic bands in cheaper garments tend to be made of rubber since it is cheaper and easier to sew than synthetic elastics. Current Federal Trade Commission rules state that manufacturers do not have to list components of a garment if the ingredient comprises less than five percent of the total make up of the product. Few manufacturers provide information concerning the contents of the waistband. Hence, it is difficult for consumers to know whether a pair of underpants has a rubber or synthetic waistband. In general, sewn-in waistbands are more likely to contain rubber threads than knitted-in waistbands.

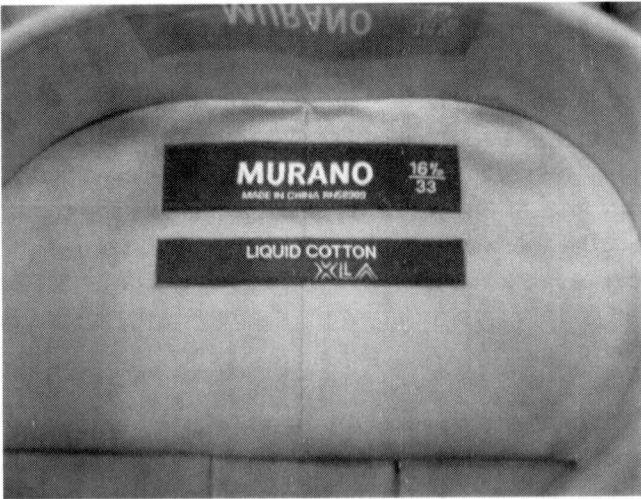

Manufacturers are producing suits, dress shirts and pants with a few percents of stretch fibers such as XLA.

46. Why wear oversized woven boxers?

Surprisingly, many men or their love ones do not know the size of their underwear, especially when the undergarments are sized in sport size, such as small, medium or large, instead of exact size, such as 34", 36" or 38". If customers are looking for woven boxers, I am inclined to recommend them to buy a slightly larger size. Most woven boxers are made of broadcloth, which has a plain weave structure and is prone to tearing. Hence, a slightly larger size will help prolong the life of the garment.

The plain weave is the simplest of the weave constructions, in which each weft yarn goes alternately over and under each warp yarn. Though the construction is simple, plain weave is the crispest weave. Nevertheless, plain weave has a shortcoming that is it tears more easily than other types of weaves such as twill and satin.

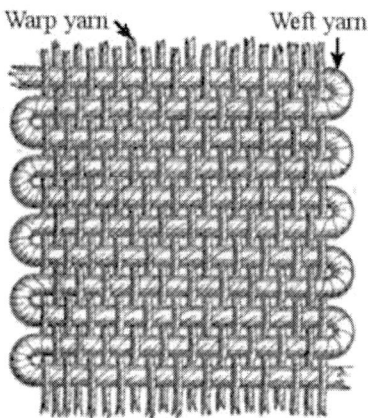

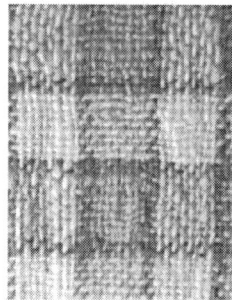

Warp yarn   Weft yarn

The tendency for a fabric to tear depends on two variables. One is the mobility of the yarns within the fabric construction. The mobility is the ease with which the yarns are able to move. The other is the number of yarns that will bear the load. The greater the mobility and the greater the number of yarns that will bear the load, the harder it will be to tear the fabric. Because a plain weave has the tightest construction and only one yarn bears the load when the fabric is torn, the plain weave has the least resistance to tearing.

The following illustration explains the concept of load bearing during tearing. It is easier to tear a single string of thread (a) than a bunch of threads (b). When a plain weave fabric is torn, only one yarn is present to resist the tear (c). Hence, it is easier to tear a piece of plain weave cloth by breaking the yarns one by one in the same direction.

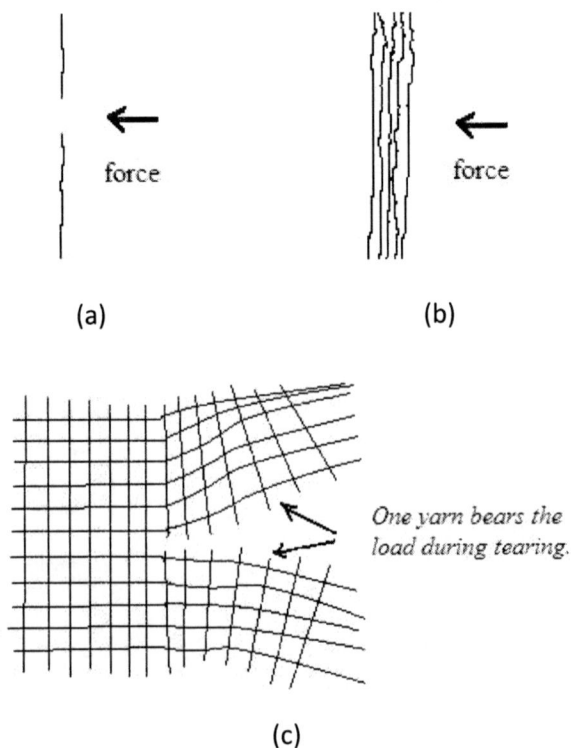

force   force

(a)   (b)

One yarn bears the load during tearing.

(c)

Because plain weave fabrics tear easily, salesclerks in the fabric shops tend to tear the fabrics by hands instead of cutting the fabrics with a pair of scissors so that the fabrics can be separated along the grain. I have advised thousands of consumers to buy a larger sized boxer to prolong the life of the underwear. None of the customers knew this fact, but they were appreciative to learn about this helpful tip.

Manufacturers often modify a plain weave to improve the resistance to tearing by inserting fewer filling yarns during weaving. Poplin is an example. The looser construction allows for more internal mobility or yarn slippage and becomes harder to tear. Nevertheless, the looser construction also weakens the structure of the fabric.

A better way to enhance performance is to combine different types of weaves. A parachute fabric combines a plain, rib, and basket weave to produce a durable fabric. The plain weave gives strength and stability to the fabric whereas the rib and basket weaves increase the resistance to tearing. Nonetheless, manufacturers are unlikely to use such complex structure to produce underwear.

In previous chapter, I have discussed the use of stretch fibers such as spandex and XLA to increase the elasticity of the undergarments. Nevertheless, stretch fibers are mostly used in knit products. The store, where I work, occasionally carries woven silk and cotton boxers that contain stretch fibers. Few customers know and appreciate the advantages of stretch boxers, forcing the company to discontinue the products. If you wear boxers but do not like the fact that woven boxers tend to wear out quickly, you may try knit boxers or stretch woven boxers. Or, you can always buy regular woven boxers in a slightly larger size. A larger size boxer reduces the stress from overstretching and helps prolong the life of the undergarment.

There are two major categories of underpants, briefs and boxers. A woman asked President Clinton whether he wears briefs or boxers because most men wear either one. Few men wear both. Whereas briefs are tight-fitting, boxers are loosely cut. Thus, it is not awkward to wear a slightly larger size woven boxer.

47.   Avoid underpants with a center seam.

Once a while, I met customers, who came to the store to buy underpants and specified that they did not want any underwear that has a center back seam. The center back seam rubs against the skin in the bottom. It is irritating and may cause a lot of pains, especially for older men. As a man gets older, his blood does not circulate as well in the rear. Constant friction owing to body movements in this area can cause great discomfort. If your skin is sensitive in this area, you may want to avoid any underpants that have a center back seam.

To cut down the cost, garment producers utilize every small piece of fabrics as they can. They sew small pieces of cloth together to form a larger piece. This is the reason that many underpants have a back center seam. You may think this will happen to large size woven or knit boxers and trunks. Do not be surprised if you find a small brief that also has a back center seam. Some designers skip the center seam but place two seams near the center instead. Most underpants have two side seams. Better made underpants have no center and side seams.

If the center seam of your underpants bothers you and you are not ready to let the pants go, you can wear your underpants inside out to reduce the irritation caused by rubbing against the stitching in the seam. I served in the Marine in Taiwan in the 1970s. We wore our underpants and socks inside out.

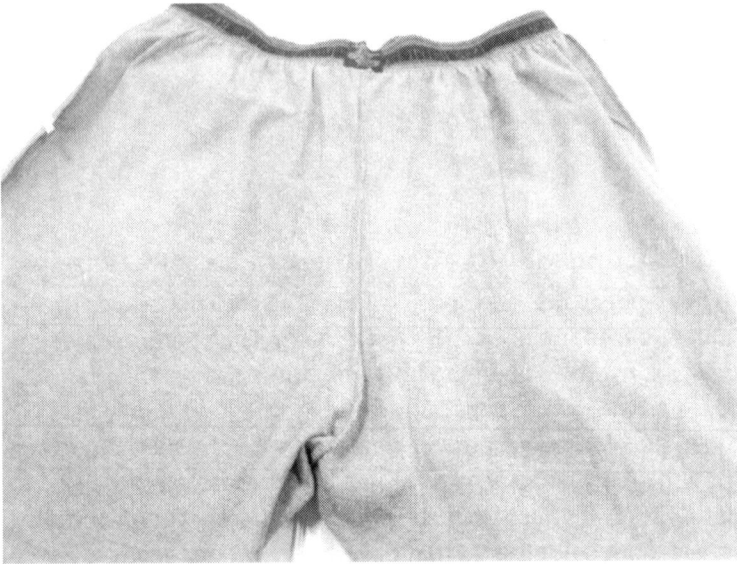

Underpants with a center back seam, which is a sign of poor construction.

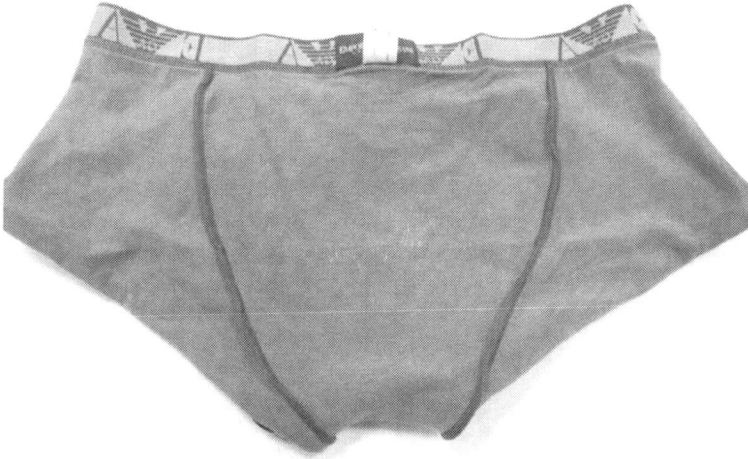

Some designers skip the center seam but place two seams near the center. The design, if done correctly, can contour to the buttocks for a tighter fit. Nevertheless, the design is often utilized simply to save material. The two curved or parallel seams are used in place of the two side seams. Better made underpants have no center or side seams.

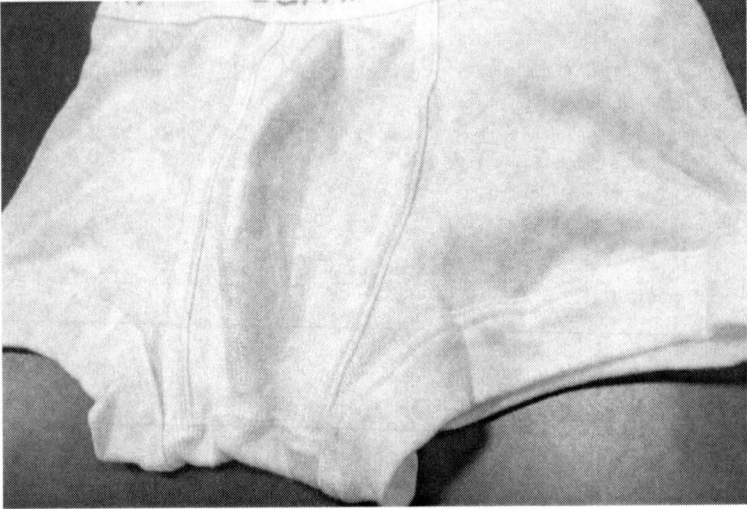

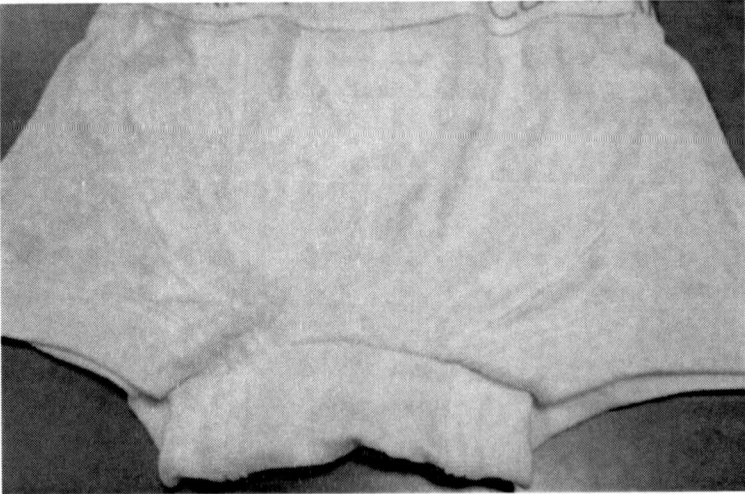

The three seams in the front of a high-priced trunk made by one leading American designer were used to produce a protruded 3D pouch to accommodate the shape of a male reproduction organ (top photo). The center and two curved side seams in the back of the exact same trunk serve no purpose, only to show its poor construction (bottom photo).

48.   Should socks match the shoes, slacks or neither?

There are two pervasive theories concerning the color of socks. One theory says that the color of socks should match the color of shoes. The other suggests that the color of socks should go with the color of pants. Both theories are unfounded. Socks are supposed to be covered until the wearer moves around or bends his leg. Why should something that is mostly hidden match anything else?

An ideal human body has a pair of legs that is one and half to twice the length of the torso. Men with long legs look more attractive. To lengthen the leg line, it is smart to include the foot as part of the leg. If the color of socks contrasts sharply with the color of pants, the socks cut off the leg line. Hence, it is wise to wear light color socks with light color pants, and dark socks with dark pants. But, it is unnecessary to wear the same color socks and pants.

Shoes are important items in an ensemble but they are too remote from the face and the center of body. It is silly to worry about how socks should relate to the shoes. Men wear only two or three different colors of shoes. It is no fun to wear few colors of socks all your life.

Fashion experts recommend that the socks should coordinate with something that is worn above the waist. When a man dresses up from head to toe, he may gradually lose the connection between his upper and lower body. The socks give an opportunity to connect both parts of the body.

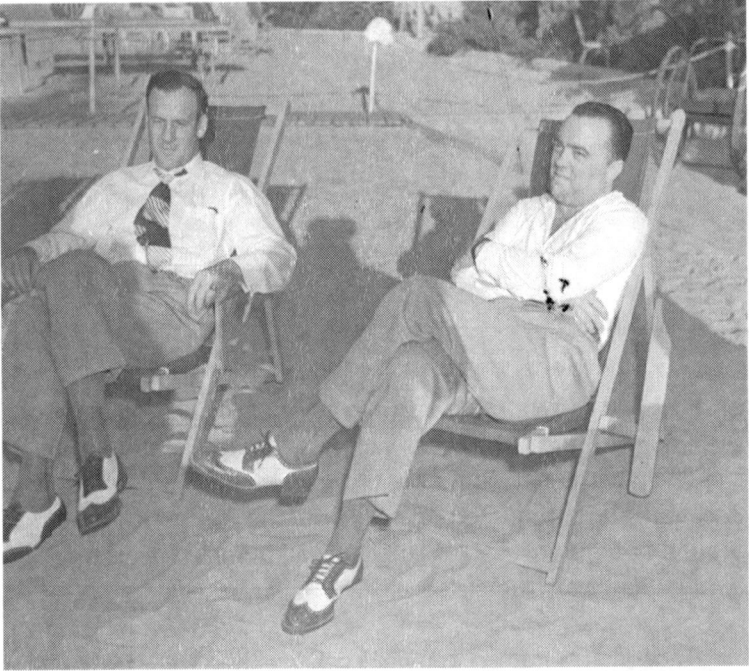

J. Edgar Hoover and his assistant Clyde Tolson

Socks are supposed to be covered under the pants until the wearer moves around or bends his leg.

I once saw Fred Astaire wear a tie that matches his socks in a photo. Rich people have the financial means to do whatever they wish. Ordinary people should not lose sleep over the colors of their socks. Some designers do produce few matching tie and socks but you may be unable to find them. If this is the case, do not worry. You can always use socks that coordinate with your shirt, jacket or pocket square, and so forth. Each season our company carries a variety of wild socks in red, yellow, orange and other bright colors by famous designers. Those socks do not usually sell until the end of the season when they are closed out and sold at 90% of the suggested retail price. I do not know why the buyers of the company never learn. Most consumers mistakenly think socks must match either the pants or shoes. Because few men wear red or orange pants or shoes, it is no wonder that few consumers will buy wild socks at $20.00 a pair, when a good quality non-iron shirt or a pair of non-iron pants is about $50.00.

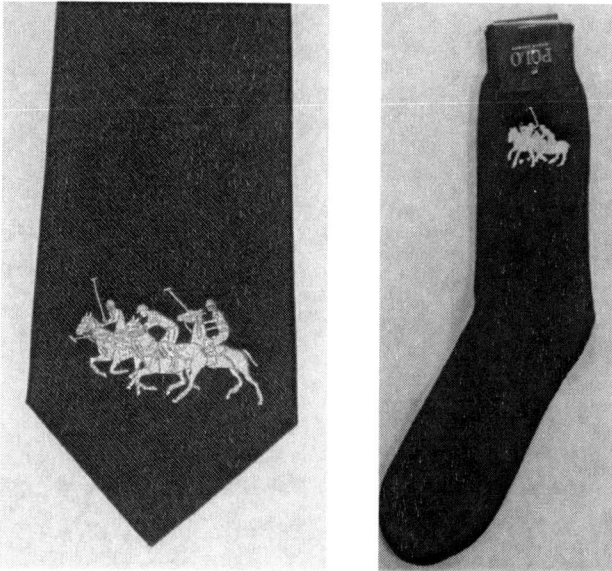

Ralph Lauren produced ties and socks
that are matched in color and pattern.

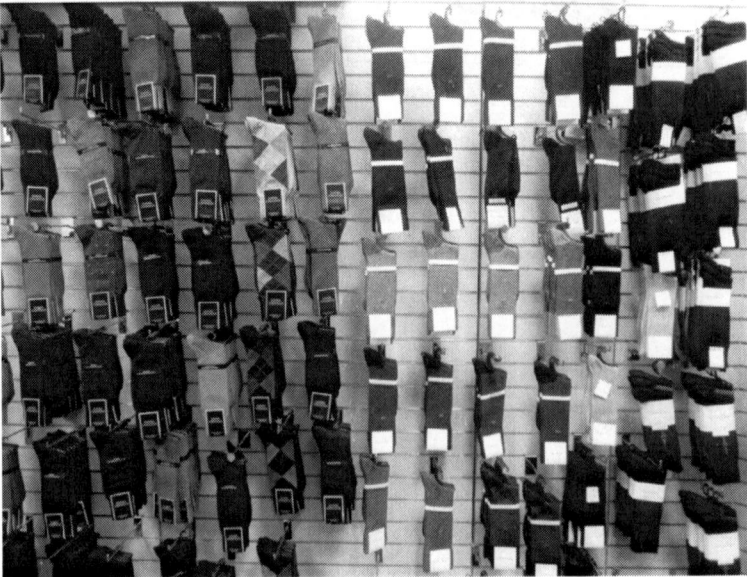

Department stores carry men's socks in a wide variety of patterns, weaves and materials, but in a limited number of colors because consumers mistakenly think socks must match either their shoes or pants.

Whereas the left foot and right foot of a pair of shoes or sandals are different in shape, the two feet in a pair of socks are identical. Each sock tends to stretch to fit the shape of the foot. Hence, both feet are interchangeable. Many men stock with a few pairs of the same socks so that they can mix and match the socks easily. Some designers put their logos on some of their socks. The logos are intended to be worn facing out. Thus, the two feet are usually not exchangeable.

49. How to buy dress socks

One of the most amazing phenomena at men's department is that many men stand in front of the dress socks wall for half an hour or more and cannot decide which socks to buy. They have difficulty choosing a few pairs of dress socks because they mistakenly think that socks must match their pants or shoes. To meet the demand, clothing stores tend to carry dress socks that may go well with men's dress outfits. This makes the selection process easier, you think. The opposite may be true. To perfectly match a color, one has to consider a range of factors, such as the tint, shade, chroma, saturation and brightness of the hue. This is what drives millions of men and women crazy. If you have read the last chapter and agreed with me that dress socks need not match pants or shoes, it will make your life much easier next time you shop for a few pairs of dress socks.

Some men wear the same types of dress socks all the time. They waste no time in selecting dress socks. If you are not one of these men, there are a few factors for you to consider.

Fitting the shoes

The first factor is how your shoes fit. Some men wear tight shoes while others wear loose ones. It is obvious that thick socks do not go into tight shoes. Most dress shoes are designed for close-fitting so that the shoe and the foot work as one unit. Hence, most dress socks are thin socks. Some men feel thick socks are more comfortable to wear because they provide more cushioning power. As technologies are improving, many dress shoes are equipped with multi layers of protective padding made of advanced materials. Separate padding and inserts are also widely available in the market. All of these technologies reduce the need for cushioned or thick socks. Nevertheless, you should try on the shoes with the right type of socks when you shop for a pair of shoes. It is easier to decide on what type of socks to wear the same time you decide on what type of shoes to wear. If the shoes you already own are too loose and the socks are too thin, you can always wear two socks to fill in the space.

Size

Most shoppers who came to the sock department in our store would ask about the sizes of socks that we carried. This reflects the reality that many men have difficulty finding socks of the right size. Unlike shoes that come in different sizes, socks sold in the market generally are in a standard size. There are several different shoe-size systems that are used worldwide. None of the systems uses the direct measurement of the foot length. Numerical sock sizes, on the other hand, are given as the length of the foot in inches. When you pick up a pack of socks, the label reads [the socks fit] shoe size 6-12 ½, sock size 10-13. You may not know which shoe size fits a foot of 10 inches, but you should know that the sock size 10 will fit a 10-inch foot comfortably.

There is a huge length difference between shoe size 6 and 12, and sock size 10 and 13. How will both size feet fit into the same size socks perfectly? It may be true that knit socks are made to stretch. But, even the most elastic socks can only stretch to some degree. A smaller sock can stretch a little to fit a slightly larger foot, but a larger sock will not shrink much to fit a smaller foot. Hence, men with small feet tend to have difficulty finding the right size socks in clothing stores unless they buy children's or women's socks. Men with large feet can buy extended sizes at Big and Tall department even though the selection tends to be limited. Some special socks such as non-elastic and compression socks will not function properly if they do not fit correctly. They tend to come in a few different sizes. But, most men do not wear such special types of socks. For those men who need odd size socks, they can order from sock specialty companies online or by mail. Most sock manufacturers produce socks in a variety of styles and designs. Not every style is made the same length, regardless of what the label says. If you need odd size socks, bring along a measuring tape when you shop.

Unlike shoes, which are usually available in several widths, from A, B, C, D to XXXE, socks are seldom labeled in width. This is because knit socks are stretchy. Manufacturers do not believe it is necessary to make socks in different width. Some socks appear much narrower than other socks. Narrow socks tend to be made of rib knit fabrics, which are stretchier and have a snugger fit than plain knits.

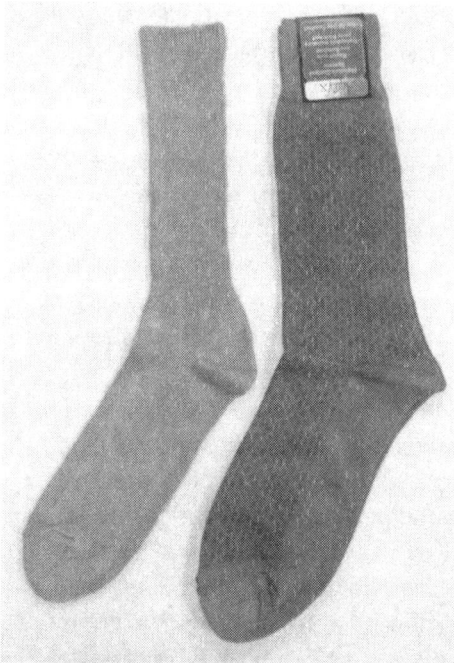

These two socks are meant to fit the same size foot. But, why does the left one appear much smaller? It is made of rib knit, which will expand to fit the foot. Ribbed socks are ideal for men with small feet.

Materials

Socks come in a wide variety of materials, including synthetic, artificial, and natural fibers, and dozens or hundreds of different combinations. Most men buy socks based on the prices, colors, patterns, textures and styles but not the contents of the socks. This is unwise, indeed.

The foot is among the heaviest producers of sweat in the body. Each foot contains more than 250,000 sweat glands and is able to produce over a pint of perspiration per day. What makes our feet smell is the bacteria on our skin. The bacteria eat the sweat and excrete waste that has a strong odor. Sweat also contributes to the breakdown of skin chemicals and has a harmful effect on other aspects of the foot health. Dr. Ken Sokolowski wrote the following.

> The excess sweat can act as a chemical vehicle and solvent extracting chemicals from the linings of your shoes. These dissolved, shoe chemicals can cause skin rashes. The sweat can also lead the more rapid deterioration of your shoes.

> Most importantly, the sweat also significantly changes the environment inside your shoes to not only dark and warm, but also damp--the perfect environment for certain yeast, mold, fungal and viral infections of the skin. Sweaty feet are thus more like to develop skin rashes, yeast infections, athlete's foot, fungus toenails and warts (common or plantar).

To eliminate or reduce the smell, we should either remove the bacteria or remove the sweat that feeds the bacteria. It is therefore beneficial if a man wears socks made of absorbent materials that can absorb large quantity of sweat so that bacteria cannot feed on it. In general, natural fibers such as wool and cotton, and artificial fibers such as rayon are more absorbent than synthetic fibers such as polyester, nylon and acrylic. Dr. Sokolowski objects the use of cotton socks in closed shoes because they "guarantees hotter, wetter feet!" I believe that he is wrong in this matter.

Many people such as those with diabetes need special socks to keep their feet dry in order to reduce the risk of foot ulcers and other infections. Nevertheless, there is great confusion concerning the best sock materials to keep the feet dry. In an article published by the American Diabetes Association, Carol B. Feldman and Ellen D. Davis reported conflicting recommendations by medical professionals, health educators, government and pharmaceutical companies, and books and magazines including professional education materials. They conducted an informal survey of physicians, podiatrists, staff nurses, and certified diabetes educators (CDEs) to explore providers' sockwear recommendations and the reasoning behind them.

Our survey of 12 physicians and podiatrists revealed that sockwear is not a subject about which physicians feel particularly concerned. Most said they never make sock recommendations. One said he was more likely to make a comment on socks if a patient had signs of tinea pedis.

Of those who do make recommendations, one said she usually asks patients to wear cotton or wool socks because they are associated with less moisture and because she prefers natural fibers. Another recommends and wears acrylic socks because these were recommended to him by staff at an athletic shoe store. A podiatrist said he prefers a cotton/wool/acrylic blend.

When we performed the same survey with 11 general staff nurses, it became clear that nurses had a different focus. Although they expressed concern that socks should be comfortable, they were also likely to recommend specific fabric types. Most of the nurses thought people with diabetes should wear cotton or wool socks. But those recommending acrylic fabrics said they were "better," more absorbent, and more comfortable.

Our third survey involved 11 CDEs, who were the most vocal group on the subject of sockwear. Like the general staff nurses, most of the CDEs thought that cotton or wool socks were preferable. The main reason for their recommendation was absorbency. Several CDEs referred to perspiring feet or excess moisture and said that cotton was better at addressing this problem.

However, some of the CDEs surveyed did recommend acrylic socks. One educator said she had changed her advice regarding cotton versus acrylic based on an article she had read in the American Diabetes Association (ADA) magazine *Diabetes Forecast*, which stated that people with diabetes should not wear cotton.

It is disturbing to know how health care professionals give their advice. Medical professionals are not textile experts. They ought to be more careful about their opinions outside their field. Feldman and Davis summarized their findings.

Clearly, diabetes educators and other health care professionals often base advice on tradition rather than on scientific evidence. The available evidence suggests that people with diabetes who have "normal" feet should be able to wear whatever socks they find to be comfortable. Socks should fit well, without constricting cuffs, lumps, or uncomfortable seams. Therefore, fitted socks are preferable to tube socks. Lighter-colored socks may alert wearers with compromised sensation to a draining wound. Patients can judge for themselves which type of fabric feels the most comfortable.

Many men do not like wearing wet socks. So, they choose socks made of moisture-wicking materials such as Coolmax. These materials are usually synthetics with poor absorbing abilities, which allow sweat to escape into the air more easily. They dry faster than materials with good moisture-absorbency. Hence, Moisture-wicking materials are widely used in sport clothing. Socks made of moisture-wicking materials are not particularly helpful if you wear them inside closed shoes. Based on the law of conservation of mass and energy, the sweat is not going to disappear because you wear moisture-wicking socks. The sweat either stays on feet or escapes into shoes if the socks do not absorb the moisture. As you already know, sweaty feet and shoes are harmful to the health of your feet. Some athletes wear moisture-absorbing socks on top of their moisture-wicking socks. This combination may help you keep your feet dry. The key is to choose shoes that ventilate. If the shoes do not ventilate well, it matters little what types of socks you are wearing. Because you do not wash your dress shoes, the smart thing for you to do is to change the wet socks as soon as possible and wash them regularly.

No one would believe you before mid 1990s if you told any rational person that you had a dress shirt that was made of 100 % cotton and it did not wrinkle. In the recent past, the only way to make a shirt wrinkle-free is to use synthetic fibers such as polyester. After the invention of non-iron treatment in the 1990s, now you can have a 100% cotton shirt without wrinkling. Similar to the development of non-iron garments, manufacturers nowadays are using chemical treatment instead of synthetic fibers to keep socks fresh and dry. In the near future, we may be able to enjoy moisture-wicking socks made of wool or cotton instead of synthetic fibers. Synthetic socks have many disadvantages. One of the most noticeable defects is that synthetic socks pill badly. Pills are the small balls formed by rubbing the loose ends of fibers. Synthetic fibers generally are not as good insulators as natural fibers. They tend to keep your skin feel warmer in the hot weather and colder in the cool weather. Some customers told me that moisture-wicking socks make them feel hot, which in turn generates more sweat.

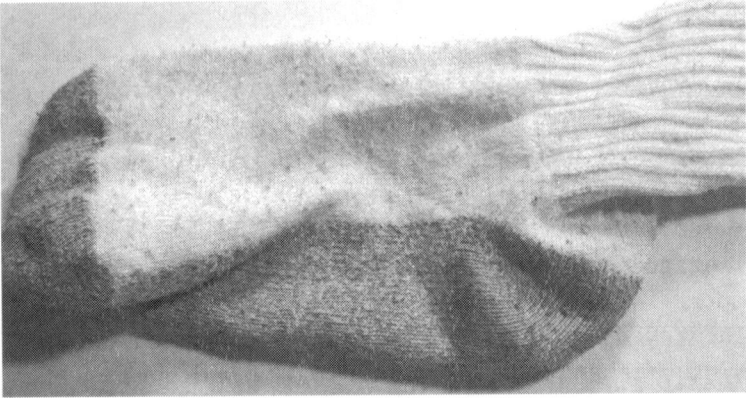

These two photos show that two synthetic socks began to pill after just one wear.

Weave and Weight

A customer came to the store where I worked to look for bamboo socks. He had a pair of bamboo socks, which he liked very much, so he would like to buy a few more. I told him that bamboo fabrics are rayon products from bamboo. There are socks made of better materials such as mercerized cotton. After speaking with the man a while, I realized what he was searching for had nothing to do with bamboo rayon. What he liked are socks with a terry cloth padded sole. He asked for bamboo socks only because his old pair of socks was labeled bamboo socks. There have been numerous researches, which compare various effects, such as moisture absorbency, blistering and vertical pressure, among socks made of different materials. I doubt the validity of many studies. There are many confounding factors that affect the performance of a pair of socks. These factors include but not limit to the size, weave, density, and construction of the sock, and also the type and fit of the shoes. Material is only one of the important factors. Unless all other important factors are under controlled, it is unreasonable to attribute certain effects to sock material alone. One study, for instance, suggests that padded acrylic socks produce less moisture at the skin surface and less blistering than do cotton socks. Nevertheless, socks made of 100% acrylic and 100% cotton seldom have the same fiber length and fineness, surface texture and weave structure. How can we be sure that socks absorb more moisture and less friction because they are made of a specific type of material rather than because they have softer fibers, looser weaves, or other reasons?

Different socks tend to have different weave structures. Gold Toe socks are one of the most popular brands in the U.S. Each pattern such as Canterbury, Metropolitan, Nassau and Fluffie has its distinct weave and texture. Some weaves have a tighter construction that produces more binding or compression effect. Some textured weaves such as terry cloth provide more cushioning power by adding bulk to the fabric. The weight of the fabric also affects the ability to absorb moisture and other characteristics. This is like that a larger or heavier towel tends to hold more moisture because of its bulkiness.

Most socks are made of a blend of different fibers. In truth, different parts of a sock are often made of different types of materials, weaves and densities, making it more difficult to identify which section of the sock, not to mention which material, makes the sock comfortable to wear.

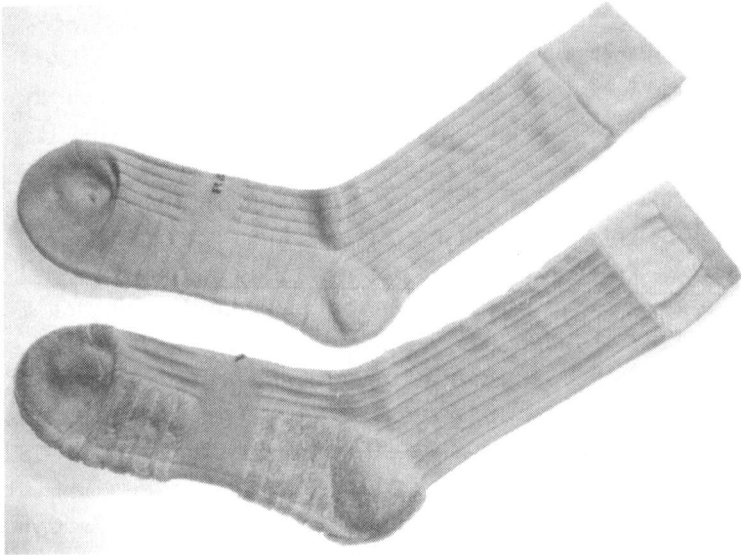

Different parts of a sock are often made of different types of materials with different type of weaves and densities. (Top one is the outside view whereas the bottom one is the inside view of the same sock.)

Height

Customarily, men do not show their legs under the dress pants, so they wear over-the-calf socks. Over a decade, I have witnessed the popularity of over-the-calf socks decreased significantly. Today, most men wear dress socks that are below the calf. Frequently, I met shoppers who complained that standard socks are too high for them. A customer told me that he just returned a bunch of socks to another department store in the mall. He came to our store to look around hoping to find some short crew dress socks. Our company offered a variety of short crew in sport socks but none in dress socks. I suggested him to fold down the socks. He said he had pulled down his socks but did not like the socks bulged above the shoes. After he saw my socks folded into half length, he commented he had never thought that tall socks could be folded into half length so nicely. So, he decided to return to the first store to buy back his socks. Most men who like short socks are unwilling to fold down the long socks. They would rather search the whole town for short dress socks.

Why do so many men prefer short dress socks? One possible explanation is that many men wear their dress pants far too long these days, making it more difficult to see their skin under the pants when they bend their legs. As the concept of compression socks is developing and gaining supports from medical professionals, I wonder it may be a miss of opportunity to provide additional health benefits to the feet. Most dress and athletic socks these days contain a considerable amount of nylon and a few percents of advanced stretch fibers such as spandex. Elastic socks offer some degree of compression, which helps improve blood circulation in the legs and feet even though the effect may not be therapeutic. Unless a man have a medical condition that prevents him from wearing elastic socks, it is generally more beneficial to wear the socks high than low.

Binding Top

To prevent the sock from falling, most socks have a binding top, which is usually made of stretch fibers such as rubber latex or spandex. Latex is cheaper and breaks down more easily. Better socks these days contain spandex, which can expand five times its length without breaking. Federal Trade Commission (FTC) requires the generic name and percentage of any fiber that exceeds 5% of the total weight be listed on the label while anything less than 5% may be listed as "others." Manufacturers tend to disclose the content of spandex on the label even though the content is less than 5%.

But they seldom mention the content of latex when it is present. FTC allows that the fiber content of trims does not have to be identified if the trim covers less than 15% of the surface of the garment, but the label must include the phrase "exclusive of decoration." When you shop for socks, it is wise to know what types of stretch fibers are used. If you do not find names, such as spandex, Lycra, elastane, XLA or other high tech terms, but find the phrases "others" or "exclusive of decoration," you may wonder what will keep the socks staying up. Notice that non-elastic or non-binding socks are specially designed for patients who cannot wear tight socks; therefore, these socks may not contain any stretch fibers.

Most socks contain a binding top, which is usually made of stretch fibers, to hold up the socks and prevent bunching and slippage. If the stretch fibers are latex or other inferior materials, they tend to break and unravel.

President Obama did not cover his leg with an over-the-calf sock.

50. Non-elastic and compression socks

Over a decade, I have observed that more and more men are looking for non-elastic or non-binding socks. Many of these men said they have swollen legs, so they wear loose socks to avoid putting pressure on their legs. Non-elastic socks are currently unpopular. Hence, they tend to be a little more expensive than regular socks. The selection is also limited. To save money and time in searching for such socks, consumers can create their own non-binding socks by stretching out regular socks. If you slip a sock over a can, the sock will lose its elasticity in a short period of time. Most socks contain advanced stretch fibers such as spandex these days. If you intend to stretch out the socks, choose those socks that contain less spandex and nylon.

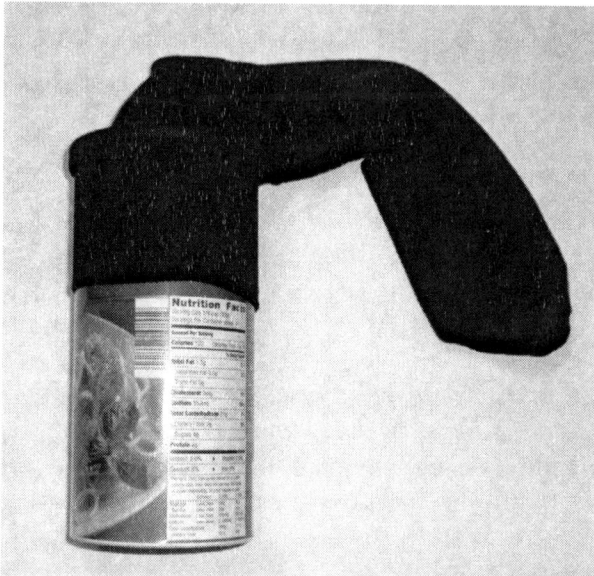

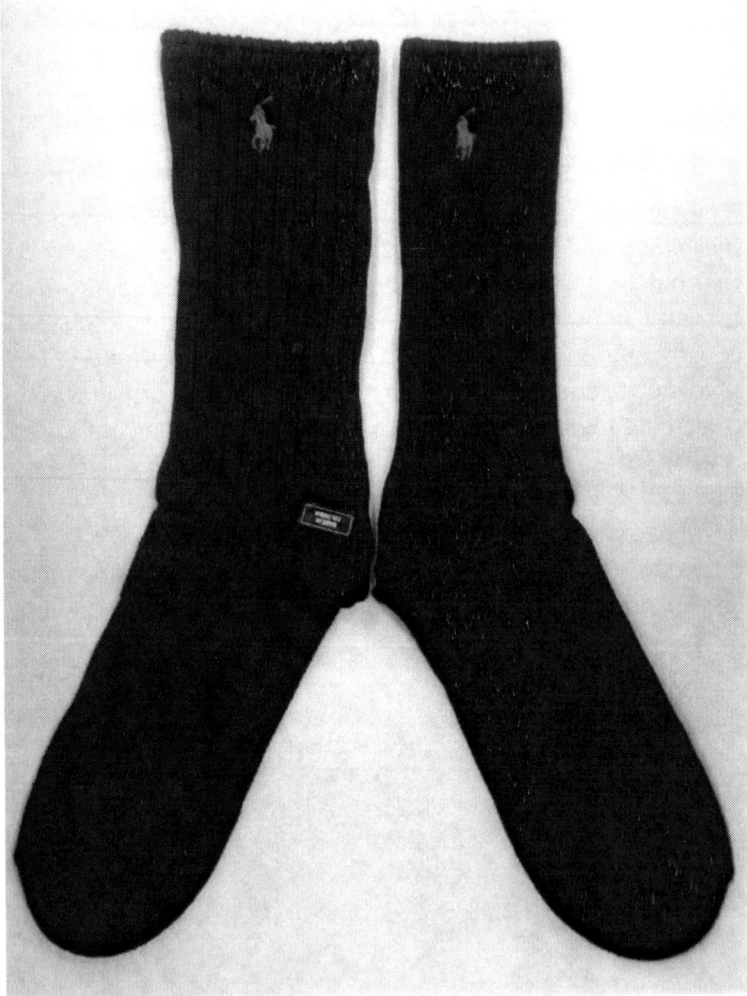

I put my hand inside the left sock in the photo for a few seconds; the sock lost its shape immediately. This demonstrates how easy it is to stretch out a pair of ordinary socks.

In the past when there are no effective stretch fibers to make socks that stay up well, manufacturers tend to make the top of the socks exceedingly tight. Consequently, tight socks often leave a sock ring imprint on the leg. As technologies progress, good quality socks these days often contain advanced stretch fibers that provide the right amount of elasticity to the top of the sock. Any normal person and even a diabetic patient can enjoy a pair of firm sock without putting too much pressure on the leg. If you feel your socks are putting too much pressure on your legs, you can always fold over your socks. This will reduce the pressure significantly.

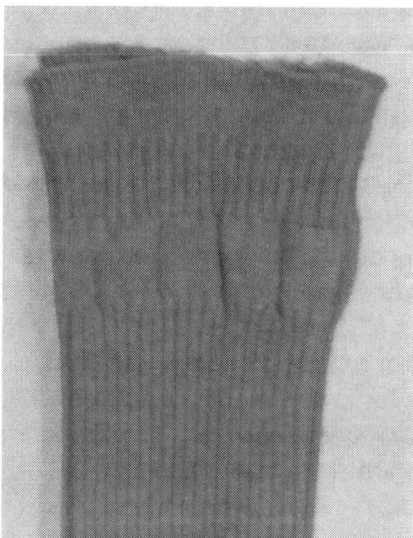

Non-elastic socks tend to have a non-binding relaxed top.

I wonder why people with poor circulation in their legs want to reduce the level of discomfort by wearing loose socks. Is it a better solution to improve the circulation in the legs? Compression socks are designed to improve circulation in the legs. What are compression socks? Michael Pollick wrote the following at wiseGEEK website.

Compression socks are specialized hosiery items designed to provide extra support and increased blood circulation for their wearers. Some compression sock manufacturers may also use the term *support socks* to describe their product. Compression socks are not to be confused with traditional dress socks or non-compression diabetic socks, although they may look similar. The main purpose of compression socks is to provide graduated pressure on the lower leg and foot. Traditional dress and athletic socks offer some degree of compression, but not enough to be considered therapeutic.

The key to understanding compression socks lies in their graduated pressure application. Throughout an average day, the body pumps blood to all of the extremities as equally as it can. However, gravity often causes blood to pool in the lower legs and feet, causing circulatory problems such as edema, phlebitis and thrombosis. At the very least, all of this blood pooling can cause fatigue and leg cramps. Elevating the legs and feet may alleviate the pain temporarily, but it often returns after a few hours of constant standing or walking.

This is where the use of compression socks can be extremely beneficial. Compression socks use stronger elastics such as lycra, rubber or spandex to create significant pressure on the legs, ankles and feet. By compressing the surface veins, arteries and muscles, the circulating blood is forced through narrower channels. The arterial pressure is increased, causing more blood to return to the heart and less blood to pool in the feet. Compression socks are tightest at the ankles, gradually become less constrictive towards the knees. The soles of compression socks may be heavily padded for better shock absorption.

Although compression socks were originally marketed to those with compromised circulatory systems, many people now find their everyday use beneficial. Experts suggest passengers on long flights should wear compression socks to prevent circulatory problems like deep vein thrombosis, leg cramps and edema. Athletes often wear compression socks to give their leg muscles additional support while running or jumping. Those with occupations requiring long periods of standing may also benefit from the use of compression socks.

In traditional Chinese medicine, the legs are considered the second heart. Special methods, such as standing Zen, are developed to help the legs pump the blood back to the heart. Most people probably do not have the time or knowledge to practice such complicated exercises. Compression socks offer an easy way to help pump the blood.

There are two types of compression socks: Gradient and anti-embolism. Wikipedia describes these two in the following.

> Gradient compression stockings are designed to remedy impaired "Musculovenous pump" performance due to incompetent leg vein valves. They are woven in such a way that the compression level lessens towards the top of the hose. Doctors will typically recommend these stockings for those who are prone to getting blood clots, edema, and blood pooling in the legs and feet from prolonged periods of sitting or inactivity.

> Anti-embolism compression stockings are commonly referred to as TED (Thrombo Embolic Deterrent) hose. They are used to support the venous and lymphatic systems of the leg. Unlike gradient compression stockings, anti-embolism hose deliver an equally distributed amount of compression at the ankle and up the leg. This compression, when combined with the muscle pump effect of the calf, aids in circulating blood and lymph fluid through the legs (in non-ambulatory patients).

It is imperative to notice that compression socks are not recommended for those people who are diabetic, who smoke or who have a decreased blood supply to the legs. Compression socks squeeze the muscles of the leg and drive blood away from the leg. They can decrease the blood supply further and worsen the disease. For these people, they can wear special diabetic socks or regular non-elastic socks.

A man with circulation problems in the foot may consult with a competent physician, podiatrist or other medical professionals for proper fitting. Non-prescription compression socks and stockings are widely available in the market, but they may not provide the adequate level of compression required to prevent blood clots or leg swelling. As technologies improve, most regular socks now contain a few percents of stretch fibers such as spandex to help hold up the socks and prevent slippage. Although the amount of stretch fibers may not be sufficient enough to provide therapeutic effects, the long term use of stretch socks may provide additional health benefits for people with normal or healthy feet.

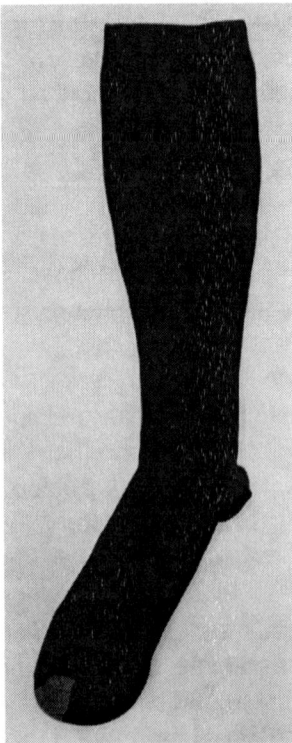

Stretch fibers such as latex and spandex are used to help hold up the socks. In regular socks, they usually exist at the top of the socks only. But in compression socks, they are built in the entire socks. Most knee-high compression socks have the shape of a lower leg to guarantee a better fit.

Standing Zen is a meditation technique, which is widely used by martial artists to utilize or manipulate "chi" or internal energy. The exercise also helps the legs pump blood back to heart.

(Photo is adopted from the *Taiki-Ken Pages* website. It is likely an illustration from the book, *The Essence of Kung-fu: Taiki-Ken*, by Kenichi Sawai, Japan Publications, Inc., 1976.)

347

51.   The problem with black socks

When yarns, fabrics or garments come out of the dyeing machine, the color may not meet the specifications of the customer. Manufacturer cannot erase the color that has been put on the materials. The only remedy is to re-dye the materials in a darker color to cover up the mistake. White yarns and fabrics are re-dyed in light colors whereas light colored yarns and fabrics are re-dyed in medium or dark colors. If dark colors fail, everything goes to black. After being boiled with chemicals several times in the dyeing machine, some natural fibers, such as cotton, linen and wool, may be weakened or destroyed.

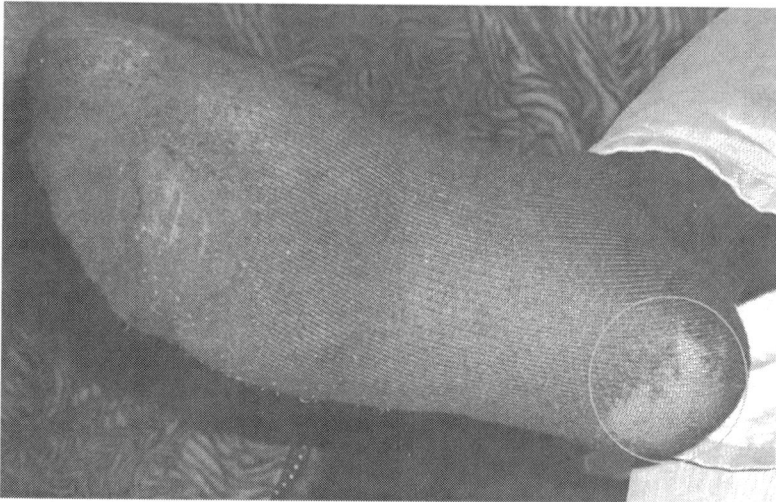

Socks are usually made of a blend of natural and synthetic fibers. The natural fibers provide comfort and absorbability while synthetic fibers add strength and holding power. After socks have been dyed and re-dyed several times, the natural fibers in the socks tend to deteriorate and break away, causing some areas of the sock to become thinner.

Many wool and olive oil products are labeled "virgin" to indicate the products were made from fresh materials for the first time. No black socks are labeled "virgin socks." You may not know whether a particular pack of dark or black socks has been repeatedly dyed. You can inspect the sock under the light to look for rotten spots in the sock. You may also complain to the vendor if the socks come apart after several launderings.

52. How to buy belts

Many men and women have heard that the size of the belt should be two inches longer than the waist size of the pants, but they do not know the exact reason. The waist size of a pair of pants is measured inside the pants. The belt is worn outside the pants. Hence, it is reasonable to assume that a person needs a couple of additional inches for the belt. Most solid belts come with five holes. Experts recommend that it is best that you wear your belt on the second or third hole from the buckle so that the extra length will pass the first belt loop or carrier without going to the second loop. Some contemporary belts come with seven holes. You may want to settle on the third or fourth hole from the buckle.

There are a few factors to consider when shopping for a belt.

Reversible vs. non-reversible belt

Traditionally, men wear the same color of belt and shoes. Hence, many men like the idea for having a reversible belt. One belt goes with two pairs of shoes of different colors. I have always discouraged customers from buying a reversible belt. When you wear one side of a belt from time to time, the other side of the belt is going to ruin by cracking or discoloring. It is pointless to wear a dress belt that is damaged. Moreover, reversible belts break quite easily. You thought you get two belts for the price of one. Actually, you probably will buy several reversible belts before you wear out one non-reversible belt.

A reversible belt tends to break at the two tiny screws that connect to the leather band, or at the middle screw that connects to the buckle.

Material

Frequently, customers brought into store their worn out belts to replace them with new ones. Many of those belts were not old. They broke down quickly because they were made of synthetic material. As required by laws, leather products made in U.S.A. must reveal which type of leather the products are made from. Many leather goods are imported from the foreign countries these days. Nonetheless, manufacturers often printed the product information on the backside of the belts since it has becomes a custom to do so. Most consumers pay much attention on the appearance but hardly ever examine the contents of the belts. Better belts are made of genuine full grain leather, which is a whole piece of leather that has not been split. Modern technologies can make fake leather look like real one. Consumers are advised to read the labels for product information.

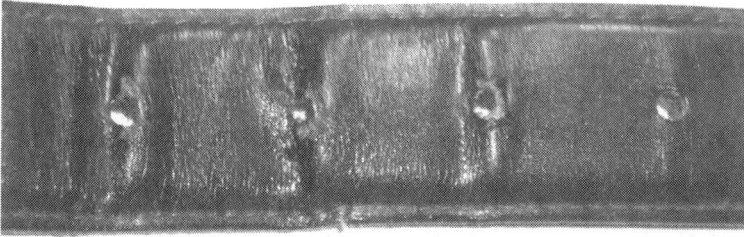

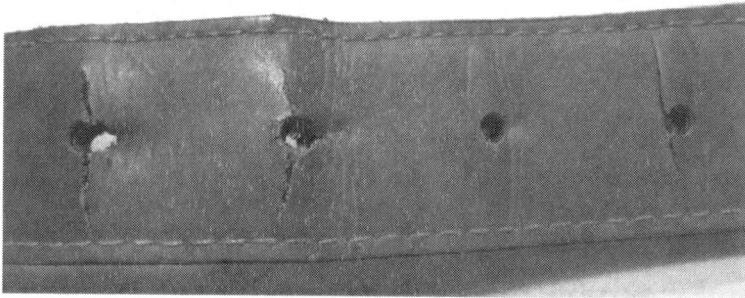

Belts made of synthetic materials tend to crack easily.

Construction

Most dress belts are made of two or more layers of leather or other materials. The layers are bonded together with adhesive and are secured with edge stitching. Sometimes designers want to create a smooth and clean appearance; they skip the edge stitching. Then, the layers come apart after repeated use. If you prefer a belt that will last, it is wise to buy a belt with edge stitching.

Some casual belts may be made of one single layer instead of multi layers. When you see the edge stitching, you are pretty sure that the belt is made with two- or multi-layer construction. But when the belt has no edge stitching, it may be difficult to determine whether the belt is one or two pieces. Manufacturers coat the edges of the belt with ink or paint, making it difficult to detect whether the belt is layered.

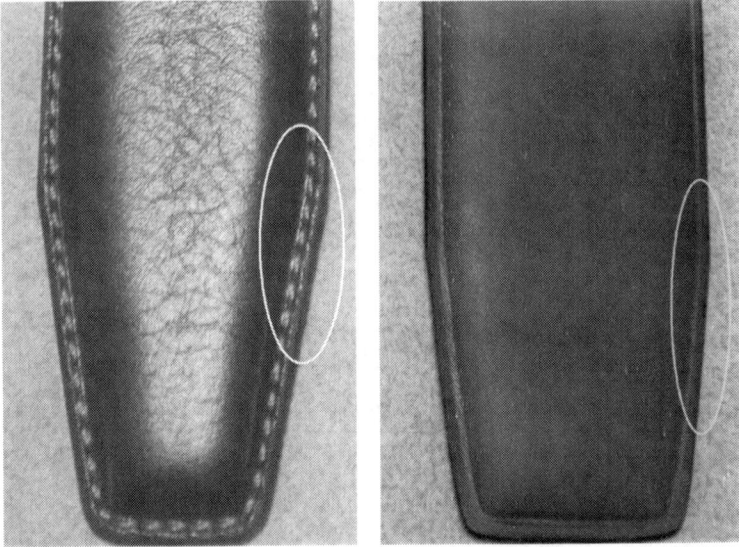

A belt with edge stitching (left) and without stitching (right).

Cheaper belts are made of synthetic materials. Some belts may be made of genuine leather upper but lined with inferior material. If you prefer a good quality belt, be sure that both the upper layer and the lining are full grain leather.

Manufacturers often line full grain leather with synthetic material. Since no manufacturer will proudly announce that they use inferior material. They often fail to mention there is lining. When the label reads "full grain," it does not necessarily mean that the belt is one piece construction.

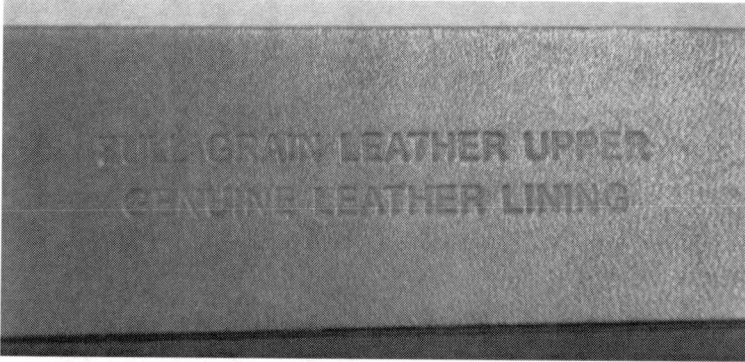

When the label mentions both "upper" and "lining," you know that the belt is made with at least two-ply construction.

Better belts are made of full grain leather upper and lining.

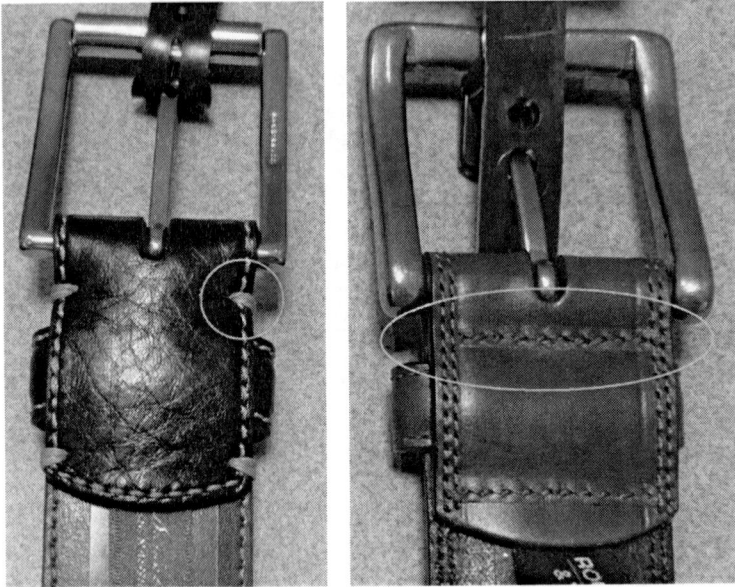

The buckle and belt loop are kept in place by a few threads in the left photo. Once these few threads are broken, the belt comes apart. A more secure way is to sew the leather fold across the band as shown in the right photo.

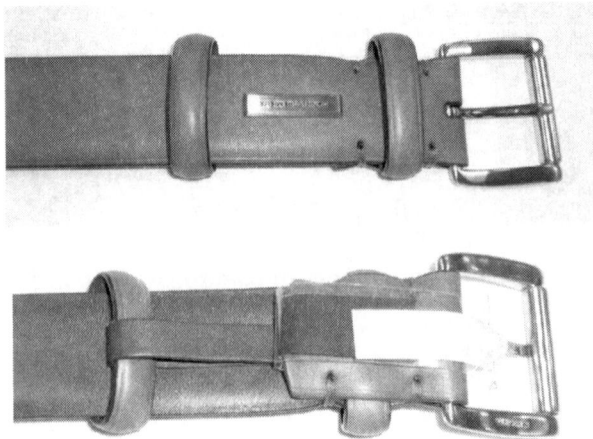

Some belts come with a movable loop.

Buckle

According to Wikipedia, "men started wearing belts in the 1920s, as trouser waists fell to a lower line. Before the 1920s, belts served mostly a decorative purpose, and were associated with the military."

In the past, belts served mainly a decorative function; therefore, they tend to have a lavish buckle.

Today, a belt becomes a part of dress code for business attire. "Within reason, there are no unacceptable belts; the buckle is the problem," wrote John T. Molloy in *the New Dress for Success.* "Big, heavy ornate buckles tend to be unacceptable; small, clean, traditional buckles with squared lines are best."

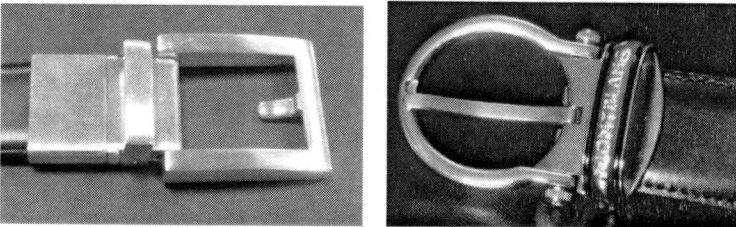

Curved buckles are less characteristic than squared buckles.

Most dress buckles come in two colors: brass and stainless steel. Brass projects the image of "warmth" while stainless steel promotes "coolness." It is advised that you coordinate the color of the buckle with your other jewelry items, such as watch, ring, cufflinks and glasses.

Color

Customarily, men coordinate the color of their belts with their shoes. Since men's dress shoes only come in three major colors, dress belts generally are available in black, cordovan and brown. Many customers stood in front of the belt racks for half an hour and were frustrated by being unable to find a perfect match. In truth, the color of shoes tends to change overtime as the shoes weather. The shoe polish will definitely change the color of the shoes. So, why should any man waste time to find a perfect match? If you insist on matching your belt with your shoes, take the color of your shoe polish into account. There is a much smaller color selection of polish than the color selection of shoes. A man may relate the color of his belt to his shoes, but it is unnecessary to be matchy-match.

Fashion experts generally recommend the belt be darker than the trousers. As brown shoes become popular in recent years, it is difficult to find a brown belt that is darker than a pair of navy or black trousers. Hence, you need not adhere to this recommendation either.

Dressiness

After losing their ornamental function in contemporary societies, belts now serve one primary purpose that is to hold up the pants. In order not to disrupt the continuity of a business suit, a belt is preferred to be as inconspicuous as possible. It seems that the invisibility becomes the chief basis for judging the dressiness of a belt. The dressiness scale is generally determined by the following criteria.

1.   Narrow belts are considered dressier than wide belts.
2.   Belts with a small buckle are dressier than those with a large buckle.
3.   Belts with one belt loop are dressier than those with two belt loops.
4.   Frame-and-prong buckles are dressier than solid buckles.
5.   Belts with contrasting-color stitching are less dressy than those with same-color stitching.
6.   Belts with metal loop, metal tipping, or other decoration are less dressy than those without decoration.
7.   Woven belts are less dressy than solid belts.
8.   Belts with multi colors are less dressy than those with single color.
9.   Black belts are considered dressier than cordovan and brown belts.

Mock

In the past, fancy belts were made of exotic skins such as eel, ostrich, sneak and alligator. Those belts wear out easily. Manufacturers therefore produce belts made of cowhide with the grain of exotic skins. These belts, called mock, have become gentlemen's favorite. A plain mock without excessive decoration is luxurious, yet suitable, for business attire.

A mock croc belt.

Woven belts

Some woven belts do not have a line of holes at the end of the strap. To wear one of these belts, the prong of the buckle must pierce through the belt from between the weave tracks. This not only looks unattractive but also damages the belt. If you desire the texture of a woven belt, you may consider one with a solid end. Or, it is even better to find a woven belt with a solid lining.

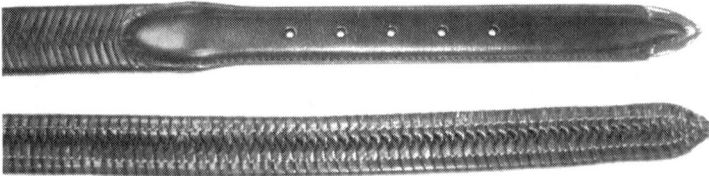

Some woven belts have a solid end (top).

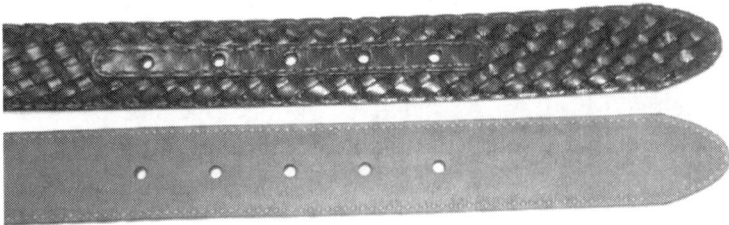

Some woven belts have a solid lining.

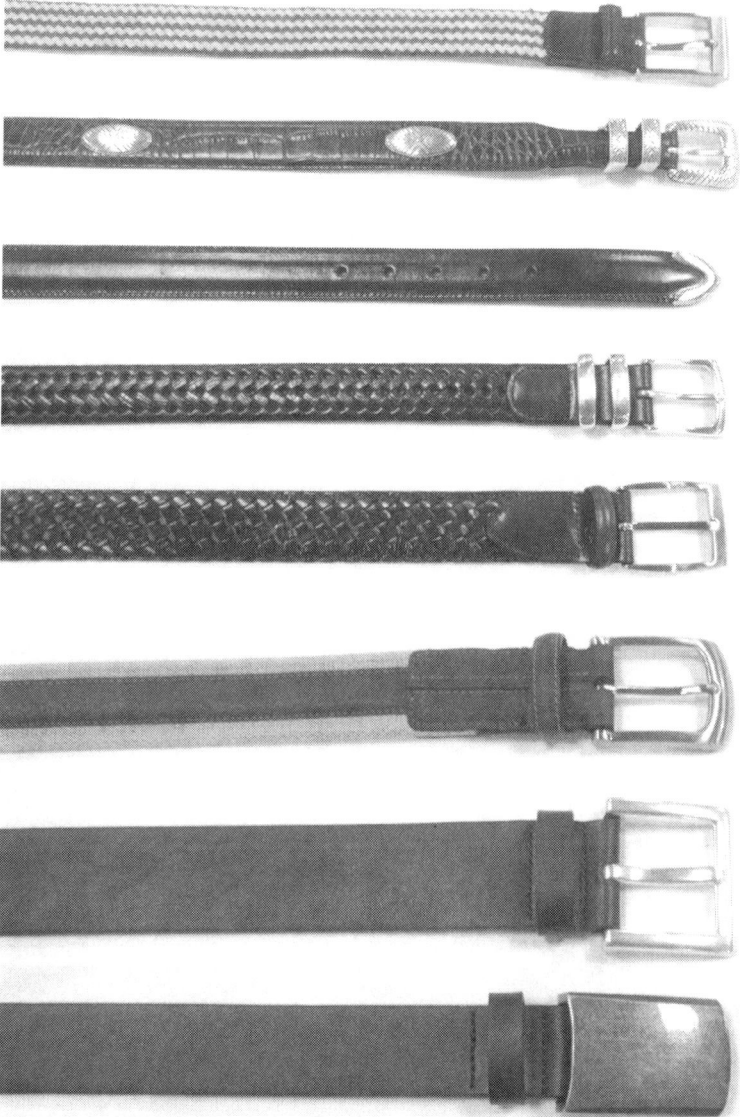

Weaved belts and solid belts with multiple colors, a solid buckle, metal loop, metal tip, or other decoration are considered sporty belts.

53.   *Money clips and wallets*

Esquire's *The Handbook of Style* advises that wallets are for credit cards only and money goes to money clips. In the past there were no driver license, and social security, insurance, credit or membership cards. All a man needed was a simple device to organize his money. The money clips serve well for this purpose. John T. Molloy once commented that people have high regards for a person who uses a money clip as a neat person.

A typical money clip is a solid piece of stainless steel or other metals folded into half. The bills and other items such as credit cards can be wedged in between the two halves of metal. There are two major problems with a metal money clip. One is that the clip must have strong "spring tension" in order for it to work. People who do not have a sturdy hand may have difficulty wiggling the bills into the clip. The second problem is that the clip tends to lose its grip once the metal fold has stretched out and become unable to return to its closed position. The damage is usually caused by inserting too much cash in the clip. If you shop for a metal clip, look for one made of titanium instead of stainless steel or brass. Because titanium is more flexible than steel, titanium money clips require less spring tension in the closed position, making it easier to push the bills into the clip. They do not stretch out or fatigue over time like many other types of metal clips can. Money clips made of non-metal materials, such as carbon fiber, have been marketed. Carbon fiber clips can open up beyond parallel without the deformation of normal metal clips. They are also scanner proof, meaning passing through metal detectors without any problem.

An improved version uses a hinge to swivel into an open and closed position. It is much easier to use but is less secure than the typical clip. Some money clips have a spring inside the clip. The spring helps clamp the bills with ease but makes the clip bulkier.

A simple money clip

Once the mouth stretches out and is unable to close, the clip is damaged and no longer able to grip thin material.

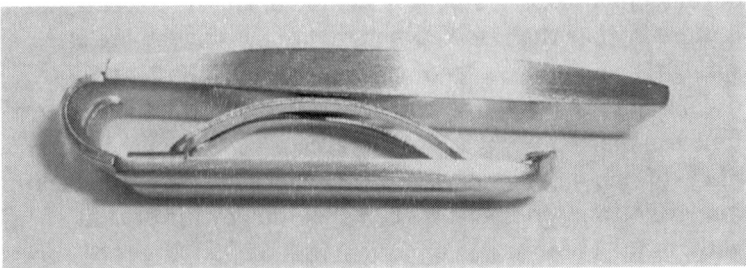

A money clip with a spring

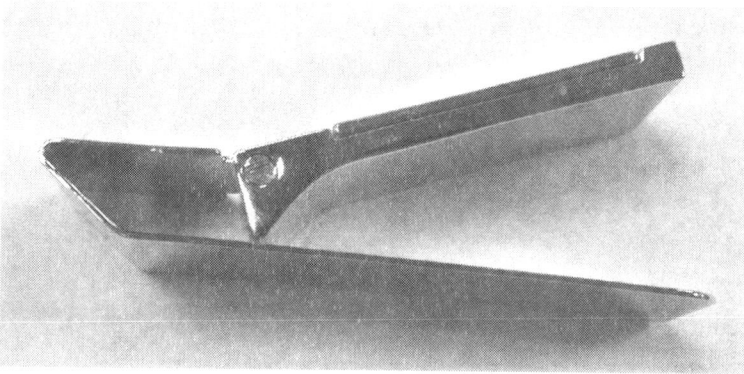

A money clip with a hinge

The magnetic money clip is usually made of two magnets encased in opposite sides of a folded leather strap. Depending on the strength of the magnets, the clip may not hold up as many bills as a hinged metal clip. A major setback of the magnetic clip is that the magnets tend to distort or erase the magnetic strip of the credit and identification cards if the clip is placed near the cards. A customer told me that he was unable to unlock the hotel room because the magnetic clip ruined the key card. The magnets are fragile. But, a broken magnet usually causes no problem since it is encased in leather.

Magnetic money clip

Marty Allen, American comedian, holding wallet with six credit, social security and union cards extended in accordion fashion.

Today, men tend to carry many items in their pockets. In addition to various IDs and credit cards, they also carry all sorts of name cards, pictures, coupons, receipts and other documents. A wallet seems necessary. Over the years, I have found that many men are fastidious about the style of the wallet. They stood in front of a tableful of wallets and could not make up their mind about which wallet to buy. Many men liked their old wallets but were frustrated for being unable to find a replacement wallet of the same style or design.

Senator Evan Bayh pulled out photos of his twins to show his supporters.

There is a wide variety of styles and designs on wallets but there is no consensus concerning which styles or designs are preferable. The tall secretary or large square wallets that can be carried only in a suit jacket pocket was once considered an upper-middle-class symbol. The styles are no longer popular as men abandon their jackets these days. Most men prefer smaller wallets that can be placed in their shirt or trouser pockets. Money clip wallets are very popular. Nevertheless, I find them distasteful. If you need both a money clip and a credit card wallet, buy two separate ones.

Three basic styles of money clip wallet

A customer bought a magnetic money clip at $30.00 in 2010. He returned to the store to buy another one a couple of months later. I asked him what happened to the one he had recently purchased. He put the money clip on the counter in a convenient store for a few seconds; someone grabbed the clip and ran out of the store. It is my opinion that money is better to be concealed. If you use a wallet, why not put the money inside the wallet. No one will know how much cash you are carrying. A blind man told me that his neighbors kept robbing him by taking large bills out of his wallet and leaving him with small bills in the wallet. I sold the customer a wallet with a hidden compartment. The blind man returned to the store a few weeks later to tell me that the strategy worked. His neighbors took small bills out of his wallet without noticing the large bills in the hidden compartment.

John T. Molloy said that "there is only one rule for the shape of a wallet; it should be thin. Regardless of what kind of wallet you carry, it should never be crammed so full that it bulges." Some men like smaller wallet; they choose a trifold. The problem with a trifold wallet is that the wallet tends to bulge and become unable to close if there is too much stuff in the wallet. A bifold reduces the thickness of the wallet since it only folds once instead of twice.

Most wallets have an ID window, which is made of clear plastics to allow the ID to be shown. I believe it is a bad idea to buy such a wallet. When someone requests you to show an ID, it is better to take the ID out of the wallet instead of handing your entire wallet over. You really do not need a see-through window made of cheap plastics to show yourself there is a photo ID in the wallet. The plastic window wears out or discolors easily. It is wasting money to throw away a wallet because of the broken plastic piece. Some wallets have a detachable ID holder, which can be taken out of the wallet. If you prefer a wallet that will last a long time, I suggest that you choose one without any plastic component. You may also choose one with a detachable ID holder. If the plastic ID window wears out, you still can keep the wallet without the ID holder. Some men do not like wallets with detachable ID holder because it adds bulk to the wallet.

Whereas a low count of "stitches per inch" is usually a sign of bad tailoring in woven or knit garments, it is unnecessarily a bad sign in leather products. Leather is a product of animal skin. Each time the needle punctures the skin, it leaves a hole, which is a form of damage. This is the reason that most leather products have a loose stitching pattern. Some wallets are made of hard leather while others are made of soft leather. The stiffness of the leather also has little to do with the quality of the products. Manufacturers can create the same products with both finishes to meet the demand of consumers. Wallet making is not like rocket science; it requires little technology to produce a good wallet. Over the years, I have found a good indicator to show whether a wallet is of top quality. Most parts of a wallet are made of full grain leather except the lining, which is usually made of fabrics of cheaper materials such as nylon, Bemberg or cotton. The very best quality wallets tend to have a leather lining, which is very rare. If you happen to find such a wallet, do not let it go easily.

A wallet with a non-detachable ID window

A wallet with a detachable ID holder

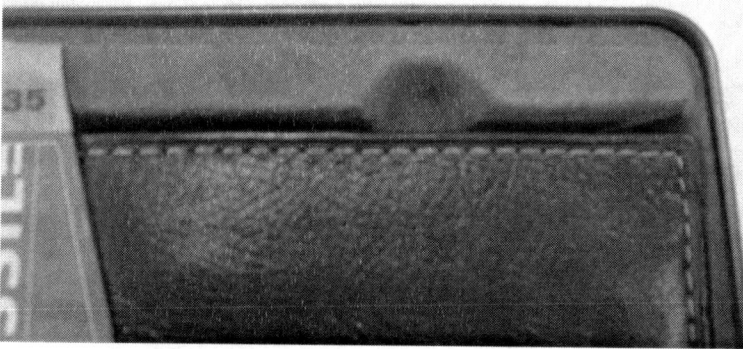

A low count of "stitches per inch" is not regarded as inferior quality in leather goods.

Frequently, customers asked me where to find a "front pocket wallet" at men's department. Wikipedia defines the front pocket wallet as "a case with no currency compartment and very few pockets for cards." Various manufacturers advertise money clip wallets as front pocket wallets. The definition is somehow ridiculous. All wallets should be carried in the front pockets of a jacket, shirt or pair of trousers. Most men carry their wallet in the back pockets of their pants. This not only ruins the wallet but also damages the back pocket of the pants. Numerous medical reports have linked some back pains to the placement of wallets in the back pockets.

Stitching weakens or damages the leather, causing the edges to chip, especially at the center fold where both sides of the wallet swivel into a closed and open position.

Some better made wallets therefore skip the unnecessary stitching along the top edge and at the center fold.

Some wallets have a coin compartment, which is very handy but increases the volume of the wallet significantly. A bulky wallet does not convey a positive image for business. I suggest a thin wallet for credit cards and bills, and a small coin purse for changes. Many men ruin their wallets by putting too much stuff in one wallet. They should reduce the number of items in a wallet, or use two or more wallets to carry all they need.

A wallet with a coin compartment

Traditionally, gentlemen reserve black color for formalwear. They avoid black clothing for business activities. They wear black shoes and belts, but reject black gloves, wallets and briefcases. John T. Molloy commented, "The best color for a wallet is a dark, rich brown—almost cordovan." An overwhelming majority of customers, whom I have encountered, prefer black wallets. I personally would stick to tradition and choose a brown or cordovan. If you prefer a black wallet, I do not find any good reason that you should not have one as long as you buy a quality one.

As explained previously, mock leather has been the favorite of sophisticate dressers. Mock wallets are less popular these days. If you prefer a wallet that appears different and elegant at the same time, mock wallets are a good choice for your consideration.

Ordinary wallets are often lined with cheaper materials such as nylon, Bemberg or cotton.

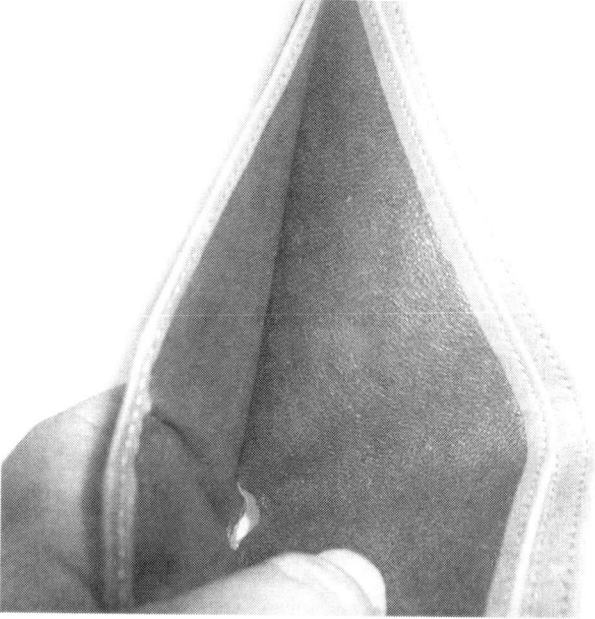

The very best quality wallets tend to have a leather lining in both sides of the bill compartment and behind the ID window.

About the Author

Dr. Ivan M.C. Chen was born in 1956 in Taipei, Taiwan. He graduated in 1977 from Ming-Chi Institute of Technology, which is a member of the Formosa Plastics Group. He retired from the Chinese Marine Corps in 1979 and worked several years as a chemical engineer. In 1983, Dr. Chen came to the United States to pursue advanced degrees. He earned an MBA from the University of Scranton in Pennsylvania in 1985 and a Ph.D. in curriculum and instruction from the University of Missouri-Kansas City in 1991. Dr. Chen is a dedicated schoolteacher. He has sold men's clothing since 1995. Dr. Chen lives in Kansas City, Missouri with his beloved wife and three children.

Dr. Chen strives for perfection on everything he does. No matter what trade or profession he is engaged in, he studies constantly and performs his jobs and duties effectively and efficiently. Dr. Chen becomes an expert on whatever he does. He has been able to share his expertise through publications in various professions. He published two articles in two issues of the annual journal Ming-Chi Institute in 1976 and in 1977 during his study at the institute. He wrote a manuscript, entitled The Psychology of Soldiers, while he served in the Chinese Marine Corps. The manuscript was recommended by the Ministry of Defense to join the Seventh Military Sciences Golden Statue Award Contest in Taiwan. He published many articles on business and management in prominent magazines and journals in Taiwan when he worked in the industry between 1980 and 1983. He was chosen as one of the keynote speakers from all over the world to present his doctoral dissertation at the Seventh Conference of Distance Education Association held at the University of Wisconsin-Madison in 1991.

After serving tens of thousands of customers in a retail department store for more than a decade, Dr. Chen has gained valuable expertise in menswear. With his multi-disciplinary educational background, experience in textile industry, and his exceptional reasoning capacity, Dr. Chen has been able to understand and explain many phenomena in men's clothing better than any fashion expert. Dr. Chen often provides surprising, yet convincing explanations. Many of his answers are thought provoking and are contrary to common beliefs.

Dr. Chen has studied men's clothing and has been disappointed by the inaccuracy of many contemporary writings. He has tried to correct many pervasive misconceptions about men's clothing by publishing a series of books. Unlike many fashion books that copy ideas from one another and keep spreading erroneous information and concepts, Dr. Chen's books are filled with original ideas and wisdom that have never appeared in previous literature. He is one of the few men in the world who can arch out a tie without using any artificial device such as a vest or collar pin. His ideas and methods have been proven practical and effective over the years by tens of thousands of customers who have trusted him with millions of dollars in purchase.

Ivan M.C. Chen, Ph.D.
Major Contributions to Men's Fashion

Contemporary writings on men's clothing keep repeating the same old information. Many of the information are incorrect. Most writers mistake yarn size for thread count and wrongly claim that fabrics made of 2-ply yarns are better in quality than those made of single-ply yarns. They also suggest that the tie should reach the waistband of the pants and cuffed pants are dressier than non-cuffed pants. Dr. Ivan Chen is an advocate of consumer education. He has written a series of books to correct the misconceptions and to teach consumers about men's clothing. Many of his ideas and thoughts are original and have never appeared in previous literature. His major contributions include but not limit to the following.

1. Wrote the world's first book on the art of arching out a tie.

2. Classified tie knots into Type-A and Type-B categories, and challenge the domination of the three most popular knots: the four-in-hand, half-Windsor and Windsor.

3. Created the Ivan Chen Knot, a Type-B version of the Mosconi diagonal knot.

4. Oppose tie knots that use the tie blade as the passive end, such as the Atlantic and Merovingian knots, for safety concerns.

5. Advocate the use of different sleeve lengths for barrel cuff and French cuff shirts.

6. Advocate the proper length of a knotted tie and the proper placement of a tie accessory be based on the length of the wearer's face.

7. Established scientific guidelines to determine the proper length of a suit jacket.

8. Provide comprehensive and innovative explanations for many phenomena in men's clothing better than other fashion writers can.

   - *Why do many men wear a crooked bow tie?*
   - *Why should the shirt collar fit the neck snugly?*
   - *Why should a man wear a spread collar with a jacket?*
   - *Why is it better to finish a pair of pants with a slanted bottom?*

9. And much, much more.

Books *by* Ivan M.C. Chen, Ph.D.

The Art of Arching Out a Tie
ISBN: 978-1438254401

The Rules of Ties
ISBN: 978-1438286600

The Essentials of Dress Shirts
ISBN: 978-1438288369

A Perfect Pair of Dress Pants
ISBN: 978-1438287102

The Etiquette of Suits and Sport Coats
ISBN: 978-1438287102

The 12 Simple Ways to Dress Differently and Better Than Other Men
ISBN: 978-1449577056

In Menswear Everything Has Two Prices One for the Fool
ISBN: 978-1439298565

The Stupid Things Men Do about Their Clothing
ISBN: 978-1438286136

Learn by Pictures
The Correct Way to Wear Men's Clothing
ISBN: 978-1448651016

What Fashion Experts Teach You Wrong
or Did Not Teach You About Fabrics
ISBN: 978-1438269818

Books can be ordered through createspace.com, other websites, or any bookseller worldwide.

The world's first and only book to teach you

The Art of Arching Out a Tie

Many men think fancy clothes help them look good. They do not realize that people are less likely to give a man credit for the quality of his clothes. People know he does not make the clothes he wears. People will, however, give the man credit if he coordinates his outfit nicely and wears his garments correctly. A good-looking tie does not suggest the smartness of the wearer, but a well-arched tie may.

As the fashion trend moves toward more casual and sporty setting, more men are dressing poorly. Many men are searching for ways to dress differently and better than other men. What is a better way to dress differently and elegantly than to arch out a tie? After all, few men in history have ever been able to do so.

There is no other article of men's clothing that requires more skill to execute than the tie. There are about 100 different ways to tie a tie. Every tie book illustrates the methods of tying the three most popular tie knots, the four-in-hand, Windsor, and half Windsor. In truth, these three knots are the main reasons why a man cannot arch out his tie.

The Art of Arching out a Tie is the world's first and only book that teaches men how to arch out a tie without using any artificial device, such as a collar pin, collar tab, or vest. The book will revolutionize the way men tie their ties. Open this book and discover the many factors that help produce an arched tie. You will become one of the few masters who can arch out a tie without the support of any device. The book also provides information, which no other book can offer, concerning the best way to determine the length of a knotted tie and the best location to place a tie tack, tie bar or tie chain.

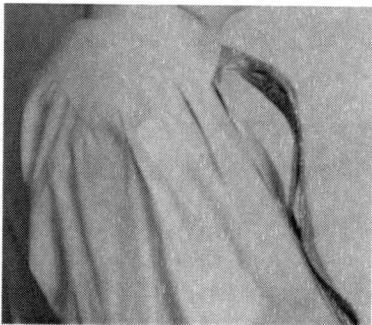

The Rules of Ties has everything you need to know about ties. Most men and women buy ties, which they think will look beautiful, sharp or will match their shirts, suits and pants. John T. Molloy considers ties the most important status symbols. Alan Flusser calls ties the icon of western culture. A key factor in selecting ties has something to do with "status" and "culture." This book offers you a paradigm shift and tells you what types of ties are proper for business and social activities. Many men wear fancy ties but wear the ties with a sloppy knot or at the wrong length.

Tie experts maintain that a well-tied tie should have a forward arch beneath the knot, but no one knows how to accomplish this goal. Every fashion book teaches its readers how to tie the three most popular tie knots, the four-in-hand, Windsor, and half Windsor. If you use one of these knots, you probably will never have a chance to arch out your tie.

The book exclusively teaches you the biggest secret in tie history--how to arch out a tie without using any artificial device, such as a collar pin or a vest. The book illustrates the method of tying the unusual diagonal knot, which will make you the envy of your peers.

The book also teaches you how to relate the width, length, and patterns of the tie to your face. The book further explains the correct way to wear tie accessories. The ideas and methods illustrated in the book are practical and effective. Many of them are thought-provoking and have never appeared in previous tie literature.

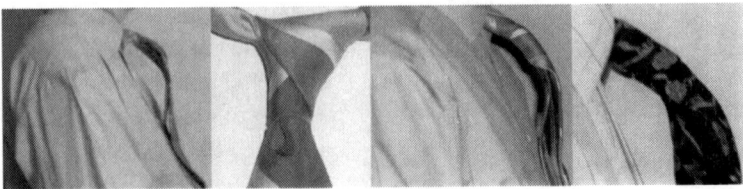

The Essentials of Dress Shirts

The great majority of men wear wrong size shirts without noticing the problem. This book is a must read if you commit one or more of the following.

❖ Do not know what "80's 2-ply" means, or you think the term refers to thread count per square inch.

❖ Desire a loose collar because it is more comfortable.

❖ Wear the same sleeve length as your arm length.

❖ Wear the same sleeve length for both barrel cuff and French cuff shirts.

❖ Do not know why you should wear a spread collar with a jacket.

❖ Do not wear a top fused shirt.

❖ Believe that fabrics made of 2-ply yarns are better.

❖ Prefer cotton and polyester blend shirts for wrinkle-resistance.

❖ Wear a collar pin or a tab collar to arch out the tie.

❖ Wear a shirt collar with tie space.

❖ Do not know that broadcloth is dressier than oxford cloth.

❖ Do not know the aesthetic balance between the collar style and the head shape.

❖ Mix fabrics and styles without matching up the dressiness scales, such as wearing a spread collar made of oxford cloth, or a button-down collar made of broadcloth.

❖ Do not know that not every non-iron shirt performs in the same way.

❖ Wear a shirt that has no crease at the pleats or folds.

❖ Wear a shirt with puckered seams.

Dr. Ivan Chen provides an insider's trade secrets and wisdom that no other fashion book can offer.

A Perfect Pair of Dress Pants
--The most misunderstood topic in men's clothing--

Dr. Ivan Chen has sold men's clothing for more than a decade. He has been disturbed by how American men buy and wear their dress pants. Clothing stores nationwide carry a variety of good quality dress shirts but stock inferior quality dress pants. Merchants do so because consumers keep buying the wrong pants.

Most men want to wear wrinkle-free and machine washable pants, so they choose synthetic or synthetic blend slacks. They are unaware that good quality wool pants are virtually wrinkle-free and can be machine-washed in water. Wool contains lanolin, a natural deodorizer, which prevents wool from absorbing odors. Hence, pants made of worsted wool require minimum care. Unless a man sweats heavily, he really has no need to clean his wool slacks. All he has to do is to air out and brush the slacks regularly, and steam them occasionally. Many men buy fancy wool pants but sent them to the dry cleaner regularly to have their expensive pants damaged quickly.

Most men do not even know how to wear a pair of pants correctly. They wear their pants a few inches below the waistline. They wear their pants too long, leaving multiple breaks in the bottom back of the pant legs. Many men mistakenly think cuffed are dressier than non-cuffed pants. They wear cuffed pants with a wrong cuff width, which is the best way to cheapen a pair of pants. Most men, including fashion experts, are indecisive about cuffs. In truth, whether a pair of pants is cuffed is insignificant. What is important is to finish the pants with a slanted bottom.

A Perfect Pair of Dress Pants tells everything you need to know about dress pants. With the secrets that no other fashion book can offer, you can now wear a perfect pair of dress pants.

The Etiquette of Suits and Sport Coats

Alan Flusser, a prominent fashion designer, claims that 90% of all men wear their jacket sleeves too long. Do you think the rest 10% of men do everything else right about their suits and sport jackets?

After buying a suit, many men have their suit pants cuffed at the wrong width, which is the best way to cheapen a new suit. Other men send their brand new suit directly to a drycleaner and have the suit damaged by over-pressing or by washing with harsh chemicals.

Most men rely on their spouse, girlfriend or salesclerks to select their suits. This is the main reason that today's men dress for failure according to John T. Molloy. Few men ever realize they need to learn something about men's clothing. This book is a must read if you commit one of the following.

- Cup your fingers to determine the length of the jacket.
- Desire longer jacket sleeves for fear that the sleeves may retreat too much when the arms bend.
- Do not know how long a jacket should be.
- Wear long size jackets because you think you are tall.
- Do not know why dress pants should not have a break in the back of the pants.
- Believe that cuffed pants are dressier than non-cuffed pants.
- Do not know why dress pants are better finished with a slanted bottom.
- Do not know that worsted wool garments require little care.
- Send your suits or jackets to drycleaners regularly.
- Do not know wool garments can be washed in water, called wet-cleaning.

The 12 Simple Ways to Dress Differently and Better Than Other Men

As the fashion trend moves toward more casual and sporty setting, more men are dressing indifferently. Dressing normally becomes an exception. Some men want to dress differently from the rest of the crowd, but they often choose the wrong approach. They wear garments of luxurious fabrics in flashy styles to boost their image.

Dr. Ivan Chen believes that any man who can wear a simple article of clothing correctly will look different from most men. The methods included in this book appear simple, yet different and better.

Open The 12 Simple Ways and discover why and how to dress differently and better than other men without additional cost.

❖ Arch out a tie without the support of a collar pin or a vest.
❖ Hang a tie that is shorter than two head lengths.
❖ Wear collars that fit the neck snuggly.
❖ Wear spread collars, especially with a jacket.
❖ Wear a jacket just long enough to cover the seat.
❖ Reduce the break on pants to a minimum.
❖ Finish pants with a slanted leg bottom.
❖ Wear the correct cuff width on pants.
❖ Keep creases sharp on shirts and pants.
❖ Wear a correct shirt sleeve length.
❖ Wear a correct coat sleeve length.
❖ Hang the pants from the waist.
❖ Wear top fused dress shirts.

In Menswear Everything Has Two Prices
One for the Fool

  Men can only wear what they buy and buy what are available to them. The way men or their loved ones shop have a great deal to do with how men dress. Alan Flusser, author of *Style and the Man*, says that during the past two decades, men have spent more money on clothing for themselves than in any other period of modern history. Most men buy the wrong clothing, which is one of the main reasons that today's men dress poorly.

  Clothing stores nationwide are stocked with mediocre products because consumers keep buying them. To avoid paying a fool's price, consumers either pay the same price for better merchandise, or buy the same quality merchandise at a lower price. Nevertheless, consumers must first know how to detect the quality of merchandise. The fashion industry has often deceived or misled consumers.

  Dr. Ivan Chen has sold men's clothing for more than a decade. He understands and explains many phenomena in men's clothing better than any fashion expert. Dr. Chen examines why consumers keep buying the wrong clothing and teaches consumers how to find the best buys in different categories of men's clothing. Dr. Chen often provides surprising, yet convincing explanations. Many of his answers are thought provoking and are contrary to common beliefs.

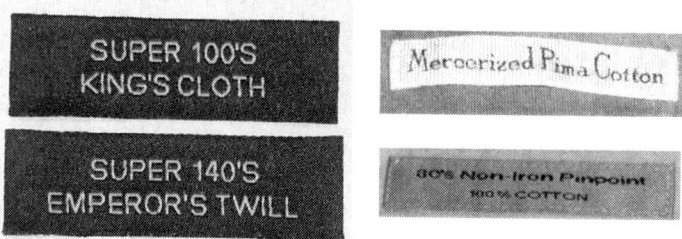

Manufacturers spend millions of dollars each year to put important product information on labels but they never educate consumers about the technical terms. Consumers often buy the wrong products because they have been misinformed or have not been informed.

The Stupid Things Men Do
about Their Clothing

Alan Flusser, a prominent fashion designer and author of many books, believes that 90% of all men wear their jacket sleeves too long. The jacket sleeve is one of the most obvious areas. If a man can make a mistake in the sleeve length, he probably will make mistakes in other areas of his clothing. The majority of men dress poorly these days. Most men do not even know they dress improperly.

Dr. Ivan Chen has sold men's clothing for more than a decade. He has spoken with tens of thousands of customers and has been amazed by the many foolish things men do about their clothing.

➢ Many men buy fancy dress pants and have the pants cuffed at the wrong length, which is the best way to cheapen a pair of pants. Some men want to buy flat-front pants with cuffs or have their flat-front pants cuffed.
➢ Many men wear oversized shirts and ask for fitted ones.
➢ Many men wear their pants several inches below the waistline and still wear longer pants, leaving multiple breaks at the bottom of the pants.
➢ The vast majority of men tie their ties using one of the most popular three knots, the four-in-hand, half Windsor, and Windsor. They do not realize these three knots are the wrong knots, which prevent the tie from arching out.
➢ Most men wear their dress shirt sleeves the same length as their arms. Few men know that the sleeve length of a French cuff shirt should be different from that of a barrel cuff shirt.

Dr. Chen collects some of the most common mistakes and offers solutions. He has been able to understand and explain many phenomena in men's clothing better than any fashion expert. Dr. Chen often provides surprising, yet convincing explanations. Many of his answers are thought provoking and are contrary to common beliefs.

Learn by Pictures
The Correct Way to Wear Men's Clothing

In an ad during WWI, Hart Schaffner & Marks urged consumers to buy the company's products and save. In truth, people waste their money more on buying the wrong size clothes or wearing the clothes incorrectly than on buying bad quality clothes.

This country can't afford waste in food or clothes—neither can you. Our clothes wear long and save

Dr. Ivan Chen has served tens of thousands of consumers in a men's department store. He has discovered that not every man has the time or is interested in reading a substantial amount of text. This book uses an effective and efficient new approach to learn how to master men's clothing by showing pictures of men wearing correct and incorrect articles of clothing. The photos in this book have impressed and changed the mind of tens of thousands of customers.

A right picture is worth a thousand words. This book will help you learn and learn very fast, and will not let you forget what you have just learned about men's clothing. Read this book in a couple of hours and save money for a lifetime by buying and wearing the right clothes.

What Fashion Experts Teach You Wrong or Did Not Teach You about Fabrics

Manufacturers spend millions of dollars each year to put important product information, such as "80's 2-ply" and "Super 120's", on labels, but they seldom educate consumers the meaning of these designations. Merchants are facing a dilemma. They wish to brag about the quality of their better-made products. But if they do so, how will they be able to sell other less quality merchandise? Clothing stores nationwide are filled with mediocre products. These products must be sold also. This dilemma may explain why merchants are not enthusiastic to educate consumers how to detect quality products. In their language, mediocre garments are made of "fine" fabrics whereas better garments are made of "finer" or the "finest" fabrics.

Fashion experts often boast of their terrific ideas on how to coordinate a set of outfit, how to fit a particular body shape or skin tone, and so forth. They rarely talk about basic technical terms perhaps because they know little about technologies. Some fashion writers, including famous ones, dare to take on this task only to give false information. They often mistake yarn size for thread count. The Federal Trade Commission recently warned that consumers "could be deceived or misled" by thread count information put out by vendors. What a surprise! Fashion experts and manufacturers have misled consumers for some time.

Dr. Ivan Chen has sold men's clothing for more than a decade. He has been disappointed with the inaccuracy of many contemporary writings on men's clothing. Dr. Chen wrote this book to correct some of the common fallacies about fibers and fabrics.

100'S TWO PLY

INNOVATIVE XILA™ COMFORT

Double Mercerized Cotton

SUPER 120'S
ROYAL GABARDINE

Index

397

CPSIA information can be obtained at www.ICGtesting.com
Printed in the USA
LVOW042249250412

279151LV00017B/142/P

9 781453 880043